T0288833

THE RULES OF SECURITY

PAUL MARTIN

THE RULES
OF SECURITY

staying safe in a risky world

OXFORD
UNIVERSITY PRESS

OXFORD
UNIVERSITY PRESS

Great Clarendon Street, Oxford, OX2 6DP,
United Kingdom

Oxford University Press is a department of the University of Oxford.
It furthers the University's objective of excellence in research, scholarship,
and education by publishing worldwide. Oxford is a registered trade mark of
Oxford University Press in the UK and in certain other countries

First Edition published in 2019

Impression: 1

Published in the United States of America by Oxford University Press
198 Madison Avenue, New York, NY 10016, United States of America

British Library Cataloguing in Publication Data

Data available

Library of Congress Control Number: 2018958839

ISBN 978–0–19–882357–5

Printed and bound in Great Britain by
Clays Ltd, Elcograf S.p.A.

FOREWORD

S ecurity plays an important part in our lives. It is also a field where mystique and obfuscation too often thrive. Sometimes this is deliberate, as it helps companies to sell products that are either unnecessary or ineffective. Sometimes it just comes from muddled thinking. In this excellent book, Paul Martin, an acknowledged expert in protective security, draws back the veil and lays out a pragmatic, proportionate, and sensible approach to protective security that reflects the best thinking of British government experts over the last thirty years.

When Sir Ian Gow MP was murdered by the Provisional IRA in 1990, the Government decided that public figures needed better protection against terrorist attacks and created a new unit in the Home Office to lead that work. I was seconded from MI5 to be the deputy head of the unit. It soon became clear that the arrangements in place were seriously inadequate. The protective security measures that were being provided were not based on a proper understanding of the actual threat the IRA posed, and each department was doing its own thing, often with little idea of what they were trying to achieve. Experts around government were doing their best, but the whole was less than the sum of its parts. As a result, some public figures had elaborate and disproportionate security at their homes and others had too little. We set about remedying this by defining a standardized set of measures that were closely based on what we knew about the IRA's intentions and capabilities. We built an integrated team of experts who worked together to a single end. And we created a clear and straightforward system for managing the design and delivery of the required security measures. It was one of the most satisfying periods of my security career, and it embodied the approach that Paul Martin advocates in this book.

Understand the threat you face, understand the vulnerabilities you are managing, create a holistic response, and be clear about who is in charge.

The approach laid out in *The Rules of Security* may seem like common sense. That does not mean that it is widely applied. Security gets entangled in issues of commercial interest, personal status, entrenched practices, poor information flows, and so-called expertise that cannot see beyond the end of its own nose. As a result, people and assets are left unprotected, money is wasted, and frustration or cynicism can flourish.

As a useful aide-memoire for the professional, or as an insight for non-professionals who want to understand what is being done in their name, Paul Martin's book deserves a wide readership.

Jonathan Evans (Lord Evans of Weardale)
Director General of MI5, 2007–13

CONTENTS

CONTENTS

CONTENTS

RULE 1

SECURITY RULES

Security is a basic human need. It enables individuals and organizations to go about their lives freely and without harm. Good security liberates us from the disruptive fear of harm and builds confidence to invest in the future.

―――――――

Why Does Security Matter?

We live in uncertain times (though we are hardly the first generation to think so). Crime has moved online, where it flourishes largely unchecked. A second Cold War is underway, in which hostile foreign states exploit the cyber domain to subvert nations and wage hybrid warfare. Determined terrorists are plotting now to kill and would kill far more, save for intense efforts to stop them. Burglars continue to burgle, spies continue to spy, and malicious insiders continue to harm their employers. There is certainly no shortage of reasons for paying attention to security. Nonetheless, attitudes towards it can best be described as ambiguous.

Security is one of those things we prefer not to need and bitterly regret not having when suddenly we do need it. As popular ideas go, the image of security is undeniably dark. Practitioners grow used to contemplating the many dreadful things that might happen, like doctors accustomed to disease, while the rest of humanity mostly prefers not to dwell on such matters. Some rely on just hoping for the best, like smokers trusting that fortune will favour them with continuing health. Quite often they get away with it as well. But despite—or more likely because of—all the blithe optimism and denial, dreadful things do happen. Criminals defraud and extort. Hackers clone identities, steal wealth, and hold data to ransom.

1

Fixated stalkers relentlessly pursue the objects of their obsession, in what one victim described as murder in slow motion. Hostile foreign states steal intellectual property, undermine democratic processes, and experiment with cyber sabotage tools capable of causing immense physical damage. Think what Russia has done to pick away at the fabric of society in the US and UK. Terrorists use guns, bombs, vehicles, and knives to dismember and obliterate randomly chosen victims. Given half a chance, some of them would attack us with biological weapons or lay waste a city. And when they are not planning attacks, they torture and execute people they accuse of being heretical or disloyal.

What to do? The answer, of course, lies in neither extreme of irrational confidence or apocalyptic despair. The answer lies in intelligent, evidence-based protective security. It works. Better still, there is more to security than stopping terrible things from happening—valuable though that is. Security frees us to concentrate on doing what we really want to do, both now and in the future; and unless you happen to make your living as a security practitioner, that does not involve fretting about security.

Security is more than just a tactical response to current worries. It is a basic building block of civil society. Individuals, businesses, institutions, and nations cannot thrive in its absence. The right kind of security enables us to live fulfilling lives by protecting us from harm, freeing us from the disruptive fear of harm, and giving us confidence to invest in the future. We take it for granted at our peril, though many people living comfortable lives do just that. History shows that most improvements in security come in response to terrible events, not as a way of preventing them.

Good security is intelligent and proportionate to the risks. It is a practical discipline concerned with safeguarding lives, property, information, wealth, reputations, and societal wellbeing. But what constitutes good security and how is it achieved? Deciding what is needed, and then making it happen, is not easy. The threats to our security are complex and rapidly evolving, as criminals, hackers, terrorists, malicious insiders, and hostile foreign states continually find new ways of staying one step ahead of us— their potential victims. At the same time, we are continually creating new vulnerabilities as we adopt new technologies and new ways of working. Furthermore, the practical application of security is often distorted by vested interests and conflicting agendas.

Those who do not understand the fundamentals of security open themselves and those around them to avoidable dangers, needless anxieties, and unnecessary costs. Inadequate security may leave them exposed to intolerable risks, while the wrong kind of security is expensive, intrusive, and ineffective. Security practitioners make understanding harder by obscuring the issues in clouds of jargon that even colleagues in neighbouring specialisms find opaque. Worse still, the jargon often conceals muddled thinking. The language barriers are particularly conspicuous in cyber security, where practitioners are in danger of forming an exclusive guild that communicates in private code. Quantum mechanics can be explained in plain English, so why not cyber security? Guiding principles that transcend the ever-shifting detail can help to navigate the complexity.

This book attempts to demystify a subject that affects every one of us in our private lives and at work. In this chapter and the following nine I have set out what I believe are the most useful guiding principles of protective security. They are expressed in the form of ten simple rules of thumb, or heuristics.[1] The purpose of such rules is to help solve complicated problems for which there are no pre-formed textbook solutions. They are 'rules' in the sense of guiding principles for dealing with situations of flux and uncertainty, rather than precise prescriptions. The good thing about rules of thumb (provided they are the *right* rules of thumb) is that they work reasonably well in many different situations. When faced with novel problems requiring complex decisions, it is easy to focus on the wrong things. Rules of thumb remind us what really matters and free our minds to deal with the most pressing tasks. The ten rules and their key underlying principles are recapped at the end of the book.

Along the way, we will explore real examples of bad things that have happened or nearly happened: the lone terrorist murdering seventy-seven people in one day, mostly one at a time; hackers stealing the details of three billion users; a rogue intelligence officer volunteering to spy for the enemy; patients turned away from hospitals because of an avoidable cyber incident; terrorists almost destroying the electricity supply to a large part of England. And yet, almost all of the really bad things that *could* happen have not happened, for reasons we will also explore.

My hope is that the ten rules and the reasons behind them will be helpful to anyone with an interest in their own security and that of their home, family, business, or society. I hope too that they may help those in positions of responsibility to understand how best to protect their organization and people. They assume no expert technical knowledge and aim to explain the ideas in terms that are clear and simple (though not, I hope, simplistic). Many of the examples are drawn from recent history but the principles are enduring.

As you will see, a recurring theme is that people lie at the heart of security. The criminals, terrorists, and hackers are social animals with emotions, experiences, and psychological predispositions. So too are the victims of those attackers and the security practitioners who strive to protect us. The human dimension is central.

What Is Security For?

The first thing to understand about security is its purpose, which is less obvious than it seems. The benefits run deeper than is commonly supposed and the penalties for failure run wider.

Security is conventionally regarded as a means of stopping bad things from happening. It does this by protecting people, property, information, or other treasures against damaging acts by malevolent forces. In view of its protective function, and to distinguish it from more rarefied scholarly disciplines like international relations and geopolitics, the subject is usually referred to as protective security. To be more specific, *protective security is the means of mitigating risks that arise directly from the potentially harmful actions of people such as criminals, terrorists, hostile foreign states, and malicious insiders.* This definition hinges on the all-pervading concept of risk, which forms the subject of Rule 2. The visible manifestations of protective security include locks, fences, and cameras. The less visible but equally vital manifestations include such things as personnel screening, contingency planning, and the paraphernalia of cyber security.

The risks that protective security is meant to mitigate are different in certain respects from many other types of risk, including those associated with safety, financial markets, and natural hazards such as severe weather and flooding. Climate change and disease pandemics probably pose even bigger risks to the long-term future of humankind, but they are not the subject of this book.

Security risks stem from the actions of purposeful adversaries and they evolve rapidly in response to defensive countermeasures. In contrast, safety risks arise from unintentional actions by people whose motivation is generally benevolent. Safety and security risks are not just different: they can be in direct conflict. For instance, fire safety regulations may require the outer doors of a building to open automatically in response to a fire alarm, allowing the occupants to escape. This safety feature creates a security risk that could be exploited by a determined intruder, who might enter opportunistically or even trigger a false alarm in order to gain entry. Transport systems and industrial plants are designed with an intense emphasis on safety. But too narrow a focus on safety can leave blind spots for malevolent adversaries like hackers and terrorists. Safety systems may fail if they are not secure.[2]

Another feature of security risks is that they are involuntary. A business can choose to take financial risks when deciding on new investments or acquisitions. You can choose to take risks when deciding whether to smoke or go skiing. Security risks, however, are imposed on us. We might decide to tolerate them or mitigate them by strengthening our security, but we rarely volunteer to have them inflicted on us. Involuntary risks like terrorism and serious crime are distributed unequally across society and fall unevenly on a few shoulders.

Security, in the broader sense of protecting citizens from each other and from foreign antagonists, is famously the first duty of any government. Indeed, it is arguably the oldest and most compelling reason for the very existence of governments. No democratic government survives for long if it fails to protect its citizens. The principle that a government must protect its citizens has been enshrined in British constitutional and legal tradition for centuries and was absorbed into American constitutional doctrine at the time of the Revolution.[3] In the seventeenth century Thomas Hobbes described the terrible consequences when people's only source of security is their own physical strength. The result is a world in which there is no society, no industry, no trade, no art, no science; only 'continual fear, and danger of violent death'. It is, he wrote, a life that is 'solitary, poor, nasty, brutish and short'.[4] Security is a basic human need.

Those of us who live safely in liberal democracies may take security for granted, but unstable and disorderly states outnumber the orderly ones.[5] It would be harder to feel complacent about security if you were living in present-day Syria, Afghanistan, South Sudan, Venezuela, Yemen, DR Congo, or regions of Mexico, for example. There are huge inequalities in security across the world, just as there are in material wealth.

The responsibility of governments to organize protective security at the national level is generally uncontroversial. It has formed part of the UK government's approach to national security since World War One, when much of the success in preventing German espionage and sabotage within Britain was attributed to MI5's protective security regime making the country a harder target. As well as stopping German spies, it stymied German attempts to bring biological warfare to Britain by spreading plague and anthrax.[6] Security was allowed to decline through benign neglect during the inter-war years, as later revealed by the Soviet Union's spectacular success in penetrating the UK government and intelligence services in the 1930s.[7] The US government consolidated its work on protective security when it created the Department of Homeland Security following the 9/11 terrorist attacks of 2001.

Protective security is of course not just something that governments provide for nations. Businesses, organizations, and individuals do much to protect themselves. Most of the protective security measures described in this book are operated by individuals or organizations.

How much protective security do we need? The world is a much less dangerous place now than it was a century ago, if danger is measured in terms of violent deaths. No western European countries have fought wars against each other since the end of World War Two, whereas for many centuries before then they started an average of two new wars a year.[8] Even so, the harm caused by crime, terrorism, and cyber attacks is immense, and it cannot be measured only in terms of deaths. Security risks are manifested in many different forms and have many different consequences. Businesses are damaged, reputations trashed, intellectual property stolen, individuals psychologically wounded, democratic processes undermined, and society's confidence sapped. Any of us could be defrauded by a criminal or have our identity stolen by a hacker. Any business could be harmed by a cyber attack, as Sony, TalkTalk, Yahoo, Equifax, and many others have found to their cost. Cyber-enabled information warfare by hostile foreign states is eroding the integrity of democratic processes, as exemplified by Russian interference in western elections. The chances of being personally caught up in a terrorist attack are very small, but the possibility is there. Those who adhere to the ideologies of IS or Al Qaeda would happily slaughter us, given the opportunity. And even when the risks do not materialize in damaging attacks, the fear of what *might* happen can still have a chilling effect. That fear may be justified or irrational, but either way it interferes with normal life.

Given the evident potential for harm, it is surely a worthy goal to prevent such events, or at least reduce the risk to a tolerable level. Then again, protective security costs money and adds friction to the conduct of life. For many businesses it is something of a grudge purchase—an expensive necessity that is at best a way of avoiding even bigger costs and perhaps gaining a competitive advantage over rivals. The financial return on investment in security is notoriously hard to quantify in ways that satisfy accountants or auditors. Security at any price is rarely an option. We might therefore conclude, as many do, that the sole purpose of protective security is to stop bad things from happening, subject to affordability and other constraints. If so, we would be missing something important.

Security Builds Trust and Confidence

Trust makes the world go round, and security risks undermine it. Trust is the basis of civil society and is even more important at times of uncertainty.[9] Protective security helps to redress the balance by reducing uncertainty.

The right protective security, intelligently applied, can have a liberating effect that is hard to quantify but nonetheless profound. By bolstering trust and confidence, it enables individuals, businesses, institutions, and societies to conduct themselves more freely than would otherwise be possible. It protects them from harm and the chilling fear of harm. As the former British intelligence chief David Omand put it, security contributes to 'a state of mind that gives confidence that the risks ahead are being managed to a point where everyday life—and investments in the future—can continue'.[10] By the same logic, there can be no simple trade-off between freedom and security because freedom is not attainable without security. With good security, we can have both. The strategic purpose of protective security is to enable individuals, organizations, and nations to thrive; and the tactical means by which it does that is by reducing the uncertainty caused by security risks.

The benefits of fostering a high-trust environment extend beyond the prevention of tragedies. Organizations with high levels of trust make faster decisions and cope better with change. They waste less time and money on bureaucratic risk-dodging, legal wrangling, and cumbersome compliance regimes. They are also more agreeable places to work.[11] Western security and intelligence agencies strive to be exemplars of high-trust organizations because without trust they are lost. They learned the bitter lessons of getting it wrong when a few insiders turned against them. When trust is betrayed, the consequences can include lasting psychological harm as well as material damage. Discovering that a trusted friend or colleague has betrayed you is deeply upsetting.

A further endearing trait of protective security is that its benefits tend to spread. Individuals and organizations that protect themselves may also help to protect others, not least by creating a more hostile environment for those who wish to cause harm. We live in a highly interdependent world, in which the risks that each of us faces depend on the actions of others. By improving our own security we may also improve the security of others, even if that was not our intention. To put it another way, *security is a common good*. The mutuality cuts both ways, however. If we neglect our own security, then others may suffer. For example, if I refuse to wear my security pass, I make it harder for security personnel to spot intruders, thereby putting others at risk. Similarly, if I connect my insecure device to my organization's network, I put every other user at risk of being hacked. Security is not selfish.

Security risks can be mitigated but they can rarely be eliminated. Even with the best protective security, some risks can never be neutralized. We must therefore expect bad things to happen from time to time. Moreover, we cannot live satisfying lives without accepting some risk. Any strategy for dealing with security risk should recognize the inevitability of some risks materializing and aim to minimize the impact of those that do. Good security means understanding which risks to tolerate, mitigating or avoiding the rest, and being resilient when bad things do occur. The following chapters explore the nature of security risk, the practical strategies for managing it, the hallmarks of good protective security, the essential qualities of resilience, the peculiar features of cyber security, and the human dimension of all of these.

RULE 2

RISK IS THE KEY

Risk is the universal currency by which security problems and solutions are judged. Security risk has three basic components: threat, vulnerability, and impact.

———

What Is Risk?

Protective security was defined in Rule 1 as the means of mitigating certain sorts of risk—namely, those arising directly from the potentially harmful actions of hackers, terrorists, and suchlike. The concept of risk is central to security and we should be clear about what it means. Much of what is said and written about risk is confused and confusing.

Security problems vary enormously in their nature and scale, ranging from minor domestic crimes to cyber warfare and mass-casualty terrorism. The risks manifest themselves in widely differing ways in both the physical and virtual domains, with outcomes ranging from tarnished reputations or illicitly copied data to dismembered bodies and demolished buildings. One thing they all have in common, however, is risk. The entire convoluted business of dealing with security problems, whether they relate to people, money, physical structures, or virtual data, can be distilled down to judgements about risk.

Risk is the universal currency of protective security and a ubiquitous concept in other walks of life as well. Financial analysts have built professions around the quantitative analysis of risk. Their methods have sometimes proved to be fallible, as demonstrated by financial crashes; they are also of surprisingly little relevance to protective security, for reasons I will explain. Risk analysts use the term 'risk' to mean different things, even within the same profession, and security practitioners are guilty on occasion of bandying terms like 'risk' and 'threat' in ways that reveal some confusion in their thinking.

What, then, is risk—or, more specifically, *security* risk? At its most basic, security risk is *the amount of harm that is likely to arise if no further action is taken*. To put it crudely, security risk is the amount of bad stuff that is likely to happen if you do nothing more to protect yourself.[1] An inherent feature of risk is *uncertainty*, because risk refers to possible future states that may or may not come to pass.[2] We use the concept of risk when trying to make decisions about possible futures, and we use risk management mechanisms like protective security to reduce the uncertain dangers.

In describing risk, I have unashamedly used subjective-sounding words like 'harmful' and 'bad'. They convey the reality that security risk ultimately depends on subjective and cultural judgements about what we value and what we are willing to tolerate in return for the things we desire. Whatever the sellers of security snake oil may claim, there is no such thing as objective security risk.[3] Pseudo-scientific efforts to quantify security risk, as though it were a precisely measurable entity like temperature or money, can be dangerous, for reasons that are explained in Rule 9.

All security risks are composed of three distinct components. They are *threat, vulnerability,* and *impact*. Threat is a product of the intentions and capabilities of those whose actions have the potential to cause harm. The people, organizations, or states in question are referred to as *threat actors*. In order to cause actual harm, threat actors must exploit gaps or weaknesses in security, otherwise known as vulnerabilities, or find other ways of defeating security. If they succeed in carrying out an attack, the amount of harm caused is the impact. Understanding security risk therefore involves assessing the capabilities and intentions of the threat actors, identifying their potential victim's vulnerabilities, and estimating the impact of a successful attack. Let us consider each of these three components in turn.

Threat

Threat is an ambiguous term with a colloquial sense of declared intent. In relation to protective security, however, it means something more specific. Threat is a product of the *intentions and capabilities* of threat actors—in other words, their desire to cause harm and their practical ability to do so. In this context, 'intentions' refers to plots or plans of action, rather than broad ideological goals or general aspirations. Supporting an extremist cause is not the same as plotting a terrorist attack (although one may lead to the other) and an intervention by the police may neutralize a terrorist plot without changing the terrorists' underlying aims.

Threat actors vary enormously in their goals, abilities, and motivation. At present, the most significant categories of threat actor are criminals, terrorists, hackers, hostile foreign state agencies, insiders, violent protesters, fixated individuals, and political extremists. We will explore their methods and motivations later. Incidentally, the categories overlap: for example, hostile state agencies use hackers and insiders to help them steal secrets.

An important point about threat is that bad intentions alone do not create risk. The intentions must be backed by practical capabilities. The level of security threat is high if, and only if, there are threat actors who possess both the intention and the capability to carry out an attack. Many would-be terrorists, criminals, and extremists have firm intentions to cause harm but fall short in their capability to convert that intention into reality. Conversely, many nation states have the capability to cause catastrophic harm but normally lack the intention unless they are at war. Threat requires both. A more precise definition of threat is *the probability that threat actors will make a credible attempt to attack*. The 'attempt' reflects their intentions and the 'credible' reflects their capabilities.

Many countries, including the UK and US, have a public system of threat levels for communicating to the population the overall seriousness of the terrorist threat. The threat levels convey, albeit in a somewhat nebulous way, the estimated probability, or likelihood, that terrorists will make a credible attempt to carry out an attack somewhere in the nation over the coming weeks or months. In the UK, the national threat level is expressed on a five-point scale, ranging from LOW ('an attack is unlikely') to CRITICAL ('an attack is expected imminently').[4] Despite the official wording, threat levels say more about the terrorists' *attempts* than the likelihood of an attack actually happening, because most terrorist plots are thwarted by the police and intelligence agencies.[5] The threat level can remain sky-high even when there have been no attacks for long periods. The point is that terrorists are trying hard to attack and will probably succeed at some point.

Vulnerability

Vulnerability, the second element of risk, refers to the *gaps or weaknesses in the potential victim's protective security defences* that could be exploited by threat actors. To put it another way, a victim's vulnerability is a threat actor's *opportunity*. To take a simple example, you would be at high risk from burglary if determined and capable burglars were sizing up your house (high threat) and you had no locks on your doors (high vulnerability). With sufficient protective security in place, your vulnerability would be low and the burglars might try but fail. Bad things happen when there is a threat *and* the victim is vulnerable. A more precise definition of vulnerability, which complements the one for threat, is *the probability that threat actors would succeed if they were to attempt an attack*.

Terrorists have so many potential victims to choose from that they are guaranteed to find some vulnerable ones, as became apparent yet again in a string of mass-casualty attacks on crowded streets, restaurants, and nightclubs in the UK, US, Tunisia, France, Turkey, Germany, Spain, Belgium, and elsewhere in the past few years. Much the same is true for cyber hackers. Any device connected to the internet has some vulnerability, no matter how sophisticated its technical defences, and could potentially be interfered with by anyone from anywhere in the world. Capable hackers, especially those equipped with the resources of a nation state, will find a gap in the armour.

New vulnerabilities emerge when defences that were once adequate fail to keep pace with improvements in the threat actors' capabilities. The vulnerabilities of organizations and individuals also vary over time, according to their circumstances. Criminals intent on defrauding have learned to target their victims when they are most vulnerable—for example, following bereavement or divorce. Another period of heightened vulnerability to fraud is soon after a financial transaction such as submitting a tax return or receiving a grant payment, when the victim is half-expecting their bank or the tax authorities to contact them. Criminals get hold of these dates and attack their victims using age-old fraudster techniques to obtain passwords and bank details. Similarly, businesses are more vulnerable to criminal scams when vigilance lapses at the end of a busy week, giving rise to the phenomenon of 'Friday Fraud', or when they are distracted by mergers, acquisitions, or restructuring.

Some victims make themselves unnecessarily vulnerable because they have other priorities and do not appreciate the risks. For instance, universities are prime targets for cyber espionage attacks. Their networks are packed with valuable intellectual property and designed for sharing rather than protecting information. Nation states steal this material on an industrial scale because it is easy pickings and highly beneficial to their economies. Why spend millions on research into new materials or pharmaceuticals when you can easily steal someone else's results? The scale of the risk is rarely apparent to the victims because the thefts are covert and the subsequent exploitation is gradual. The victims see no obvious evidence of harm, leaving them unmotivated to protect their data. To give just one example, in 2018 the US Department of Justice indicted a number of Iranians for undertaking a long-running cyber espionage campaign against universities around the world, many of them in the US and UK, which resulted in the loss of information derived from research costing several billion dollars. The Iranians were accused of attacking at least 320 universities and more than 100,000 individual academics.[6]

Impact

Impact, the third basic ingredient of risk, is a measure of *the consequences of a successful attack*. It is the 'so what' component of risk. We care about security because its absence or failure has bad consequences.

As a general rule, the impact component of security risk cannot be measured adequately in terms of a single quantity like dollars or numbers of dead bodies. Impact is *multi-dimensional*, meaning that it is composed of many different elements, or dimensions, which vary according to the nature of the threat and the victim. Any successful attack will produce a range of different consequences, some more obvious than others, that materialize over different timescales and vary in their perceived significance. The impact of a terrorist bombing, for example, could include deaths, physical injuries, psychological injuries, damage to buildings, financial costs, disruption to businesses and financial markets, declines in business confidence and tourism, societal fallout, and political turbulence, in varying proportions and over timescales ranging from seconds to decades. The societal impact of deaths caused by terrorism is different from that of deaths caused by, say, road crashes or heart disease. The geopolitical repercussions of the 9/11 attacks of 2001 are still being felt. A major cyber attack will typically produce a different pattern of consequences, such as the compromise of sensitive data, loss of intellectual property, disruption to business processes, reduced customer confidence, reputational damage, regulatory fines, and legal costs. However, even something as virtual as a cyber theft of digital data can still have a fatal impact. For instance, in 2015 hackers stole the personal data of individuals who were using the Ashley Madison website, which specialized in enabling extramarital affairs. The hackers threatened to publish the names of the users, several of whom committed suicide.

Impact is difficult to quantify because some of its most important dimensions do not easily lend themselves to precise measurement.[7] Any meaningful assessment of the impact of terrorism, for example, must take account of its political, psychological, and social effects. The impact of losing intellectual property through cyber espionage is also hard to quantify: putting a financial value on intellectual property is more art than science. Assessing the multiple dimensions of impact requires qualitative judgement, and there is nothing wrong with that.

The Risk Chain and the Risk Matrix

A security risk is said to *materialize* when an attack or incident occurs and produces an impact.[8] For that to happen, there must be threat actors with the intention and the capability to carry out an attack and security vulnerabilities for them to exploit; otherwise the attack would not succeed. (That said, even a failed terrorist attack will have some impact by stoking fear, generating media coverage, and absorbing resources.)

The threat, vulnerability, and impact components that combine to make security risk may be thought of as forming a temporal chain of cause and effect. The causal chain starts with the intentions and capabilities of the threat actors and culminates in bad things happening, as illustrated below.

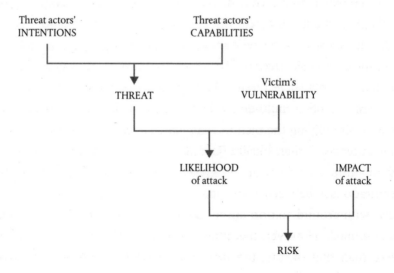

As we saw, threat may be defined as the probability that threat actors will make a credible attempt to attack, and vulnerability as the probability that they would succeed if they tried. Therefore, the combination of threat and vulnerability determines the *likelihood* (probability) that an attack will be attempted and succeed. If an attack does occur, the *impact* is the amount of harm that would arise as a consequence. It follows that the combination of likelihood and impact determines the amount of harm that is likely to arise if no further action is taken—otherwise known as risk.[9]

The UK's longstanding national strategy for countering terrorism (known as Contest) uses a broadly equivalent framework of tackling the threat, vulnerability, and impact elements of the risk chain. The strategy comprises four strands, called Prevent, Pursue, Protect, and Prepare.[10] The Prevent strand addresses the threat: it aims to stop people from becoming terrorists by tackling the underlying social, political, and psychological causes of terrorism. The Pursue strand, which mainly comprises the work of the intelligence agencies and police, also addresses the threat. It aims to pre-empt attacks by identifying and disrupting the terrorists. The third strand, Protect, aims to reduce the vulnerability of potential terrorist targets, especially critical national infrastructure and crowded public places. Finally, Prepare is about reducing the impact by preparing to cope with the aftermath of attacks that have not been stopped.[11]

Decisions about protective security should be based on an understanding of the actual risks faced by the potential victim. The trouble is that each potential victim is subject to its own particular mix of crime, cyber, insider, terrorism, and other multi-dimensional security risks. Nonetheless, there is a way of simplifying the picture. All security risks, whatever their nature, differ in terms of their likelihood and impact. Some are high-likelihood and low-impact, others are low-likelihood and high-impact, with all permutations in between. Conventional crime, for example, is remarkably likely, with around 30,000 crimes committed every day in England and Wales alone.[12] However, the impact of most conventional crime is less severe than that of, say, terrorist attacks, which are less likely. Cyber attacks are happening all the time and vary hugely in impact. How might an organization balance its protective security response to deal with these very different types of security risk? The answer lies in the assessment of *relative risk*.

A useful way of comparing different sorts of security risk is to plot them on a *risk matrix* showing their relative likelihood and relative impact. The example below illustrates how ten different types of security risk (R1, R2, etc.) might be compared. For instance, R1 might represent the risk from cyber attack, R2 disruptive protest, R3 serious crime, R4 terrorist attack, R5 unauthorized intrusion, and so on.

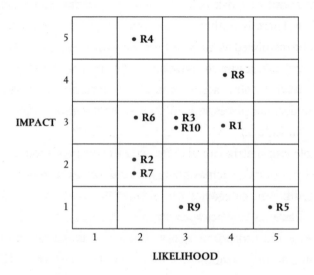

Each type of risk, such as 'cyber attack' or 'unauthorized intrusion', encompasses its own spectrum of severity, ranging from relatively minor incident to outright disaster. The convention is to consider the *reasonable worst-case scenario* (as distinct from the worst-case scenario or the most likely scenario). So, for example, the 'terrorist attack' risk might refer to a marauding attack by several assailants with firearms and explosive devices (rather than, say, a lone attacker with a kitchen knife or a highly trained team with a stolen nuclear weapon). The risk matrix can be prettified by presenting it as a *heat map*, in which the background colour changes from relatively comforting green in the bottom left, through anxiety-provoking amber in the middle, to nerve-jangling red in the top right-hand quadrant.

The judgements embodied in the simple risk matrix are relative, not absolute. In the example above, Risk 1 is judged more likely to materialize than Risk 2, and Risk 4 has a bigger impact than Risk 2. However, there is no attempt to quantify the differences in likelihood or impact. As noted earlier, impact is multi-dimensional and some dimensions, notably the psychological and social effects, are hard to quantify. The likelihood of some security risks can also be hard to estimate because they represent events that happen infrequently. However, it is easier to make *relative* judgements about one risk being more likely, or having a larger impact, than another. There is nothing wrong with relative judgements and they should not be dismissed as 'unscientific'. Psychological research has shown that *relative risks are easier to assess than absolute risks* and convey useful meaning.[13] If you come across a security risk expressed in numerical form to two decimal places, my advice would be to run away. (We return to this issue in Rule 9.)

The simple risk matrix can also be used to compare security risks with other categories of risk, such as financial, legal, safety, or reputational risks. Comparing different categories of risk in this way helps to counter the undesirable tendency to place security in its own special niche, separate and apart from the other corporate risks that are normally of greater interest to those running an organization. Security risks should be considered along-side other corporate risks as part of normal business.

The risk matrix approach is used by the UK government for its national risk assessment process, which analyses the biggest risks facing the nation over the coming five years. An unclassified public version covers the biggest risks arising from natural hazards, accidents, disease epidemics, and societal problems, as well as malicious risks like terrorism and cyber attacks. Among the former categories, the biggest risks include pandemic influenza, severe cold weather, flooding, widespread electricity failure, heatwaves, space weather, poor air quality, and emerging infectious diseases. Of these, the biggest is pandemic influenza. It is worth remembering that the 1918

Spanish flu pandemic killed between 50 and 100 million people, which far exceeds the number killed in World War One. The biggest malicious risks on the national risk matrix include CBRN (chemical, biological, radiological, and nuclear) attacks, terrorist attacks on transport or crowded places, and cyber attacks on services.[14]

When constructing a risk matrix, it is crucial to identify the *right* risks at the outset and review them regularly to check they are still the right ones. A common mistake is shortcutting the identification of risks and expending huge effort on debating their relative likelihood and impact. Judgements about relative risks are of little use if the wrong risks are being assessed. The rigour with which a risk matrix is constructed can be improved by systematic information gathering, interviewing experts, and brainstorming. The resulting matrix should then be subject to regular and searching reviews—as distinct from superficial and ritualistic reviews that achieve little more than ticking a compliance box and producing a warm glow of false assurance.

Many organizations maintain *risk registers*, often in the form of spreadsheets that list numerous risks and the actions being taken to mitigate them. A common problem with risk registers is their tendency to fossilize. The risks on the register remain the same but the actual risks keep evolving. Before long, the risk register parts company from reality. Another pitfall is the tendency for risk registers to accumulate far too many overlapping risks, leading to loss of perspective, confusion, and inertia.

Some of the nastiest security risks, such as certain ultra-high-impact forms of terrorism or cyber attack, materialize very infrequently or have never happened at all (so far). Their likelihood is very low but their impact, were they to occur, would be truly catastrophic. These risks are statistical outliers that are hard to assess because there is little empirical data about them.[15] In contrast, assessments of conventional crime, safety, and financial risks can be based on data-rich normality. The likelihood and impact of a domestic property being burgled or someone's credit card being cloned can be estimated with reasonable confidence, drawing on masses of historical data about comparable events. The insurance industry has been accumulating actuarial data on fire risks for more than 350 years and has more than a century of data on vehicle and aviation risks. There is much less data about terrorism or high-impact cyber risks and both are rapidly evolving—which brings us to two more distinctive features of security risks.

Security Risks Are Dynamic and Adaptive

Security risks are *dynamic*, which means they can change rapidly over time as new ways of thinking, new attack methods, new targets, and new vulnerabilities emerge. Compare that with fire safety. The risk of your house burning down will remain roughly constant, other things being equal. You can reduce the risk to some extent by installing a fire alarm and, once you have done so, the risk should then remain at the lower level. The same does not apply to security risks like terrorism or cyber crime. If left unattended, they tend to get worse.

A clever lawyer once pointed out that as many people in the UK died each year from insect stings as from terrorism, and therefore perhaps the UK's counter-terrorist laws could be relaxed.[16] He said this in 2012, when there had been no successful terrorist attacks in the UK for two years, while an average of five people a year were being killed by stings from bees, wasps, and hornets. An obvious fallacy in this argument (which the clever lawyer surely understood) is that throttling back on the counter-terrorism effort would result in more people dying from terrorism, whereas the risk from insect stings is unchanging. His argument seemed less compelling a few years later, after five terrorist attacks occurred in the UK in 2017, killing thirty-six people and seriously injuring many more.[17] The death toll would have been much higher had the police and intelligence agencies not prevented many other planned attacks. In the year following the March 2017 attack on Westminster, the police and MI5 thwarted a further twelve Islamist terrorist plots.[18]

Another significant feature of security risks is that they arise from the actions of purposeful threat actors. Terrorists, criminals, hackers, hostile foreign states, and the rest adapt their behaviour in response to the defensive reactions of their intended victims and vice versa. The result is that *security risks are adaptive*. As victims build stronger defences to protect against the latest threats, the threat actors in turn develop new ways of overcoming or bypassing those defences, and so on.

The adaptive nature of security risks means that threat actors and their potential victims are participants in a perpetual *arms race*. Like the Red Queen and Alice in *Through the Looking-Glass*, they must keep running to stay in the same place. Those who stand still become vulnerable. To put it another way, *protective security is an enduring process, not a state*. We will never reach those sun-lit uplands in which full security has been permanently attained and efforts can cease. With that in mind, it seems unfortunate that the cyber security industry is so fond of the term 'maturity', as in assessing the 'cyber maturity' of organizations. The assessment process itself is fine, because it is always good to review one's current state of security, but the language of 'maturity' implies an ideal end state that does not exist. In reality, the risks keep moving and no cyber security will stay 'mature' for long unless it too keeps moving.

Another awkward feature of arms races is the presence of multiple feedback loops and gaps in knowledge on both sides. The defenders act on the basis of partial and often inaccurate information about the threat actors, and vice versa, leading both sides to behave in ways that are not always optimal. The imperfect knowledge and feedback loops make it hard to predict what will happen next. There is always scope for nasty surprises.[19]

The adaptive nature of security risk was displayed in a terrorist attack that took place in the UK in 2017, when an Islamist suicide bomber attacked a crowd leaving a pop concert in Manchester. His bomb killed twenty-two people and seriously injured dozens more, many of them children and adolescents. The security for the event had been based on previous known risks and was designed primarily to prevent a bomb being brought *into* the arena as it filled up. The terrorist had apparently realized that it would be easier to attack the crowd on their way *out*, when the security would be much looser and the crowd density higher, because everyone leaves at the same time. He could loiter near a main exit without having to go through security checks and without looking too suspicious. To put this atrocity in clinically abstract terms, the risk had adapted to defeat the security defences. Naturally, those responsible for the security of public events have recognized this innovation and responded adaptively to the new risk. And so it goes.

Another example of adaptive risk, this time from 2006, was a foiled Al Qaeda suicide plot to destroy at least seven airliners over the Atlantic on the same day while en route from London to US and Canadian cities. Al Qaeda planned to bring down the planes using improvised explosive devices disguised as bottles of soft drinks. The plot was foiled by MI5 and the police. Had it succeeded, the death toll could have been even greater than that of 9/11. The terrorists had worked out how to build effective bombs that would circumvent the security screening processes then in use at airports. The contents of the soft drinks bottles were replaced with homemade liquid explosive and the detonators were disguised as batteries. The discovery of this plot led to the sudden introduction of the now-familiar restrictions on taking liquids or gels onto planes in hand luggage.[20] Since then, terrorist groups have continued their quest for new ways of breaching aviation security, including making bombs containing little or no metal, hiding them in laptops or tablets, inserting them into body cavities, and experimenting with surgically implanting them inside the bomber's body.[21]

The rate of adaptive innovation by threat actors is especially high in the cyber domain, where new attack methods and new security countermeasures often emerge on timescales measured in days or weeks rather than years. No sooner does the cyber security industry develop the latest piece of protective technology than hackers find smart ways of bypassing it and even exploiting it to their advantage. This phenomenon is so prevalent across the security domain that the subject of *malevolent creativity* has become an established field of research in its own right.

A well-documented case that illustrates the dynamic and adaptive nature of security risks is that of the Norwegian solo terrorist Anders Breivik, whose ruthless attacks in 2011 killed seventy-seven people in one day. Breivik's subsequent interrogation and trial revealed much about his preparations and planning, which remained highly changeable and often chaotic right up to the last minute.[22]

On 22 July 2011 Breivik detonated a vehicle bomb outside a government building in Oslo, killing eight people. He then travelled to the small island of Utøya, where a summer camp was being held for youth members of the Norwegian Labour Party. After landing on the island disguised as a police officer, Breivik spent seventy-five minutes systematically hunting down and shooting everyone he could find. His victims had few options for escape, beyond jumping into the water, and most were forced to hide. Breivik shot many at point-blank range, including victims he managed to trick into leaving their hiding places. Some managed to survive by concealing themselves in buildings.[23] By the time armed police arrived on the island and arrested him, more than an hour after the massacre commenced, Breivik had killed a further sixty-nine people, many of them teenagers.

During his long preparation for the attacks, Breivik considered many different potential targets, including individual politicians, the Norwegian Parliament, Oslo City Hall, and a government ministry, before eventually choosing the two he attacked. Breivik's plans changed many times, either because he changed his mind or because of altered circumstances. In common with many other terrorist plots, the chain of events leading to the final attacks was dynamic and adaptive, with numerous diversions and hasty decisions along the way. During his trial Breivik claimed he had changed his plans twenty to thirty times, often reluctantly, because of unexpected developments. He originally planned on making three bombs within a month but it took him three times as long to make just one, forcing him to proceed with a single bombing. On the day of the attacks, Breivik's plans unravelled further. He was late in starting and found that his primary target, the government building, was largely empty because it was a Friday afternoon.[24] The highly changeable nature of Breivik's attack planning and implementation is a common feature of Islamist terrorism. An analysis of hundreds of documented plots and attacks worldwide found they were characterized by highly dynamic and adaptive planning, resulting in outcomes that would have been hard for anyone, including the terrorists, to predict at the outset.[25]

One practical consequence of the dynamic and adaptive nature of security risk is that time becomes a significant factor. A serious security risk like terrorism or hacking is analogous to a ticking time bomb: the longer you metaphorically sit on one without defusing it, the more likely you are to be blown up (metaphorically, if not literally). This important variable may be thought of as *time on risk*. It means that urgency is a salient concern when planning security, and defensive measures should be implemented with minimum delay. Striving after perfection could result in the risk materializing before the defences are implemented. Security practitioners sometimes have to explain this principle to lawyers or accountants, for whom it may be less self-evident.

Catastrophes Are Non-Linear

Finally, let us consider what might happen if one of those very high-impact security risks were to materialize and a full-blown disaster unfolded. We are talking here about hugely damaging events on the scale of 9/11 and worse— perhaps a massive cyber attack that cripples great swathes of critical infrastructure, or a mass-casualty terrorist attack with biological weapons. Any such disaster would be unique and almost certainly not foreseen in detail. The event might be of a qualitatively new type, depriving the responders of historical data. Nonetheless, we can do better than guesswork when contemplating such possibilities. Basic principles borrowed from science can help to illuminate the nature of catastrophic events and hence improve our ability to manage the risks.

The principles in question derive from the science of *complex systems*.[26] A complex system, in the scientific sense of the term, is a set of interacting components whose collective behaviour is greater than the sum of its parts. In this context, 'complex' means something more profound than 'complicated'. Things that are merely complicated can be designed, predicted, and controlled; complex systems cannot. The weather, financial markets, ecosystems, living animals, the internet, and national economies are complex systems in this sense. So too are businesses, organizations, terrorist networks, organized crime syndicates, human societies, and nation states. Security incidents take place within complex systems, and large-scale incidents are complex systems in their own right. Complex systems have interesting properties, the most relevant of which are as follows.

The first notable feature of complex systems is that they have *emergent properties* which cannot be predicted by adding together the properties of the component parts. For instance, the ability to speak Spanish is an emergent property of the human brain, which cannot be inferred from the properties of individual brain cells. Emergence is one of the primary differences between complex systems and systems that are merely complicated. *Security risks are emergent properties of complex systems.*

A second relevant feature of complex systems is that, under certain conditions, they behave in radically *non-linear* ways. The science tells us that complex systems tend to evolve towards a state that mathematicians refer to as *chaos*. (The 'chaos' of mathematicians has a technical meaning that is quite distinct from the colloquial 'chaos'.) Complex systems that are on the borders of a chaotic state are prone to sudden and dramatic change, which can be triggered by a tiny disturbance. Mathematicians refer to this sudden change within a chaotic complex system as a *catastrophe*, again defining the word in a distinctly different way from its colloquial sense. A physical analogy is a large and unstable conical heap of sand, onto which single grains of sand are added one by one. At some critical point, adding one more grain of sand will cause an avalanche, when the conical shape suddenly collapses and sand cascades to the bottom.

Non-linear change is strange. Most things in everyday life vary gradually in a broadly linear fashion, where the rate of change remains roughly the same. When you walk, for example, your position changes linearly: if one step moves you one metre, then two steps will take you two metres, three steps three metres, and so on. In sharp contrast, complex systems can behave non-linearly, shifting rapidly away from their starting point in an accelerating manner. Suppose your walking was non-linear, such that each step covered twice the distance of the previous step. In this case, you would have travelled one metre after one step, three metres after two steps, and seven metres after three steps. With linear walking, ten steps would carry you ten metres, whereas ten steps of fantastical non-linear walking would carry you 1,023 metres. An example of non-linear change is illustrated in the diagram below, which shows how a function (F) varies over time (T) in a linear system (the straight line) and in a non-linear system (the sharp curve).

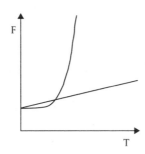

The science of complex systems has implications for how we think about high-impact security events. When the risk starts to materialize, events may unfold non-linearly with alarming speed. A prolonged period of business-as-usual, characterized by gradual change or moderate fluctuation within familiar limits, is suddenly interrupted by an abrupt shift to a new state that lies far outside the normal range of variation. To put it more graphically, *catastrophes are non-linear*. Major security incidents can cause system failures—for example, breakdowns in business processes. The ideal form of failure is *graceful degradation*, in which the system fails gradually and with plenty of warning. Non-linear failures can be extremely grace*less*.

One example of non-linear change in cyber security is the spread of so-called wormable malware—that is, malware which actively spreads copies of itself across networks without any intervention by users.

Infections caused by wormable malware can spread extremely quickly, causing major systemic failures. (Some recent examples are described in Rule 8.)

A third relevant characteristic of complex systems is their exquisite *sensitivity to initial conditions*. A very small change in the initial conditions is capable of triggering a very large event. This phenomenon is the origin of the famous butterfly effect, whose name derives from the title of a 1972 paper by the mathematician Edward Lorenz, called 'Does the flap of a butterfly's wings in Brazil set off a tornado in Texas?' Lorenz intended the title to convey the idea that in a complex system on the border of chaos, like the global weather system, a tiny change in the initial conditions (the flapping of the butterfly's wings) could produce dramatic outcomes.[27] The same concept of small events triggering big events is conveyed in the old rhyme: 'For want of a nail, the shoe was lost; for want of a shoe, the horse was lost; for want of a horse, the rider was lost; for want of a rider, the battle was lost; and for want of a battle, the kingdom was lost.' By the way, pointing out that a small event can trigger a big event in a complex system is not the same as saying the small event *caused* the big event. All interesting phenomena have multiple causes, and a dramatic outcome can rarely be attributed to a single cause. The small event is more like pulling the hair-trigger on a very large gun that is already assembled and loaded and aimed, or Gavrilo Princip shooting Archduke Franz Ferdinand and pre-cipitating World War One.

A fourth interesting feature of complex systems is that when they undergo catastrophic non-linear change, *the exact outcome is impossible to predict*. Think of a pencil balanced precariously on its tip: we can safely predict that the tiniest disturbance will make it fall over, but we cannot predict the exact direction in which it will fall. In the case of social systems, economies, or even large projects, it is possible to go further and state that *most of the possible outcomes will be worse*. The logic here is simple. In complex technology-dependent systems or societies there is an almost infinite number of ways in which things could go wrong, but very few ways in which everything can combine to work smoothly. To misquote Tolstoy, all successful enterprises resemble each other; each unsuccessful enterprise is unsuccessful in its own way.[28] If a business or economy or system is functioning well and then undergoes a catastrophic non-linear change, the vast majority of potential end states will be worse than before.

The sorts of complex systems that are most relevant to protective security have an additional property that makes their outcomes even harder to predict, which is their adaptive nature. *Complex adaptive systems* are made up of entities (which mathematicians call 'agents') that adapt their behaviour in response to their interactions with other entities. Security risks arise from complex adaptive systems: threat actors and defenders are locked in an arms race in which the actions of one side affect the actions of the other, and vice versa. Politics and financial markets are also complex adaptive systems. They involve players who continually monitor, learn, and respond to the actions and statements of others. The science strongly suggests that the notion of governments precisely controlling economies or social changes, or financiers consistently making money through sheer skill, is delusional.

Putative real-world examples of complex adaptive systems undergoing catastrophic non-linear change include the collapse of the Soviet Union in 1991, the UK fuel crisis of 2000, the Great Financial Crash of 2008, the Arab Spring uprisings of 2011, and the London riots of 2011. In each case, a relatively small perturbation pushed a complex system into non-linear change, with outcomes that were not predicted because they were impossible to predict. And even if the outcomes *had* been predicted, they would not have happened in the same way because these were adaptive systems. Faced with precise predictions of massive disruption, the authorities would have responded adaptively by intervening at an earlier stage and changing the outcome. Large-scale security risks, in common with political revolutions and spontaneous uprisings, involve the adaptive behaviour of sentient threat actors, making the precise outcome impossible to predict.

So, how does all this abstract theory help those charged with managing security risks? One implication from complex systems behaviour is that we should invest in building the *resilience* of our systems and organizations, because unexpected bad things will happen. The inherent unpredictability makes it unfeasibly difficult to pre-empt every possible eventuality by erecting defences to stop them all happening. A better strategy is to complement protective security with preparations for dealing with unexpected major disruptions and strengthening the ability to recover quickly. Resilience forms the subject of Rule 5.

The potential for rapid non-linear change also implies that decision-makers should be prepared to intervene rapidly and radically at an early stage if they think they might be on the brink of a 'big one'. Taking quick and decisive action on the basis of uncertain information requires a different mind set from business-as-usual. It does not come naturally to people who have no personal experience of severe events. History shows that individuals and organizations tend to under-react when things start going seriously wrong, especially when events fall outside their normal range of experience. They watch what others are doing and wait to see what happens next. Although watching and waiting is often a rational response in conventional small-scale incidents, it could be calamitous if a non-linear catastrophe is looming.

After Anders Breivik detonated his bomb in Oslo, the authorities were slow to react. Norway was not used to such horrific events, making it harder to comprehend what was going on. Breivik was able to travel unhindered to Utøya island, where he proceeded to massacre a further sixty-nine people. A detailed analysis of that day concluded that the Norwegian authorities were slow to 'push the big button'.[29] Of course, knowing when to push the big button is easier said than done, and most decision-makers in an incipient crisis are painfully aware of the criticism they would face if they sounded a false alarm. One area where further research would be illuminating is identifying the subtle warning signs that a system is on the verge of catastrophic change—if you like, the equivalent of the crackling sound that a polar ice sheet makes before it breaks up. Meanwhile, we must rely on the experience and wisdom of those on the spot.

RULE 3

THINK LIKE AN ATTACKER

*Judgements about risk and security require an understanding of the
current and likely future intentions and capabilities of threat actors.*

———

Know Your Enemy

At present, the biggest threats to the security of individuals and organizations in developed nations stem from organized criminals, hostile foreign states, terrorists, hackers, malicious insiders, fixated individuals, and right-wing extremists, in no particular order. These threats are profusely diverse. They are fuelled by widely differing motivations and, as we saw in Rule 2, they keep changing as threat actors apply their malevolent creativity to invent new ways of causing harm. The threats are expressed in many different forms in both the physical and virtual worlds. A criminal is much more likely to try stealing your money online than by snatching your wallet in the street. Hostile foreign states have become past masters at exploiting the cyber domain to do what they could once do only by physical means. Fixated individuals and trolls use social media to deluge their victims with torrents of bile, while feeling personally immune from any blowback. Terrorists remain wedded to the physical effects of bombs, guns, vehicles, and knives, and find innovative ways of deploying them despite the security.

Some types of threat are the subject of extensive reporting and research. There is no great shortage of people writing about terrorism, for example. Other threats are less widely aired. Take the threat from fixated individuals. Evidence dating back more than a century shows that the biggest violent threat to politicians in many western countries has come from fixated loners pursuing intense personal grievances, most of whom have a history of mental illness.[1]

Dealing with the manifold risks that flow from these diverse threats requires an understanding of the intentions and capabilities of the threat actors. Who are they? What do they want? What are they capable of doing now and what are they aiming to do in the future? If they were to attack, how would they do it? What is their perception of me or my organization? It pays to know your enemies, some of whom may not know that they *are* your enemies. The most successful gamekeepers are those who understand how poachers think.

Yes, They Really Would Do That

A mass of information is publicly available about the security threats that beset us. Some of the information is quite reliable. Even so, developing a solid understanding of the threat environment is not straightforward. First there is the problem of knowing which of the many sources to trust. Much of the information comes from people who are trying to sell things and should therefore be approached with healthy scepticism. Then we must make sense of the many disparate elements—crime, cyber, terrorism, and so on—before working out what it all means in practical terms for our own particular circumstances. And beyond these practical matters lie barriers to understanding that arise from our own psychology. Individuals and organizations are inclined to misread the cogency of threats for good psychological reasons, which are explored in Rule 7.

One obstacle to forming reliable judgements about threat is that we have short memories and even shorter attention spans. Our sense of the world is heavily swayed by our recent impressions and the memories that most easily spring to mind. The shocked reaction to the latest terrorist atrocity or crippling cyber attack quickly subsides and we start to feel safe again, much like motorway drivers who slow down after passing a nasty crash before speeding up a few minutes later. As David Omand put it: 'People forget . . . and "it must never happen again" elides into "it can never happen again". But it can and it does.'[2]

A common pitfall is accepting at an abstract level the existence of general threats such as hacking and terrorism, but nestling in the comforting delusion that they somehow do not really apply to *us*. One reason is that we find it inherently easier to believe things that we would *like* to be true, as distinct from uncomfortable things that actually are true. Another factor is our unconscious tendency to assume that our adversaries are essentially like us—a phenomenon known as *mirror imaging*. During the Cold War, western intelligence analysts sometimes fell into the mirror-imaging trap by mistakenly assuming that hostile foreign states would make decisions in similar ways according to similar criteria.[3] We are all capable of deluding ourselves in this way.

Mirror imaging makes it harder to absorb the distressing reality of some security threats. Most people have never had a close personal encounter with violent crime or terrorism and lack the altered perception that comes from the visceral experience. They may find it harder to accept emotionally, as distinct from intellectually, that there exists a small minority of ruthless individuals who do terrible things without hesitation. In much the same way, people who have only ever read about vehicle crashes may take a more relaxed attitude to road safety than those who have personally experienced one.

Thanks to mirror imaging, many nice, well-behaved people find it hard to absorb that some of the dreadful things they read about actually happen in real life. The uncomfortable truth is that some threat actors do disgusting things without compunction and then lie about it. If it suited their purposes, they would rob you or kill you and your loved ones. Afterwards, they would lie and deny, and some well-meaning people would half-believe them. Take Islamist terrorism, for example. A striking feature of some of its manifestations, especially IS, is the absence of self-imposed political or ethical constraints on the amount of harm it aspires to cause. The only real constraints are the interventions of state agencies and the practical limitations on the terrorists' capability to cause harm. No other threat actors at present aspire to cause death and destruction on such a scale.

The lack of self-imposed constraints is all too easily illustrated by events from relatively recent history. For instance, Islamist terrorists in Iraq and Pakistan have carried out suicide bombings specifically targeted against children, including one attack in which a truck bomb was detonated in the playground of an elementary school, killing thirteen children and badly wounding many more. In 2014 the Taliban murdered 132 children in a school in Peshawar.[4] It is at least conceivable that some future attacks in western countries might be aimed at schools or hospitals. Adherents of IS in Iraq and Syria have carried out public executions of alleged traitors and heretics by means of burning alive, drowning in cages, crucifixion, decapitation with explosive collars, shooting, and crushing with bulldozers. Women have been forced into sexual slavery. Men accused of being gay have been executed by throwing them off tall buildings.[5] In 2015, IS murdered Muath Al-Kasasbeh, a captured Jordanian Air Force pilot, by burning him alive inside a steel cage. Their official video of the murder ran for more than twenty minutes.[6] The extreme violence is intended to horrify and intimidate their enemies.

Islamist terrorist groups have tried for many years to acquire CBRN weapons. Al Qaeda worked on developing a chemical weapon for use in underground railway stations and other confined spaces. The *mubtakkar*, as it was called, was designed to generate a cloud of poisonous hydrogen cyanide gas.[7] More recently, Islamist terrorists have used chemical weapons in Syria. So far, terrorist groups have not managed to deploy the worst sorts of biological weapon, which have the potential to cause even greater harm. To give some sense of the risk, a limited accidental airborne release of anthrax from a Soviet bioweapons facility in 1979 killed at least seventy people, even according to the official figures. A deliberate release of weaponized anthrax in a large city could bring death on a much greater scale.[8] The UK government has taken the precaution of stockpiling small-pox vaccines, despite the very small likelihood of terrorists acquiring the virus, because of the potentially catastrophic impact.

State threat actors are also capable of ruthless brutality and brazen lying. In 2006 the Russian state murdered a former Russian intelligence officer, Alexander Litvinenko, in central London. Litvinenko died a slow and agonizing death after being attacked with a radiological weapon, polonium 210. The public inquiry concluded, to judicial standards, that Litvinenko was murdered by the FSB Russian intelligence service.[9] In 2018, the Russian state attempted to murder another of its former intelligence officers, Sergei Skripal, in England—this time using a military-grade nerve agent.[10] It was the first use of a nerve agent in Europe since World War Two. The willingness of the Russian state to murder its enemies on foreign soil should come as no surprise. Indeed, Russian federal law includes legislation that legitimizes the extraterritorial assassination of enemies of the state.

Criminals are also capable of ruthless opportunism and a disregard of ethical boundaries. For example, one of the most lucrative targets for cyber criminals has been the charity sector, including medical charities providing critical care to people dying of cancer. Charities hold money and lots of valuable data, and many of them are highly vulnerable to cyber attack.[11]

Failing to absorb the uncomfortable reality that some threat actors are willing to do extremely bad things can result in a tendency, metaphorically speaking, to believe the comforting reassurances and blink first when confronted with a serious threat. We sometimes need reminding that, as Shakespeare put it, a villain may smile and smile and yet still be a villain.[12] Or, as a former diplomat said of confronting the Russian state: 'Never engage in a pissing match with a skunk: he possesses important natural advantages.' All of which said, it would be a mistake to use the 'otherness' of threat actors as an excuse for not trying to understand and influence their behaviour. They are not a breed entirely apart, and we are more like them than we perhaps care to believe.

One useful technique for countering the mirror-imaging bias is *red teaming*, in which one group of players (the red team) consciously tries to place themselves in the threat actor's shoes, while a second group (the blue team) plays the role of the defenders. For this technique to work, the red team must be equipped with an evidence-based understanding of the threat actor's known intentions and capabilities. They must also understand that whereas the defenders are constrained by ethics and the law, they are not.

A further reason why security threats are often misread is the tendency to assume that bad things happen for a reason, and therefore no one would attack *you* unless they had some reason to single you out. If you do not fit the target profile, so the argument goes, there is surely no reason to worry. Where this comforting belief falls down is in failing to recognize the importance of chance and opportunity. A criminal, hacker, or terrorist might attack you or your organization because you happen to be in the wrong place at the wrong time and the opportunity presents itself. Any of us could suffer collateral harm from being in the vicinity of an attack aimed at something else. As noted in Rule 2, terrorists often behave opportunistically and follow a path of least resistance.

Both Sides Have Secrets

Staying ahead in the protective security arms race requires an up-to-date understanding of the threats, which are continually changing as adaptive threat actors find new ways of overcoming their victims' defences. The best ways of acquiring this understanding are by obtaining authoritative advice from those who know, learning from the experiences of others, sharing information, and actively gathering intelligence about the threat actors. The first three are relatively straightforward, but gathering intelligence is easier said than done.

Competent threat actors, including successful terrorists, professional criminals, and foreign state agencies, work hard to keep their plans and dispositions secret. For obvious reasons, they try not to advertise precisely who they are, where they are, or what exactly they are planning to do next. Technology makes this easier by providing them with ready access to an expanding range of passably secure communications media. Terrorists and criminals also use violence to deter and punish anyone who reveals their secrets to the authorities. Covert human intelligence sources ('agents') whose role is uncovered are in mortal peril. The Provisional IRA (PIRA) had a long and bloody history of hunting down and murdering individuals it suspected of being 'touts' for the police or intelligence agencies.

The covert behaviour of serious threat actors makes it hard to obtain reliable information about their plans. Sometimes there is no information at all. This simple fact has an important implication for protective security, which is that *absence of evidence of a threat does not constitute evidence of an absence of threat.* You might think this was a statement of the blooming obvious, but the behaviour of some authorities suggests otherwise. It is not uncommon to encounter the faulty logic that 'there is no intelligence of a threat to X and therefore X does not need security'. In fact, the absence of intelligence means just that—the absence of intelligence.

A more measured approach is to recognize that there might be a threat that has not yet been detected (possibly because no one is looking for it). In the absence of any specific intelligence in either direction, it is safer to *assume* a certain level of underlying threat and provide protective security on that basis, based on the general threat environment, known vulnerabilities, and the likely impact of an attack. To put it another way, *the defender's general security posture should be based on risk rather than threat.* To give a simple example, most people rightly assume that there is at least some risk of their home being burgled, even in the absence of intelligence about the intentions and capabilities of local criminals. They act accordingly, taking account of general levels of crime in their area (the threat environment), the existing security of their home (vulnerability), and a sense of how much they have to lose (impact). If there *is* intelligence of a specific threat— perhaps because neighbouring properties have recently been burgled— then the security can be adjusted accordingly. To put it more concisely, *judgements about the appropriate level of protective security should be risk-based and intelligence-led.*

The risk-based, intelligence-led approach works for cyber security too. Many organizations adopt it even if they are not conscious of doing so. They start by recognizing that there is a lot of cyber threat about and some of it might come in their direction. Some organizations go further, by collecting (or paying a specialist provider to collect) information about cyber security threats that directly affect their organization. The providers collect such information by trawling through open sources and less easily accessible sites on the dark web. Sometimes they find a smoking gun in the form of data or passwords that have been stolen from the client organization. Following such discoveries, the victims are usually stimulated to review their cyber defences. But even if the collectors find no such evidence, it would be wrong to conclude that there is no threat. It may be that the collectors just haven't found it.

The protective security planning for the London 2012 Olympics was explicitly risk-based and intelligence-led. Planning for this gargantuan event—the UK's biggest ever peacetime security operation—began in earnest on 6 July 2005, the day the International Olympic Committee announced their decision to award the next Games to London.[13] Twenty hours later, London was struck by the multiple suicide bombings of 7/7 in which fifty-two people were killed and more than 700 were physically injured. At that point the Games were seven years in the future and there was, not surprisingly, precious little specific intelligence about the security threats to the Games, whether from terrorism or any other source. Nonetheless, it was all too obvious that the terrorist threat environment for the UK was grim and set to remain so for the foreseeable future. The decision was taken at the outset to plan the protective security for the Games on the assumption that the UK national threat level for terrorism in the summer of 2012 would be SEVERE ('an attack is highly likely'). This planning assumption shaped multi-million-pound decisions about the design of new Games venues that took years to build, with security designed into them from the beginning.[14] The security planning could not possibly have relied only on intelligence about the threats. By the time such intelligence began to flow, it would have been too late to make major changes to the infrastructure. A risk-based and intelligence-led approach was the only credible option.

The covert nature of the most serious threats means that intelligence is not the same as information.[15] Intelligence may be regarded as *information that threat actors want to keep secret*. To reinforce this distinction, intelligence practitioners sometimes refer to it as 'secret intelligence'.[16] The distinction between intelligence and open-source information is well understood in the national security arena, where they are subject to different legal controls, though it is not always fully appreciated elsewhere. There is no doubt that powerful conclusions can be drawn from open-source data. Nonetheless, the sorts of security issues that national governments have to worry about must also be informed by secret intelligence. The answers are not all waiting to be plucked from the internet. For those outside the government bubble, good security advice that is based on secret intelligence is readily available online from government agencies.

The secret intelligence needed to counter the most serious threats to national security is obtained by state agencies through covert means such as electronic and physical surveillance and human sources. In democratic states, this requires rigorous checks and balances to ensure that the use of intrusive powers is legal, necessary, and proportionate. The states that pose the biggest threats, notably Russia, China, Iran, and North Korea, are less fastidious. Threat actors understand in general terms that they may be subject to surveillance, but seldom know exactly when or how it is done. Criminals, terrorists, and hostile foreign states have benefitted enormously from industrial-scale leaks of sensitive information by Edward Snowden and other former government employees in recent years. Knowing precisely which communications media can and cannot be intercepted by government agencies has enabled threat actors to keep more of their secrets secret, putting the rest of us at greater risk.

Threat actors are not the only ones who need to keep secrets. Good security depends on ensuring that sensitive information—especially anything that reveals specific vulnerabilities—is kept away from potential attackers. A precautionary rule of thumb is that *whenever a new vulnerability is revealed, a threat actor will eventually try to exploit it.* A list of security vulnerabilities is in effect a how-to manual for attackers. So, think twice before revealing information that might unintentionally inform threat actors about your vulnerabilities. Therein lies another difference between safety and security. Mature safety regimes, notably those in aviation, healthcare, maritime transport, and the civil nuclear industry, are characterized by a culture of extensive sharing of information about safety risks. In the case of security, however, the widespread sharing of information about specific security vulnerabilities should be approached with circumspection to prevent it escaping into the hands of threat actors.

Businesses and institutions of all sorts clearly benefit enormously from sharing information, both internally and externally, in line with the well-established principle of *need-to-share*. However, some have thrown the security baby out with the information-sharing bathwater by neglecting the less conventional principle of *need-to-know*. Websites and social media postings often reveal details that seem innocuous to the originator but are of real value to criminals or other threat actors. A recurring example is the marketing material published by companies selling IT systems or security equipment. Their websites sometimes display technical descriptions of how their systems work, together with a list of their prestigious customers, thereby providing threat actors with guidance on how to attack these potential victims. Secrecy is not universally bad and the measured use of discretion has its place.

Avoiding inappropriate sharing will not be enough to protect the most sensitive information, which a threat actor might try to obtain covertly, probably by cyber means. Such information requires additional protection, both when it is at rest on a database and when it is in motion across communications channels. A standard form of protection is robust *encryption*, which should prevent any stolen or intercepted material from being read by prying eyes. Not all encryption is robust, however.

Poor communications security can have deadly consequences, as the British found to their cost in World War Two. During the Battle of the Atlantic, Nazi Germany came close to severing Britain's vital maritime supply chain from North America. Although the British had enjoyed success in penetrating the German naval Enigma codes, thanks to cryptanalysts at Bletchley Park, they had taken less care over securing their own naval communications. The Germans broke the British encryption and routinely read them. As a consequence, German U-boats were able to find and sink more than a thousand allied merchant ships in 1941 alone. A confidential British report written after the end of the war noted that 'this leakage of information through inadequate codes and ciphers...not only cost us dear in men and ships but very nearly lost us the war'. The Germans made the same mistake of believing that their own coded communications were secure, even though they had penetrated their enemy's communications.[17] Both sides were complacent about their own protective security and underestimated the capability of their adversary. The same error is still being repeated today. Sometimes, the best form of defence is defence.

Contemplate the Future

Protective security is not only a matter of staying safe now; it is also about *preparing to stay safe in the future*. Thinking ahead is crucial because today's threats will inevitably change and new ones will emerge. Detecting and understanding new threats and then devising security countermeasures takes time. Unless we think ahead, we will find ourselves perpetually fighting yesterday's battles and lagging behind in the security arms race. It pays to form the habit of systematically contemplating the future, despite the immediate pressures of dealing with the here-and-now.

Various techniques that are well established in other spheres can help to explore the possible futures of security threats. Horizon scanning, wargaming, red teaming, modelling, computer simulation, and gamification can all stimulate creative thinking about the future threat environment. But no matter how good they are at painting interesting pictures of possible scenarios, they cannot reliably foretell the future of security threats, just as they have demonstrably failed to foretell the futures of geopolitics, financial markets, or national elections.

The feeble success rate of future-watching cannot be blamed solely on inadequate intelligence or faulty analysis. There are more fundamental reasons why predicting the future of security threats, political movements, or other complex systems is a mug's game. Many threat actors would struggle to articulate their *own* plans beyond a relatively short time horizon. They might be clear about their broad aspirations, but what they end up doing on a given day is another matter. Much of what happens is a product of chance and necessity, as we saw with the Anders Breivik attacks described in Rule 2. As in many other terrorist plots, the events that eventually unfolded were heavily influenced by unforeseen circumstances and bore only a loose relationship to the original plan.[18]

In addition to the powerful variables of chance, circumstance, and the capriciousness of threat actors, any would-be future-watcher must contend with the inherent unpredictability of complex adaptive systems (as also described in Rule 2). Predicting the future behaviour of dynamic and adaptive security threats is a prime example of a so-called *wicked problem*—meaning a problem that is hard to describe, has many inter-dependent causes, and does not have a right answer.[19] Other examples of wicked problems include climate change, poverty, and political conflict. Attempts to solve wicked problems sometimes have unintended conse-quences that make matters worse. *The only thing that can be predicted with confidence is that there will be surprises.* And the trick, as David Omand has pointed out, is not to be surprised by surprises.[20]

Despite the inherent obstacles and the dismal track record, pundits in many fields persist in making confident predictions and being endlessly surprised by the surprises. They overanalyse past events and use this as the foundation for overconfident predictions about future events. They fall prey to the universal human predisposition of seeing patterns even where there are none. Having seemingly made sense of the past, they feel confi-dent to do the same for the future, and hence plausible narratives about what *has* happened segue into plausible assertions about what *will* happen.

The confidence with which such predictions are made should be a warning sign in itself, because psychological research has shown there to be little or no correlation between being confident about a judgement and being correct.[21] (In marked contrast to the pundits, good scientists habitually draw attention to the uncertainties in their judgements.) There is a world of difference between being confident about future events and being right.

Having got that off my chest, I am going to speculate about possible futures. Despite knowing that our actual future will differ in surprising ways from our predicted future, it is still useful to contemplate the sorts of threats we might have to confront, so that we can take prudent precautions. Wicked problems may not have solutions, but they can at least be tamed.[22] This highly tentative form of crystal ball-gazing can be approached in three ways: extrapolating from current trends; learning from history; and considering the potential misuses of emerging technology.

The simplest and commonest way of contemplating the near-term future is by *extrapolating from current trends*—in other words, forecasting more of the same. Of course, current trends will not continue indefinitely, new threats will surely emerge, and reliable long-term predictions will remain beyond our reach. Nonetheless, there is value in identifying clear trends in the current threat environment and considering where they may lead. To use a meteorological metaphor, it may be easier to forecast the general threat climate than the precise threat weather. At least then we can decide whether to buy more umbrellas or more air conditioning. A second way of contemplating the future is by *learning from history*. In particular, this means considering old forms of threat that are no longer in play but which could plausibly re-emerge in new forms. We will look at some examples of what might be called 'blasts from the past'. A third approach is examining how threat actors might *exploit emerging technologies*. Most technology is dual use: fire, knives, aircraft, and computers can be used to do good or cause harm. A precautionary rule of thumb is that if a new technology *could* be misused to cause harm, it *will* be misused to cause harm. It is therefore prudent to contemplate the possibility in advance and consider what might be done to prevent it.

How might the future threat environment look, based on the judicious application of these three approaches? Some existing trends seem firmly set to persist for the foreseeable future. We can be fairly confident, for example, that Russia will continue to conduct hybrid warfare by deploying its potent cocktail of covert and semi-covert cyber attacks, information warfare operations, cyber subversion, tactical and strategic deception, military provocation, and old-fashioned espionage in order to gain political and economic advantage. It has served them well since 1917 and shows no signs of fading. Another existing trend that is virtually certain to persist for at least a generation is the evolution of Islamist terrorism in its various guises.

In a different sphere, we should expect more protective security effort to be directed at space. Society is critically dependent on space-based global navigation satellite systems (GNSS) for vital functions including telecommunications, navigation, industrial processes, weather forecasting, agriculture, transport, and mapping. Financial markets depend on them for the precise timings required for audit trails, and most forms of air, land, and sea transport depend on them for navigation.[23] The risks to satellites and other space-based infrastructure arise from both natural hazards (space weather and space junk) and hostile action through cyber or physical means.[24] A satellite is vulnerable to even the tiniest piece of orbiting junk, and its connectivity with terrestrial systems creates opportunities for hacking. There have been strong indications that Russia has experimented with spoofing GNSS signals to alter the apparent locations of vessels and places. The security threats to space technology seem set to grow.

What about learning from history? What 'blasts from the past' might we face if old threats were to return in new forms? The history of terrorism shows that various attack methods have swung in and out of favour over time. Two in particular stand out: attacks on infrastructure and assassinating individuals in public life.

During its terrorist campaigns in the final quarter of the twentieth century, PIRA demonstrated the effectiveness of sabotaging infrastructure—a type of attack that is not currently in widespread use by terrorist groups in western nations. Normal life depends on the continued functioning of critical national infrastructure (CNI), which includes facilities vital for the provision of energy, communications, food, water, government, healthcare, emergency services, and financial services. Of these, energy, and particularly electricity, is the most fundamental. Without electricity we have no tele-communications, no government, no banking, no emergency services, and no traffic control. Before long, we would have no food or water because their supply is also dependent on electrical power. Sabotage attacks against CNI, whether by physical or cyber means, have the potential to cause severe disruption, economic damage, and large-scale loss of life.

PIRA repeatedly targeted energy infrastructure and sites of economic importance. One highly significant episode was a 1996 plot to simultan-eously destroy a ring of six electricity substations serving Greater London using custom-built explosive devices. The plot was discovered and foiled by MI5 and the police.[25] Had PIRA succeeded, they would have cut off the electricity supply to millions of people for months. The sudden loss of power to a large region would have had cascading effects on the rest of the national supply grid. It had the potential to force a so-called Black Start, which is the difficult and as yet thankfully unused procedure for recovering from a large-scale or total shutdown of a national grid.[26] An electricity distribution network is a delicate beast; once it is knocked over, standing it up again takes time. Strange as it may seem, many power stations need to draw power from the grid to start up their generators. If most or all of the grid suddenly collapses, the resulting Black Start requires painstakingly restarting individual power stations and reconnecting them to the grid one by one, then reinstating the supply to small areas, and finally joining up these 'power islands' across the country. Had PIRA achieved its aims, the results would have been devastating.

At the trial of the PIRA terrorists it was claimed that they had based their plan on information gleaned from an electricity industry handbook, which they had found in a public library. It was a salutary reminder of how seemingly innocuous information can reveal key security vulnerabilities.[27] Much has changed since 1996, partly in response to the PIRA plot, and a great deal has been done in the UK, US, and other nations to make CNI more resilient. Remarkably, the 1996 PIRA plot was not the first attempt by Irish republicans to sabotage Britain's energy infrastructure. In 1939, the Irish Republican Army (IRA) targeted the electricity supply system and carried out an attack that cut off power to 25,000 people in north London.[28]

A second possible lesson from history is the strategy of assassinating politicians, officials, and other individuals in public life. Former terrorist organizations such as PIRA and the Irish National Liberation Army (INLA) demonstrated the corrosive effects of systematically targeting and killing public figures and senior officials. INLA assassinated Airey Neave MP in the House of Commons car park in 1979 and PIRA assassinated Ian Gow MP at his home in 1990. In 1984, PIRA came close to killing the then Prime Minister, Margaret Thatcher, in the Brighton hotel bombing. After the Brighton bombing, which killed five people but narrowly missed its main target, PIRA issued a statement that came to epitomize the advantage enjoyed by threat actors in asymmetric conflicts. It said: 'Today we were unlucky, but remember we only have to be lucky once. You will have to be lucky always.'[29] PIRA came close to killing a British Prime Minister again in 1991, when they fired mortar bombs at Ten Downing Street during a Cabinet meeting. On this occasion, protective security made a difference: the windows of Number Ten had recently been fitted with reinforced glass.[30] Even so, the bombs would probably have killed half the Cabinet had they landed a few metres closer.

The current generation of Islamist terrorists have carried out assassinations in Iraq and Syria, and in 2016 a lone Islamist killed a French military officer at his home in France. However, targeted assassinations of individuals in public life in western states have not so far featured prominently among their attack methods. Of all the Islamist terrorist attacks that were launched in western Europe between 1994 and the end of 2016, very few were aimed at prominent individuals and none was aimed at state leaders.[31] It remains to be seen whether Islamist terrorists will in future launch a systematic campaign of assassination. If they do, they might be expected to attack the more vulnerable individuals who do not receive armed protection from the state, reflecting the Islamists' general track record of choosing soft targets.

Two more possible blasts from the past would be the resurgence of state-sponsored terrorism and terrorist attacks against western targets by secular

Palestinian groups. Both phenomena were prevalent in the 1970s and 1980s, when Iran, Syria, Libya, Iraq, and East Germany used terrorist groups as proxy weapons against their western enemies, and secular Palestinian terrorist groups such as the Abu Nidhal Organization carried out major terrorist attacks in Europe. Arguably, the Russian assassination of Alexander Litvinenko and attempted assassination of Sergei Skripal in the UK were instances of state terrorism.

Finally, how might emerging technologies upset the established order by presenting threat actors with interesting new ways of causing harm? Many commentators agree that among the newer technologies with clear potential for malicious use are the Internet of Things (IoT), synthetic biology, artificial intelligence (AI), blockchain, drones, robots, and quantum computing. There are others. We will look at the IoT in Rule 8.

Synthetic biology, which enables bacteria and viruses to be designed and built to order, could provide a means for terrorists to acquire biological weapons, though it is not easy. AI and machine learning will create many new ways of causing harm, both deliberate and unintended. The first inklings of what might lie ahead have already been seen. In 2016, for example, Microsoft unveiled an online chatbot that turned into a racist Holocaust-denier after it was subverted by mischievous trolls. Hostile foreign states and cyber criminals have been exploring how AI can greatly increase the scale, speed, and ferocity of cyber attacks. On the other hand, AI is already providing the potential victims of cyber attacks with tools for defending themselves by automatically identifying and responding to malware.

Blockchain technologies will continue to offer new ways of enabling crime. In recent years, criminals and hostile foreign states have unleashed waves of cyber attacks using ransomware, a form of malicious software that encrypts the victim's data, rendering it unusable. The attackers often offer to unlock the data in return for a ransom payment in the form of a crypto-currency such as Bitcoin, which is based on blockchain technology.[32] Some victims pay up, though they seldom get their data back. Cryptocurrencies are attractive tools for threat actors because they offer the prospect of moving money or other forms of digital data without going near a bank or central authority. As you would expect, the authorities have been developing ways of tracing cryptocurrencies and the criminals who use them.[33] On the positive side, blockchain technologies offer new ways of protecting the integrity of data, as we shall see in Rule 8.

Unmanned aerial vehicles (UAVs, or drones) have already become practical tools for invading privacy and conducting terrorism. Jihadist groups have used them in Syria. UAVs can present a formidable threat when deployed in large, coordinated swarms that overwhelm a target's defences. Another unappetising prospect is autonomous killer robots that have found their way into the hands of terrorists or criminals.[34] One disconcerting scenario is the use of 'slaughterbots': swarms of armed and AI-enabled drones that could locate and assassinate specific individuals.[35] The precedent for using a robot offensively in a civilian environment has already been set. In 2016, police in the US used a remotely controlled bomb disposal robot, equipped with an explosive device, to kill a sniper.

Quantum cryptography could make it possible for threat actors to communicate covertly in ways that are physically impossible to intercept and read. On the other hand, doomsayers have been predicting the end of governments' ability to intercept communications ('going dark') since the 1970s, and yet here we are, decades later, with intelligence agencies around the world still going strong. Moreover, the emerging technology of quantum computing could greatly improve the ability of defenders to decrypt the threat actors' encrypted communications.[36] Or the balance of advantage might swing the other way, with threat actors using quantum computing to breach our information security defences. Time will tell. New technologies like these and others will continue to present new threats and new opportunities, both for threat actors and defenders. The protective security arms race will go on.

RULE 4

THERE ARE THREE WAYS
TO REDUCE RISK

*The three ways to reduce security risk are to reduce the threat, reduce
the vulnerability to attack, or reduce the impact of a successful attack.*

———

Managing Risk

The purpose of protective security is to manage certain types of risk.
The concept of managing risk is a relatively modern one, historically
speaking, but it works. What does it entail in practice?

At its bare simplest, the process of managing security risks (and indeed
other sorts of risk) involves three basic steps. The first is to *understand* the
risks you are facing. For protective security to work well, it must be shaped
according to the particular risks it is expected to confront. Each individual
and each organization faces its own combination of security risks, which
change over time. For many, the biggest risks stem from conventional
crime or cyber attack, while for some terrorism is the biggest concern. The
second step is to *decide* the extent to which you are willing to tolerate those
risks. Assuming you have properly understood the risks, you might conclude that the current situation is acceptable, in which case you need do
nothing further for the time being. If, however, the risk exceeds your
tolerance, then step three is to *act* to reduce it to an acceptable level.[1] As
we are about to see, there are three ways of acting to reduce security risk—
namely, by reducing the threat, reducing the vulnerability, and reducing the
impact. Implicit in this approach to managing security risk is the principle

that *not everything that could be done should be done*.[2] And even if everything that could be done were to be done, it is rarely possible to eliminate the risks altogether.

Security risks are continually evolving and therefore these steps need to be repeated cyclically, as shown below. Even if you decide to tolerate today's risks, you might have to take action tomorrow, when they change.

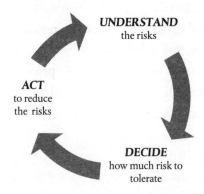

UNDERSTAND
the risks

DECIDE
how much risk to
tolerate

ACT
to reduce
the risks

This simple three-step process has wider applicability in other spheres besides protective security. It is not perfect, however. One significant drawback with this model, if it is applied simplistically, is its potential to keep the defender permanently on the back foot, always waiting to react to the threat actor's latest move. If the defender presents a static target, and the threat actor is always allowed to take the initiative, then the defender will remain at least one step behind in the security arms race.

One way of countering this drawback is by contemplating the future (as discussed in Rule 2) and planning ahead. Another way is by not presenting a static target—in other words, continually varying the protective security regime to make it harder for threat actors to find ways of defeating it. Security regimes that vary in this way are described as dynamic, as opposed to static. The concept of *dynamic security* is especially relevant in the cyber domain, where the cycle of threat and countermeasure moves very rapidly.[3] Dynamic security is discussed in Rule 9, along with other distinguishing features of good protective security. There are other strategies for gaining advantage over threat actors. One is deterrence, which is discussed below, and another is resilience, which forms the subject of Rule 5.

Know What You Are Trying to Protect

Back to step one, understanding the risks. A prerequisite for understanding security risks is knowing what you are trying to protect—that is, the people, information, money, intellectual property, buildings, infrastructure, reputations, or other assets that would be compromised if the risk were to materialize. Any organization or individual will have a range of assets that vary in significance, face different levels of risk, and require different levels of protection. Some assets, such as money and buildings, are more obvious and easier to value than others, like intellectual property and reputation. It is a cliché, but nonetheless true, that an organization's most precious asset is its people.

Trying to protect every asset to the maximum extent is impractical and unaffordable, making it important to identify the most treasured assets and ensure that they at least receive adequate protection. For instance, a company might make a reasoned choice to concentrate its finite cyber security resources on protecting a business-critical IT system and accept that it will do less to protect its public website from embarrassing defacement because it matters less. Comprehensive protection is hard to provide without a comprehensive knowledge of the assets to be protected. One example is updating software and digital devices with the latest security patches. You cannot comprehensively patch your systems if you do not know what systems you have.

Security practitioners often find that organizations have only a limited understanding of their assets. This can make them prone to underestimating the potential impact of a security breach. Some organizations have blind spots which leave them reeling at the consequences of a big breach. A financial services business that concentrates its entire security effort on protecting its money could still suffer serious financial and reputational harm if hackers stole its customers' personal records and sold them on the dark web.

Identifying the totality of assets can be difficult when it comes to digital data. Multiple copies and supposedly deleted data often lurk unseen in hidden corners of archives, end-user devices, cloud services, and suppliers. Few organizations know where all their data is. According to various estimates, at least half of all the data held by organizations is so-called *dark data* that does not appear on any inventories or registers. Dark data is effectively invisible to its owners unless they take active steps to track it down. The hackers who make money from stealing personal information or intellectual property do not care whether they steal it from an organization's main database or one of its unseen dark repositories. The damage to the victim's reputation and finances will be the same. *Data discovery* tools have been developed for rooting around in networks and identifying all the data.

In addition to sitting on large quantities of dark data, most organizations also have significant amounts of *shadow IT*—that is, digital devices and software that are unauthorized and do not belong to the organization but which nonetheless connect to its network. Shadow IT often includes personal devices that employees attach to the corporate network. Sometimes, contractors or internal teams install shadow IT without the knowledge of the corporate IT department. Their motives are usually well intentioned, but the mere existence of such unknown assets creates risk, and the fact that shadow IT is usually even less secure than corporate IT adds to the problem.

Having identified the assets you wish to protect, a desirable but widely neglected next step would be to *classify* those assets according to their value—or, more precisely, according to the amount of harm that would be incurred if they were lost, stolen, or compromised. The simplest classification system would divide physical or virtual assets into just two categories: the most valuable (crown jewels) and the rest. Finer gradations allow a more nuanced approach, at the cost of a bigger administrative overhead. The archetypal examples of asset classification are the marking schemes that governments have used for more than a century to classify official information.[4]

Systematically distinguishing between the most sensitive and less sensitive information has a number of advantages. It allows the most valuable assets to be singled out for suitable protection. The act of classifying assets also helps to raise security awareness, by reminding people to think about the value of the material they are handling. It is easy to become blasé if you are handling sensitive information every working day.

Once you know what you are trying to protect, you can decide who should have access to it. Protective security can then be used to block unauthorized access. Access to digital networks and data is controlled through *authentication credentials* such as passwords, while physical access requires a physical pass or key. A basic rule, known as the *principle of least access*, is to limit access to those who need it. This principle is valid in both the physical and digital domains. However, it runs counter to a predominant organizational culture of maximizing access to information and facilities. Implementing the principle of least access usually requires some trade-off between security and ease of working.

Mind Your Third Parties

When identifying the assets that you want to protect, you should consider whether people who sit outside your organization or trusted network have access to those assets or hold them on your behalf. Any organization or individual will be exposed to some extent to indirect security risks arising through third parties to whom they are connected in some way, such as suppliers who provide outsourced IT or cleaners who have unrestricted access to buildings out of hours. This form of risk is known as *third-party risk* (or supply chain risk).

Third-party risk is ubiquitous in the cyber domain, because pretty well every organization and business is connected digitally to suppliers, customers, or other third parties. Some external connections may not even be apparent to the asset owner. The problem is akin to giving strangers the keys to your house without always knowing that you have done so. Many organizations pay scant attention to the problem. For example, a UK government survey of over 1,500 businesses found that barely one in seven (13 per cent) had placed any requirements on their suppliers to adhere to cyber security standards.[5]

Third parties are often the soft underbelly. Hackers have long understood that the easiest way to attack a well-defended target is often through one of its less well-protected third parties. Having penetrated the more vulnerable cyber security of, say, the accountant or legal adviser, the hacker finds an easier route through the cyber defences of their primary target. A notorious third-party cyber attack took place in 2013, when the unfortunately named US online retailer Target suffered a huge security breach in which hackers stole the credit card details of more than 40 million customers. The hackers did this by first attacking the more vulnerable IT system of a small company that was supplying Target with heating and air conditioning services.

Third-party risk becomes even fruitier if the third party in question is a supplier of security services—for example, an outsourced cyber security or physical guarding company. Good security vendors tend to be more conscious of security than the average supplier, but they are seldom perfect. They also tend to have greater access to their customers' assets. The upshot is that if threat actors manage to penetrate a security supplier, the resulting impact on its clients is likely to be even worse.

Third-party risk applies to terrorism too. Weak security in one place can impose risks on others. Consider the Lockerbie disaster, for example.[6] On the evening of 21 December 1988, a PanAm 747 airliner en route from London to New York fell out of the sky over the small Scottish town of Lockerbie, killing all 259 people on board and eleven on the ground. It remains the deadliest ever terrorist attack in the UK. A huge international investigation established that the plane was destroyed by a bomb inside a suitcase in the luggage hold. A Libyan intelligence officer in Malta had loaded the suitcase onto a flight from Malta to Frankfurt, from where it was transferred to London and then loaded onto the PanAm flight to New York. The bomb was designed to destroy the plane over the Atlantic, leaving no trace, but weather forced the plane further north and it exploded over Scotland. The transferred suitcase was not security-screened at Frankfurt or London because it was assumed to have been screened in Malta. Thus, a flight from London was destroyed because of inadequate security in Malta.

Decide How Much Risk to Tolerate

Step two of the basic risk management cycle is deciding how much risk you are willing to tolerate. This entails weighing the security risks against the costs and risks of taking action to reduce them. Managing any form of risk involves making decisions about competing priorities and finite resources. Protective security costs money and can add friction to the conduct of normal life. A decision to tolerate a certain amount of security risk may therefore be entirely rational, provided the decision is based on an adequate understanding of the relevant factors. That is not always the case.

A bit of terminology cannot be avoided here. The level of security risk that applies with the existing protective security measures may be referred to as the *current risk*.[7] The willingness of an organization or individual to accept a certain level of risk is known as its *risk tolerance*. If the current risk exceeds your risk tolerance, then you should act to reduce the risk to a lower level that would be acceptable, which is known as the *target risk*. Once the risk has been reduced to its target level, the target risk becomes the new current risk, and so on.

Risk management specialists and consultants often refer to *risk appetite* when discussing other sorts of risk, such as financial or project risk, and the term has gained currency in the security world. Some managers talk boldly about having a big risk appetite—by which they really mean having a big appetite for success—while privately banking on the security risk never materializing on their watch. The notion of risk appetite makes sense when deciding about financial investments or business processes.

It underlines the reality that any new venture carries risks that must be recognized and accepted. However, the language is less helpful in the security domain, where most people are, with good reason, highly risk-averse. Nasty security incidents tend to have a chilling effect on talk of 'risk appetites'. Arguably, no one should have an 'appetite' for security risk; it is, at most, something we reluctantly decide to tolerate. A risk appetite is what you have when you *choose* to take a risk; a risk tolerance is what you are forced to decide when risk is imposed on you.

It is an awkward fact that it often takes a serious security incident to bring about improvements in protective security, even when the risk has been identified in advance. Why must we always wait for something bad to happen before acting? Why can't we act on our judgement rather than having action forced upon us after the event? Perhaps a small sliver of blame lies with the self-assured language of 'risk appetite'. Most of the blame, however, lies with an inherent human predisposition towards excessive optimism. This and other forms of psychological bias are described in Rule 7.

Managing risk requires judgements about risk tolerance. However, the notion that risk tolerance can be determined objectively, using quantitative formulae, is a myth. Judgements about risk tolerance are ultimately a matter of values and beliefs, not accountancy or hard science. Risk tolerances vary among individuals, organizations, and societies according to their experiences, cultures, personalities, and circumstances. Mathematical formulae that purport to reveal an organization's risk tolerance according to objective criteria turn out, on closer scrutiny, to be built on subjective judgements about values. Quantitative analysis can certainly add value to the assessment of risk tolerance, but it cannot substitute for the underlying judgements about what really matters. The measurement and mismeasurement of risk are discussed in Rule 9.

The intrinsically values-based nature of risk tolerance helps to explain why governments around the world have always been reluctant to quantify their tolerance of the risk from terrorism. No democratically accountable government would willingly announce that their policy is to accept, say, five more terrorist attacks a year in return for reduced spending on counter-terrorism. By implication, their risk tolerance is zero. In reality, of course, governments recognize that zero risk is unachievable. They accept pragmatically that it comes down to achieving the best possible outcomes within the constraints of societal acceptability and finite resources. The question then arises as to how much security a society will accept and at what cost—and that is a political judgement, not an accounting calculation. The stance of most governments is to reduce the terrorist risk to as close to zero as practicable. A similar stance is formally established within the civil nuclear industry, where the regulations require the safety risk of a major radiological release to be 'as low as reasonably practicable' (ALARP).

It has been suggested that we are all becoming less tolerant of bad things happening, and that this may be because science and technology increasingly offer potential solutions to almost any problem. This proposition is superficially plausible, as why would anyone want to tolerate risks if there are ways of banishing them? The snag, of course, is that the means of banishing risks are not always affordable or acceptable.[8]

Reducing Threat, Vulnerability, and Impact

Having understood the risks, and decided how much to tolerate, you can then act to mitigate the risks that are not tolerable. How is this done? If you enjoy Byzantine complexity and arcane jargon, then the worlds of physical and cyber security can provide them in spades, with a long menu of intricate policy frameworks and technical standards. But there is a much simpler way. As we saw in Rule 2, all security risks are composed of three basic elements—threat, vulnerability, and impact. Consequently, there are essentially *three ways to reduce risk*—by reducing the threat, reducing the potential victim's vulnerability to attack, or reducing the impact of a successful attack (or some combination of the three).

Reducing the threat element of risk is generally a tough proposition, especially for the most serious types of threat. Making a big dent in the intentions or capabilities of terrorists, organized criminals, or hostile foreign states is beyond the ability of most businesses, let alone private individuals. Disrupting dangerous threat actors requires the combined efforts of the police, intelligence agencies, and in some cases the military. That said, there are feasible ways of tilting security threats in the right direction.

One proven approach to mitigating threat is through *deterrence*. In the context of protective security, deterrence means influencing the intention element of threat. It works by persuading threat actors to abandon their attack plans, or go elsewhere, because they reckon that their attempts are likely to be too hazardous, too costly, or unsuccessful. Deterrence is commonly achieved, sometimes unintentionally, by having visible security defences that threat actors find sufficiently daunting. During their planning for what became the 9/11 attacks of 2001, Al Qaeda considered attacking nuclear plants in the US, with the aim of causing large-scale radiological contamination, but abandoned the idea because they judged the targets to be too hard.[9]

Deterrence can be subtly amplified through *deterrence communications*, which are public-facing communications that have been designed to influence threat actors in the right ways. For instance, an organization might use its website to convey the impression that it has a proficient and dynamic security regime. This can usually be done in ways that are both reassuring to customers and off-putting to criminals or terrorists.

In the cyber domain, the concept of deterrence is somewhat less mature but developing rapidly. As nations acquire cyber warfare weapons capable of inflicting serious harm, they are increasingly pushing out classic deterrence communications. The UK government's national cyber security strategy makes it clear that the principles of deterrence are as valid for the cyber domain as they are in the physical domain. It promises to treat a major cyber attack on the UK as seriously as it would a conventional attack. Even so, the threat of retaliation may be insufficient to deter some non-state actors, such as cyber criminals or politically motivated hackers, while the more aggressive state actors may be tempted to test the boundaries. History suggests that Russia, for one, will continue to rattle the cage in order to gauge the determination behind the deterrence. More interestingly, the UK cyber strategy has an explicit aim of increasing the economic, political, diplomatic, and strategic costs to the threat actors, increasing their risk of being found out, and reducing the benefits of attacking. This more nuanced approach is intended to deter all types of cyber threat actors.

Deterrence is aimed at influencing would-be attackers' specific plans, not dispelling their general aspirations. A terrorist group might be deterred from carrying out a planned attack, because they have been spooked by security force activity, yet retain their desire to conduct similar attacks in future. In many cases, deterrence causes attackers to turn their attention to other, more vulnerable targets. When this happens, it results in *threat displacement* rather than strictly threat reduction. The threat may be displaced in terms of target choice (going somewhere softer) or attack method (switching to easier, often cruder weapons). Much of the protective security for countering terrorism results in some threat displacement, though it still reduces the overall risk.

There is good empirical evidence that deterrence can reduce or displace some forms of conventional crime such as theft and burglary. One of the main reasons why vehicle theft fell markedly in the UK, US, and other countries from the late 1990s was because of widespread improvements in vehicle security following the introduction of central locking, alarms, and immobilizers.[10] There is also evidence that deterrence makes a useful contribution to countering terrorism. One of the reasons why there was no successful terrorist attack on the London 2012 Olympics is thought to have been the deterrent effect of visibly high levels of security, reinforced by strong deterrence communications from the UK authorities. (That was not the only reason, of course.) The visible physical security was not sufficient to deter the cyber threat actors who caused a stir on the day of the Olympics opening ceremony, when the authorities discovered signs of a covert cyber intrusion into the electricity infrastructure supplying power to the Olympic stadium.[11] The opening ceremony nonetheless proceeded without a hitch, watched by a global media audience of around three billion people.

One aspect of threat is particularly amenable to deterrence. When criminals plan to burgle a house, terrorists plan to attack a public place, or hackers plan to breach an IT system, they usually start by studying their intended target in order to find its vulnerabilities. Threat actors do this physically, by going to look at the target, or virtually, by researching the target online. Terrorists often do both. It is remarkable just how much threat actors can find out about people, places, and organizations simply from sitting at a computer. (We will return to this issue later.) This pre-attack information gathering is known as *hostile reconnaissance* and it is often susceptible to deterrence and disruption.

Targets facing a high threat from terrorism or conventional crime tend to have visible physical security such as cameras and uniformed guards. The most highly protected sites may additionally deploy security personnel to conduct covert patrols of the surrounding areas and actively search for the subtle (or not so subtle) signs of hostile reconnaissance. If such signs are detected, the covert security may become overt in order to deter, disrupt, or detain the potential attackers. The intention is to create a hostile operating environment for threat actors and disrupt their ability to plan attacks. These tactics are used successfully in airports, train stations, and public places. Furthermore, by protecting sensitive information about a target's vulnerabilities, good security may force the threat actors to rely more on physical reconnaissance, which in turn creates opportunities to spot the would-be attackers and disrupt their plans.

The ability of visible security to deter and disrupt hostile reconnaissance was evident in the case of the solo terrorist Anders Breivik, whose attacks were described in Rule 2. Breivik's subsequent interrogation and trial revealed that he had prepared extensively, using media sources, the inter-net, and physical surveillance to conduct hostile reconnaissance of his targets. Breivik claimed he had been afraid of being detected during his online and physical reconnaissance. He made eight reconnaissance visits to the government building in Oslo that he eventually attacked and abandoned his original plan to drive his vehicle bomb under the building when he found the entrance was controlled.[12]

Deterrence is not the only way of weakening the intention element of threat. Another tactic is deliberately lowering the public profile of the potential target, or obscuring its true significance, in order to make it less attractive to threat actors. The idea is that if threat actors are not thinking about a particular target, or do not regard it as important, they are less likely to attack it. This tactic is known as *security through obscurity*. Some of the UK's vital national infrastructure is housed in buildings that are made to appear nondescript and uninteresting. A degree of obscurity can also be achieved in the cyber domain, by ensuring that revealing information is not published on websites or social media. There is little point in physically obscuring the significance of a sensitive facility if the truth can easily be discovered online.

Security through obscurity is obviously a fragile commodity and not to be relied upon by itself. Once the cat is out of the bag, and the identity or location of a target has been revealed, there is no going back. When that happens, the potential victims feel much safer if they have previously invested in more durable forms of security like locks, alarms, firewalls, and encryption. The nineteenth-century cryptographer Auguste Kerckhoffs made this point specifically in relation to secret codes, when he asserted that a system of cryptography should be designed to remain secure even in the event of everything about the system (except for the actual key) becoming public knowledge.

The principle of enhancing security through obscurity is especially relevant to the *personal security* of individuals who might be the targets of terrorists, criminals, stalkers, internet trolls, or fixated individuals.[13] Threat actors of all types routinely conduct hostile reconnaissance using digital media to identify, locate, and spy on their potential victims. A breed of malicious software known as stalkerware enables abusive partners or stalkers to monitor their victims by loading a covert app onto the victim's phone. Quite often, though, threat actors need not go to the trouble of spying because their victims make it easy for them.

We all broadcast large amounts of information about ourselves through social media and other online activity, often unknowingly. Some of that information can heighten the threat by drawing threat actors' attention to an individual, while other information makes their job easier by revealing the victim's vulnerabilities.

Internet-connected mobile devices and indiscreet social media activity can easily reveal information that makes an attack more likely to succeed, such as the victim's current or future location. Someone whose social media postings display their personal habits, such as their regular use of a particular gym or coffee shop, may be inadvertently helping a stalker who wants to confront them in person. Potential victims do not always appreciate how easily their use of technology can guide a threat actor to their doorstep. A recurring example is the householder who broadcasts their holiday photos on social media, only to find on returning home that observant criminals have exploited this helpful information by burgling their unoccupied house. For instance, in 2017 a rich footballer told the world that his mansion was empty by posting photos of his skiing holiday on Instagram. Burglars seized the opportunity to steal several hundred thousand pounds' worth of luxury items.

In a more insidious example from late 2017, a software company published a global 'heat map' displaying the routes used by millions of people who had been running or cycling with a GPS-enabled smartphone or fitness monitor. An observant student noticed that the heat map also apparently exposed the locations of covert allied military bases in Syria, Afghanistan, and Somalia, along with the jogging routes used by personnel stationed there. A presumed Special Forces forward operating base located inside the Syrian border appeared on the map as a bright spot of light in an otherwise dark space, joined to a bright line running along the top of a nearby dam, where the soldiers presumably went running. Cross-referencing to other sources led researchers to further sensitive places of interest, including western military bases in Niger and Djibouti. A researcher claimed to have used the live data to track a French soldier back to his home in France following an overseas deployment.[14] One take-home message appears to be that if you are a solider on a sensitive foreign mission, you should probably leave your Fitbit or Apple Watch at home.

Anyone who is even mildly concerned about their personal security should find out what information about them is already available online, otherwise known as their *digital footprint*. They should then think about how their digital footprint might affect the intentions and capabilities of criminals, hackers, and other relevant threat actors. Thereafter, they should remain mindful of their personal security, and that of their family and friends, when deciding what information to reveal online, including locational data broadcast by personal devices. Prominent individuals who think they are maintaining a tight grip on their digital footprint often fail to realize how much personal information about them is leaching out through the social media activity of family and friends.

If you fall into the large and expanding category of people who might be targeted by threat actors, you should pause to consider before broadcasting personal information that might stoke their intentions or help them locate you. The availability online of your personal details might not worry you now, but it could come back to haunt you if the threat were to change. One feature of the digital world is that *there is no such thing as 'delete'*. Once your personal information is out there on the web, you can never get it back or control who sees it.

The need to be careful about digital footprints applies with particular force to public figures, police and intelligence officers, military personnel, and others who might be targets for terrorists or violent extremists. At present, terrorists appear to be making relatively limited use of digital media to hunt down named victims, but that could easily change. In the pre-internet era, PIRA ran a frighteningly effective intelligence department, one of whose functions was acquiring personal information about targets for assassination, such as home addresses, vehicle numbers, and patterns of movement. The stirrings of something comparable have been seen more recently in the IS practice of *doxing*, which involves publishing online the personal details of individuals they regard as attractive targets, in the hope that local jihadis will go and kill them. Much of the personal information that IS have exploited in this way was already in the public domain, having been placed online by the targets themselves. A variant on this theme is *cat phishing*, in which threat actors use fake social media profiles of attractive women (or men) to lure men (or women) into revealing personal details or other sensitive information. The Taliban have used this tactic on Facebook to identify serving soldiers. Doxing, in the more general sense of breaking internet anonymity, can also be used *against* threat actors, as seen in the growing practice of revealing online the personal identities of internet trolls.

A different and more robust way of enhancing security through obscurity is by using bespoke or unusual security hardware or software that is unfamiliar to threat actors. Most security systems are relatively standardized and come from a limited number of suppliers. Threat actors can buy them, dismantle them, and reverse-engineer them. Once they know how to bypass a particular system, the threat actors potentially have access to all of its many users. However, if your security system is unique or uncommon, threat actors are less likely to have an established means of breaching it. They would have to invest time and effort in finding a solution, which would work only for the small number of targets using that technology. In this way, bespoke security increases the up-front cost to threat actors and reduces the benefits of developing a capability. The threat actors are better off fishing in the much larger pool of conventionally secured targets. This principle, which could be thought of as *security through peculiarity*, is especially relevant in the cyber domain. Hackers have vast numbers of targets to choose from, most of which use common types of software. The obvious downside of security through peculiarity is that bespoke systems tend to cost more and may be less desirable in other ways than standard products.

A third tactic for reducing threat is *distraction*, which borrows an age-old technique of pickpockets, cardsharps, and fraudsters. Distraction works by diverting the threat actor's attention away from the real target by presenting a more conspicuous but sham target. Nation states also play the distraction game on the military and geopolitical stages.

Distraction is much talked about, but less often practised, in cyber security. Naturally, threat actors also make use of it. A common ploy by hackers is mounting a highly visible denial-of-service attack on an organization's public website and then, while its cyber security staff are distracted, conducting a covert attack against the corporate network, where bigger prizes are found. A variant of cyber distraction is the *honeypot* tactic, in which a vulnerable network is deliberately set up to attract hackers away from real targets and capture information about their methods. The Japanese government announced in 2017 that it was planning to build decoy computer systems resembling the real systems used by the government and well-known companies. As well as diverting attacks away from the real targets, the decoys would enable the authorities to analyse the hackers' techniques and convert this knowledge into better cyber defences.[15] A few years earlier, the descriptively named Honeynet Project set up a series of computer systems specifically to learn about the capabilities of hackers.[16]

The level of threat can be made to go up as well as down. Potential victims sometimes unwittingly attract additional threat through their own behaviour, in a sort of reverse deterrence. One example, which applies mainly in the cyber domain, is the unfortunate practice of goading threat actors. Organizations that publicly boast about the excellence of their cyber security sometimes find they have shot themselves in the foot. Rather than deterring cyber attacks, they attract more threat by presenting hackers with an irresistible challenge. The personal satisfaction of defeating supposedly impregnable cyber security is a powerful motivation for some hackers, who enjoy proving that there is no such thing. (And there *is* no such thing.) With the cyber world's usual flair for steely labels, this sort of hacking challenge is known as 'capturing the flag'. Similar motivation lay behind the first documented instance of hacking, which took place in the 1960s, when enthusiasts discovered how to 'crash' the mainframe computer at MIT. These trail-blazing hackers were motivated by curiosity and fun, not malice.[17]

Boasting about *bad* cyber security is also likely to attract threat. Hackers of all stripes are naturally attracted to self-proclaimed soft targets. One widely publicized instance took place in 2017, when three British Members of Parliament declared on social media that they routinely shared their parliamentary login passwords with their staff. The publicity prompted the

Information Commissioner to issue a warning about their legal obligations under data protection legislation.[18] The MPs' pronouncements made cyber security practitioners groan at the behaviour of the very people who are responsible for making the data protection laws. One commentator reiterated the sage advice that passwords are like toothbrushes—you really shouldn't share them, not even with friends. The publicity no doubt attracted a swarm of amused hackers.

A threat-enlarging phenomenon that is hard to avoid is the misleadingly named *copycat effect*, when a successful terrorist attack stimulates other terrorists to carry out further attacks. The effect seems to work by encouraging radicalized individuals to believe that they too could be successful and should have a go. As such, it is more of an 'inspiration effect' than a 'copycat effect'. The phenomenon may help to explain why attacks sometimes occur in clusters. In 2017, for example, the UK was hit by three major terrorist attacks within less than three months, which were the first successful attacks since 2013.[19] Of course, other factors also contribute to the clustering of attacks, including world events, directions from terrorist leaders, and random chance. Statistically, events will cluster to some extent even if they occur independently of one another.

As we have seen, then, threat-reducing tactics such as deterrence, distraction, and obscurity can help to take the edge off the overall risk, but they are unlikely to suppress it completely. Fortunately, there are two other ways of reducing risk—by reducing vulnerability or impact. There is usually plenty of scope for defenders to make a substantial difference to both.

Most conventional protective security measures, including locks, fences, alarms, personnel screening, firewalls, and anti-virus software, are designed primarily to reduce *vulnerability*. They harden the target and reduce the likelihood that an attempted attack will succeed. The main ways of reducing personnel and cyber vulnerabilities are explored in Rules 6 and 8.

Finding and fixing vulnerabilities is obviously desirable. But it is easier said than done, especially for cyber security, because the number of potential vulnerabilities is huge. Moreover, threat actors are unaware of some of those vulnerabilities and incapable of exploiting others of which they are aware. Therefore, trying to find and fix *all* vulnerabilities would be a questionable strategy. By spreading security resources too thinly, it would dilute effort on the vulnerabilities that matter most. Instead, the priority should be to fix the vulnerabilities that threat actors have the intention and capability of exploiting. This is done by using an understanding of the current threat to concentrate efforts on reducing the most serious vulnerabilities—or, as some practitioners might say, dealing with the sharks nearest the boat.

An example of how an understanding of the threat has *not* informed efforts to reduce vulnerability is the dubious practice of searching the undersides of vehicles for under-vehicle improvised explosive devices (UVIEDs, or booby traps). This long-established procedure can still be observed at the entrances to some high-security sites, where it is performed by security personnel using mirrors on sticks. In the UK, the practice dates from the era of Northern Ireland-related terrorism in the 1970s, when UVIEDs were a major risk. It became further entrenched after Airey Neave MP was killed by a UVIED that exploded as he drove his car out of the underground car park at the House of Commons in 1979.[20] Thereafter, vehicles driving into Parliament and other high-security sites had their undersides searched for attached bombs as a matter of routine. Four decades later, the procedure is less common but still in use.

There are two reasons, both related to the nature of the threat, why searching under vehicles no longer makes sense as a priority method. The first is that the terrorists who are currently operating in the UK and other western countries are, by and large, not using UVIEDS any more (although that could of course change).[21] A second reason is that the intention behind UVIEDs is to kill the driver of the vehicle. The devices are therefore normally designed to explode when the victim starts their vehicle and drives off. Detonation is usually triggered by some form of movement detector or tilt switch. Therefore, it is unlikely that a victim would arrive at a high-security site, having driven some distance, with a viable device still attached to the underside of their vehicle. If UVIEDs were to become a significant threat once again, then the best place to search for them would be outside the victim's home before they start their journey to work, not when they arrive at their destination.

The unusual circumstances of the Airey Neave assassination may have distorted subsequent thinking. If the device that killed him was placed under his car outside his home, then it presumably malfunctioned and did not detonate as intended when he drove off. Only later, when he was driving up the steep exit ramp of the underground car park, did the tilt switch finally set it off. Alternatively, the device might have been placed under his car while it was parked in the House of Commons car park, in which case the appropriate security response would have been very different. Either way, an understanding of the current threat suggests that the finite security capacity would be better directed at searching the *insides* of arriving vehicles, where explosive devices are more likely to concealed.

Any substantial review of protective security should include a *vulnerability assessment*, which aims to identify the main gaps or weaknesses that could plausibly be exploited by the relevant threat actors. Given sufficient time and effort, vulnerabilities can be mapped in more depth than is generally the case for threats, because your vulnerabilities are yours to explore, whereas the intentions and capabilities of threat actors are theirs to conceal. The concept of vulnerability assessment can also be applied to people. It is one of the functions of personnel security, which is explored in Rule 6.

The third way to reduce security risk is by reducing the *impact* of a successful attack, should the defensive measures prove insufficient. Reducing the impact element of risk is the main way in which organizations and individuals strengthen their *resilience*, making them better able to withstand disruptive events and maintain normal functioning. Resilience in general, and impact-reduction in particular, form the subject of Rule 5.

The three ways to reduce risk can be illustrated by the protective security regime for a hypothetical high-risk building. The building is of national significance and subject to a range of threats, including international and domestic terrorism, cyber attacks, hostile foreign state activity, fixated individuals, violent protest, and insider action. It houses hundreds of employees and public figures, some of whom are targets in their own right, along with valuable assets and IT systems that process sensitive data. What sort of protective security regime might be needed?

As we know, there are three ways to reduce risk, and the first is to reduce threat. A good starting point would be a *threat assessment* to take stock of what is known about the intentions and capabilities of the various threat actors with regard to the building, its contents, and the institution it houses. The purpose of a threat assessment is to understand the overall level of threat and the sorts of attack methods that might be used against the target. This understanding informs the design of protective security measures to counter the threat.

The threat might be reduced somewhat through deterrence, by combining visible security with overt and covert patrolling to deter, detect, and disrupt hostile reconnaissance. Online deterrence communications could be deployed to discourage would-be attackers. As the building is well known, there is limited scope for security through obscurity or distraction. Even so, there is no sense in unnecessarily advertising where the most sensitive physical assets are located internally. The institution's cyber security would benefit from both tactics.

The second way is to reduce vulnerability. The range of options here is huge, drawing from the extensive catalogues of physical, personnel, and cyber security measures. Obvious examples would include perimeter fences, vehicle security barriers, physical access control systems, locks, CCTV cameras, automatic intruder-detection systems, blast-resistant glazing, search and screening of visitors, pre-employment screening of pass-holders, post-employment personnel security measures, firewalls, anti-virus software, and protective monitoring of digital networks. A vulnerability assessment should identify any significant gaps or weaknesses in existing defences.

Impact, the third component of risk, could be reduced through business continuity planning, incident management procedures, disaster recovery facilities, data minimization, secure backup of data, and insurance.

Measures like these are aimed at softening the effects of a successful attack in the event that the security defences are breached.

Managing by Outcomes

Recent decades have seen a shift in the general approach to managing security risk. That shift has been away from prescriptive rules and towards an *outcomes-based* approach, in which those responsible for security have more latitude to decide how they achieve the desired results. The old world of prescriptive rules was populated with fat security manuals specifying what types of lock must be fitted, how high the fences must be, and so on. The rules were explicit and required relatively little exercise of judgement. However, they were also liable to be permanently out of date in the face of evolving risks. In the new world of outcomes-based risk management, prescriptive rules have largely been superseded by policies that are more genuinely risk-based, in the sense that the specific security measures are meant to be determined by judgements about risk. So, for example, rather than specifying a particular type of lock or height of fence, the policy would mandate a package of physical security that reduced the risk to an appropriate level. Those managing the risk would have some leeway in deciding precisely how to achieve that outcome in practical terms.

The outcomes-based approach is superior to the old prescriptive approach in one important respect. If done well, it gives security professionals the flexibility to apply the best available means of managing dynamic and adaptive security risks. This improves their chances of staying ahead in the security arms race and avoids wasting money on excessive or out-of-date defences that might previously have been required by prescriptive rules. There is, however, a large 'but'. An outcomes-based approach relies on expert judgement about what is required and how best to achieve the desired outcomes. In reality, many organizations lack the in-house expertise to make such judgements reliably, especially in the complex and rapidly changing field of cyber security. People responsible for managing security sometimes secretly wish they could just be told what they must do.

The most recent European data protection and privacy legislation is explicitly framed in terms of outcomes. The General Data Protection Regulation, which came into effect across the European Union (including the UK) in 2018, places a legal obligation on organizations to protect personal data by implementing 'appropriate' technical and organizational measures to ensure a level of security 'appropriate' to the risk. The law does not specify what is meant by 'appropriate', beyond stating that it should be judged by 'taking into account the state of the art' (also undefined). The interpretation of these principles will evolve through case law, as national regulators take enforcement action against those they judge to fall short.

Other Ways of (Not) Managing Risk

If you are unable or unwilling to reduce the security risks you are facing, then what other options are available? In a nutshell, there are three: risk avoidance, risk transfer, or risk acceptance. They are superficially attractive but mostly too good to be true.

Risk avoidance, as the name suggests, involves avoiding the circumstances that give rise to risk in the first place—for example, avoiding the risk of losing sensitive data by not having any sensitive data. For obvious reasons, it is rarely possible to dodge security risk altogether. However, risk can often be partially avoided—for example, by holding only the data you actually need.

One form of security risk where avoidance *is* a valuable tactic is the risk of violence against individuals. We are talking here about risks that are up-close and personal, notably those stemming from violent crime, terrorism, and fixated stalkers. For most people, the chances of being attacked by terrorists are very low, leaving crime and stalking as the most likely forms of violent risk. If you live in the US, the probability of being caught up in a conventional (non-terrorist) shooting incident is not negligible, with an average of one mass shooting taking place every day (where a mass shooting is defined as one in which at least four victims are killed or injured). One of the worst mass shootings in recent history took place in Las Vegas in 2017, when a lone shooter armed with an arsenal of automatic weapons killed fifty-eight people and wounded many more from the window of his hotel bedroom. Fixated individuals with mental health problems can also pose a significant physical risk to their victims. Further risks emanate from people who are enraged about something that has been said publicly or online. According to research published in 2017, almost half of the 3.2 billion people worldwide who have access to the internet are living in countries where individuals have been attacked or killed for their online activities since mid-2015.[22]

The most basic tactic for dealing with an acute risk of physical violence is to *run away* from it. That is exactly what the public in the UK and US has been advised to do in the event of a marauding terrorist attack, such as those in Mumbai, Nairobi, Tunisia, Paris, and Orlando. For example, in the 2015 attack on western tourists on a beach at Sousse, Tunisia, a lone gunman killed thirty-eight people before he was shot. The simple advice, which has been pushed out by the UK authorities under the mantra *Run-Hide-Tell*, is to escape from the threat as fast as you can by running in the opposite direction from the sound of gunfire. Run away. If, and only if, you cannot run away, because you are trapped, or the shooter is too close, the fall-back is to hide. You should then phone the police and tell them your whereabouts, provided you can do this without giving yourself away. The official advice in the US is broadly similar, with its primary emphasis on running away. Unlike the UK, however, it floats the possibility of confronting the shooter, and hence the US equivalent of *Run-Hide-Tell* is *Run-Hide-Fight*. Very rarely would it make sense for a member of the public in the UK to confront an armed terrorist unless there was no other choice and they had an effective weapon which they genuinely knew how to use. The situation is different in the US, where there are more shooters and many more members of the public with their own guns.

A crucial technique for detecting and avoiding an acute risk of physical violence and some forms of conventional crime is to maintain *situational awareness*. If you know what is going on in your surroundings and can spot the danger signs, you will be better placed to avoid a violent confrontation. Situational awareness is a skill that, like all skills, develops with practice. The first step is to form the habit of looking around you, not down at your phone, when out and about. With practice, situational awareness becomes second nature, leaving your conscious mind free to dwell on happier matters.

If you cannot avoid the risk of physical violence, then your next tactic is to try reducing the threat actor's intention by defusing their aggression. That requires a little knowledge of psychology and a way of thinking known as dynamic risk assessment, which essentially involves making rapid risk assessments on the hoof and acting quickly when necessary. Violent encounters may erupt in seconds, so there is no time for laboured analysis. To be effective, the potential victim's response must be semi-automatic.

Risk transfer, which is similarly self-explanatory, means transferring the risk to someone else. One company might pay another company to look after its data and expect them to shoulder the blame if the data is lost. Or an organization might outsource the guarding of its building to a security company and expect them to carry the risk. Insurance is sometimes described as a means of transferring risk, but it is really more of a mechanism for softening the financial impact of loss. (More on this in Rule 5.)

Transferring security risk may sound attractive to lawyers and senior managers but it seldom works smoothly in practice, especially when dealing with the most severe types of risk. If things go badly wrong, the problem usually returns to haunt the original owner regardless of what the contracts say about transferring risk. Reputational risk is especially hard to shift. In sum, risks can be shared but they can rarely be transferred in totality, and a shared risk is still a risk.

When planning the overt physical security for the London 2012 Olympics, the UK government believed it could transfer much of the risk to the private sector by outsourcing the guarding of venues. Not long before the opening ceremony, however, it emerged that the main contractor was unable to recruit enough guards, sparking a mini crisis in which the government found itself holding a risk that it thought had been transferred. The contractor suffered some financial and reputational harm, but the government had to sort out the mess. To borrow another metaphor, the government found it was the banker of last resort for an event that was too big to fail.

A third option (of sorts) is *risk acceptance*, which simply means accepting the current risk and hoping it does not materialize. This option is much favoured, widely used, and often regretted. Deciding to do nothing, when it would be possible to do something, is often based on the dubious belief that maintaining the status quo is generally the safest option. Maintaining the status quo is, of course, almost always the easiest and cheapest option, because improving security will cost money and carry risks of delays and overspends. However, the 'do-nothing' logic is flawed because there is no such thing as doing nothing when it comes to managing dynamic and adaptive security risks. The risk might actually materialize while you are maintaining that status quo. And if it does materialize, there is a good chance that it will have got worse during the time it was neglected. Avoiding one seemingly risky course of action, by doing nothing to improve security, inevitably means choosing another course of action, which might turn out to be worse. The basic principle is that, when it comes to protective security, *doing nothing is doing something*.

RULE 5

BUILD RESILIENCE

Purely defensive security can never guarantee protection. The most enduring way to mitigate risk is by building resilience. Passive resilience comes from reducing the impact of disruptive events and returning quickly to normality. Active resilience goes beyond that and involves becoming progressively tougher by learning from adversity.

As we have seen, there are three ways to reduce risk and the first two have limitations. Threat actors can be formidable adversaries, making serious security threats hard even for governments to tackle. Conventional security is aimed mainly at reducing vulnerability, but threat actors are adaptive and find ways to penetrate most defences. In the cyber domain, in particular, it will never be possible to stop every attack. Tackling threat and vulnerability alone cannot guarantee protection. This brings us to impact—the third element of risk, and one that deserves more attention.

The impact of a successful attack can usually be reduced, sometimes substantially, by the right sorts of planning and preparation. Individuals and organizations that strengthen themselves in this way suffer less harm if their security is breached. They are also better able to recover quickly and return to normality with less disruption. To put it another way, they are more *resilient*. There is more to resilience, however, than returning to normality after an attack. As we shall see, resilience can also entail becoming progressively stronger over time by actively learning from experience.

This chapter explores the concept of resilience as it applies to risk and security, explains why building resilience is a smart strategy, and outlines ways in which organizations and individuals can achieve it. But first, what is meant by 'resilience'?

Resilience, Passive and Active

Resilient people, businesses, and institutions cope well when things go wrong. They roll with the blows, deal effectively with the adverse consequences, and return quickly to a stable equilibrium.[1] Being resilient puts them at an advantage over those who are more fragile and should give them greater confidence. That, at least, is the conventional view of resilience. However, resilience can mean something even more substantial than recovering from disruption, desirable though that is. Resilience comes in two distinct forms, which I shall refer to as passive and active.

Passive resilience is the ability to absorb disturbance, recover quickly from a setback, and return to normality. This is the colloquial sense of the word, and the one most commonly used in relation to security. It equates roughly with being robust. To many practitioners, a resilient organization is one that copes effectively with a breach of its security and rapidly restores business-as-usual. Expressed in terms of risk, passive resilience is about *reducing the impact* of a disruptive incident or attack by reducing the size or the duration of its harmful consequences. Passive resilience is definitely a good thing and we should all aspire to have more of it. However, there can be more to resilience than absorbing blows.

Active resilience means growing progressively tougher by learning from adversity and becoming better able to manage future stresses. Actively resilient people or organizations do more than just return to their prior state after an adverse event: they learn from their experience and develop stronger defences, making them better able to resist the next time. They are less likely to suffer a security breach and cope better if they do. One of the few official definitions that captures the sense of active resilience is the US National Academy of Sciences definition of engineering resilience, which describes it as the 'ability to plan and prepare for, absorb, respond to, and recover from disasters and adapt to new conditions'.[2] The operative words here are 'plan', 'prepare', and 'adapt'.

The concept of active resilience is similar to what the writer Nicholas Nassim Taleb calls *antifragility*. Taleb argues that complex systems, including national economies and living organisms, become tougher as a result of coping successfully with moderate amounts of stress.[3] He likens these antifragile systems to the Hydra of Greek mythology: each time one of its many snake-like heads is cut off, two more grow back, making it stronger than before. Antifragility, or active resilience, is different from resilience in the conventional sense of robustness, or passive resilience. Passively resilient people or organizations absorb shocks and return to their previous state; actively resilient ones become tougher. Taleb does not pull his punches in emphasizing this difference: 'antifragility is … a ubiquitous property of every system that has survived … We didn't get where we are thanks to the sissy notion of resilience.'[4]

A biological analogy is physical exercise. Strenuous exercise causes mild damage to muscle tissues, which respond by repairing themselves. However, the muscles do not merely recover to the state they were in before they were damaged: rather, they over compensate and grow stronger. They become better able to cope the next time they are stressed, and hence strenuous exercise makes us physically stronger. To use another analogy, passive resilience is like being burgled, recouping the financial loss from your insurance policy, and carrying on more or less as before (albeit with heightened anxiety and a bigger insurance premium). Normal life resumes, after a fashion, but you remain just as vulnerable to the next burglar who comes along. Active resilience is like being burgled, recouping the loss from your insurance policy, upgrading your locks, installing an alarm, getting a dog, joining the neighbourhood watch scheme, and resuming normal life with greater confidence. Writers and philosophers have been making essentially the same point more succinctly for two millennia. 'Difficulties strengthen the mind, as labour does the body,' said Seneca 2,000 years ago. 'Sweet are the uses of adversity,' wrote Shakespeare. Nietzsche put it more starkly: 'That which does not kill us makes us stronger.'[5]

The concept of active resilience is illustrated below. The first diagram shows how a victim (for example, a business or a computer network) is affected by three disruptive attacks, indicated by vertical arrows, over a period of time (T). Each attack temporarily impairs the victim's functionality (F)—that is, their ability to perform a crucial function such as conducting normal business transactions or processing data. However, the impairment in functionality gets smaller each time, as the actively resilient victim becomes progressively tougher in response to each attack.

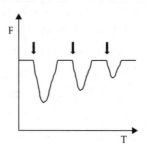

The second diagram shows the same thing in a different way, by depicting how the target's ability to resist attack (R) varies over time (T) in response to the same three attacks. Here we see that the ability to resist gets progressively bigger, somewhat like muscles growing stronger after repeated bouts of vigorous exercise.

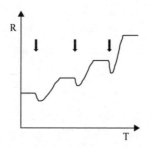

When assessing resilience, it is crucial to take account of the resilience of suppliers and other third parties on whom you may depend. To reiterate one of the guidelines from Rule 4, *mind your third parties*. It is all very well having your own sophisticated fall-back facilities, but if your business depends on a fragile small supplier for critical services, then *their* lack of resilience could suddenly become *your* lack of resilience. *Supply chains should be resilient too.*

Most organizations have moved some or all of their IT into the cloud, rightly reckoning cloud services to be generally cheaper, more secure, and more resilient. However, few organizations have evaluated the impact of a sudden and widespread loss of service. Now that most businesses rely on a small number of large cloud service providers, the loss of one of those providers could have a huge impact. An organization that really wanted to maximize the resilience of its cloud-based IT would have fall-back facilities with another cloud provider or in-house.[6]

In the following sections we will consider how passive and active resilience can be developed, and how we as individuals can strengthen our own psychological resilience—a vital commodity when the going gets tough.

Reducing Impact

Passive resilience amounts to reducing impact by reducing the severity or duration of harm. There are many ways of achieving this, depending on the nature of the risk in question. For instance, the impact of a cyber attack could be reduced by keeping a secure copy of data, while the impact of a domestic burglary could be reduced by having insurance.

The impact element of security risk generally involves some form of loss, whether that is lost lives, lost money, lost data, lost business, or lost reputation. The impact will be worse if the victim responds too slowly or makes bad decisions during and after an attack. Further losses can arise from the disruption that follows an attack. By following the temporal chain of events, we can see that impact could, in principle, be reduced by:

- reducing the amount of time that threat actors have to cause harm (early detection and rapid response);
- reducing the victim's assets so that they have less to lose (asset minimization);

- building in plenty of alternative ways of working and minimizing single points of failure (redundancy);
- keeping secure copies, so that losing the asset causes less harm (secure backup);
- sharing the loss with others (insurance);
- improving the victim's ability to cope effectively with an attack (incident management and crisis management); and
- accelerating the process of returning to normality (business continuity planning and disaster recovery).

Let us consider each of these in turn. The first line of defence in reducing impact is *early detection and rapid response*. If an unfolding attack is spotted and thwarted quickly, the threat actors will have less opportunity to cause harm. It may even be possible to halt an attack before any significant harm is done.

Early detection is especially relevant in the cyber domain. In 2017, according to one study, the average time that elapsed between an organization's network being compromised and the victim discovering the compromise was 101 days.[7] (If you think that is bad—which it is—the average in 2012 was 243 days.) If a hacker has been covertly sitting on your network for several months before they are noticed, it is safe to assume that the damage is already done. If, however, you can detect an attempted intrusion almost immediately, you have a fighting chance of limiting the damage. Speed is vital. The average time taken to detect an intrusion is one of the more meaningful performance indicators for protective security, in both the cyber and physical domains. (More about measurement in Rule 9.)

Many protective security systems for detecting incipient attacks work by identifying anomalous events, which trigger a response. A simple example is an intruder alarm, which detects a movement indicating that an unauthorized person has entered a secure area. Once triggered, it automatically alerts the guards who can then respond. A primary form of cyber security involves monitoring the digital network to look for anomalous activity that could be symptomatic of an unauthorized intrusion or malware. An inherent problem with trying to detect anomalies in complex systems like a digital network or a human workforce is the difficulty of knowing what *normal* looks like. Without a good understanding of what constitutes normal behaviour, it is hard to determine reliably whether an apparent anomaly is indeed anomalous. The less accurate the discrimination, the larger the number of false positives (innocuous behaviour triggering alarms) and false negatives (attacks going unnoticed).

A powerful but under-used strategy for reducing the impact of an attack is reducing your holding of assets. The principle of *asset minimization* means getting rid of any assets you do not need, on the simple grounds that *you cannot lose what you do not have.*

The principle of asset minimization is especially relevant in the cyber domain, where it entails keeping only the data that is actually needed and securely erasing the rest. *Data minimization* runs counter to a prevalent culture of retaining everything. Organizations are mindful of possible future inquiries, reviews, litigation, regulatory scrutiny, or tax investigations. Individual users are wary of deleting material in case it comes in handy one day. The temptation to keep everything is reinforced by the tiny financial cost of storing digital data and the deeply tedious nature of selectively deleting it. When viewed through the lens of security risk, the equation looks rather different. The more data you have, the more there is to lose. Data that might genuinely be required for business or accountability reasons should of course be retained for as long as might be necessary. But the risk of discarding potentially useful data should be balanced against the pain of losing unnecessary data.

The tendency to accumulate data is partly a reflection of organizational cultures that value data and ignore the downsides of keeping it. It also has roots in psychology. The propensity to hoard items of all kinds is a common human characteristic. In a small minority of individuals, hoarding becomes pathological: they accumulate items like clothing or newspapers to the extent that it interferes with normal life.[8] Well, something similar happens with the hoarding of digital items such as emails, photos, files, and apps. A significant minority of people accumulate digital items to an extent that disrupts normal life, a phenomenon known as *digital hoarding*.[9] The accumulation of digital items to a less extreme extent is remarkably common, both at home and in the workplace, with only a minority of us regularly deleting emails and other digital items. The main reasons people give for not deleting emails are that they might come in useful some time, they worry about accidentally deleting something important, or they see no benefit in spending time on weeding.[10]

Digital hoarding might seem innocuous, but the picture changes if we consider security risks. Given the imperfect state of most cyber security, those troves of largely redundant data are at significant risk of being stolen. The stolen data could be used to clone their owner's identity, rob their bank account, embarrass them on social media, or defraud their employer. The users whose behaviour poses the biggest security concerns are those whom psychologists have dubbed *digital collector-hoarders*. These are individuals who keep everything, know what they have, know where to find it, and think about how they might use the data.[11] You would not want your organization to be harbouring a malicious insider who is a digital collector-hoarder. (More on insiders in Rule 6.)

The principle of data minimization is highly relevant for people travelling overseas. Business travellers can reduce the risk to their personal and corporate data by taking with them only the data and devices they strictly need for the trip. In practice, many expose themselves and their employer to unnecessary risk by travelling with personal or corporate devices packed with data and connected to their corporate network. The threat is particularly high in Russia and China, where state agencies have remits to conduct cyber espionage on a prodigious scale. Ordinary business travellers are well within their scope. The risks can be further reduced through the use of security measures such as virtual private networks and end-to-end encryption. But the most robust precaution of all is simply not taking the data or devices overseas in the first place. When travelling to high-threat countries, the safest option is to take a disposable mobile device and dispose of it afterwards. Most people, however, succumb to convenience.

A general design principle for reducing impact is to build in *redundancy* in order to reduce the severity of failure. The presence of multiple alternative ways of working, or just a stock of spare parts, can reduce the risk that a computer network, business process, or other system will fail badly following an attack. Redundancy improves reliability under pressure, whereas the presence of multiple single points of failure does the opposite.

An essential strategy for reducing impact is maintaining *secure backups* of data, such that a cyber attack or other compromise would not result in its permanent loss. Everyone should do this as a matter of course, both at home and at work. The government of Estonia (or 'e-Stonia' as it is sometimes called), which is one of the world's most technologically enabled nations, is creating secure backups for the entire nation. Having suffered major cyber attacks from its Russian neighbour, Estonia is creating secure backup copies of its national repository of information about its citizens, including birth records, banking details, property deeds, and electoral rolls. Data is also being backed up at Estonian embassies and 'data embassies' in other countries to further protect it from attacks at home.[12]

Keeping a backup copy of data is a precaution that works only if the copy is up to date, secure, and retrievable. Some organizations believe they have backed up their data only to find, come the day, that they have not. To their consternation, they discover that the backup data is lost, overwritten, corrupted, out of date, impossible to retrieve, or impossible to reload onto the system. A cyber attack that compromises an organization's primary data could also compromise the backup if the two are connected in any way, so the backup must be kept fully insulated from the main system. Moreover, a backup is only useful if it can be reliably recovered. The only way to know if a backup will work in anger is to test it regularly in peacetime.

A good guiding principle for secure backup is the *3-2-1 rule*: keep at least three copies of your data (the primary plus at least two backups); store the copies on at least two different types of storage device (e.g. hard drive and cloud); and keep at least one backup copy off-site so that it will survive even if your office burns down. Magnetic tape, once a relic seen only in technology museums, has been staging a comeback as a backup medium, thanks to its long shelf life and relative invulnerability to remote hacking.

Another basic strategy for reducing impact is *insurance*, whereby financial loss is reduced by compensation. Insurance is the most common means of reducing the impact of ordinary crime. It works well when the impact of an attack or disruptive incident is mainly financial. But other dimensions of impact, such as reputational damage, loss of confidence, interruption of business, and psychological harm, are less easily washed away with cash— even assuming the insurance policy purports to cover such things.

The insurance industry works by spreading large numbers of relatively small risks across many customers. It has struggled to deal with the very high-impact risk of terrorism. The 9/11 attacks in New York and Washington created insured losses of around 40 billion dollars.[13] In the UK, a series of PIRA large vehicle bombs in the early 1990s caused hugely expensive damage in the City of London. One of these attacks, which destroyed the Baltic Exchange in 1992, led to insurance claims of around £800 million, another caused damage estimated at £350 million, and several more on a comparable scale were narrowly thwarted.[14] In response to the burgeoning claims, the insurance industry set up a pooled mutual fund, known as Pool Re, for reinsuring against the property damage caused by terrorism. It was called upon in 1996, when PIRA bombed the centre of Manchester, generating insurance claims of £400 million.[15] Pool Re is underwritten by the UK government because the market could not cope alone. The US Congress passed legislation in 2002 which similarly provided government support following a major attack.

Terrorism is still with us, of course, and now we have cyber attacks as well. The insurance industry has responded to the demand, and cyber security insurance has become a rapidly expanding market worth several billion dollars a year.[16] Once again, though, there is the problem of multi-dimensional impact. The consequences of a major cyber attack are not just financial. In addition to the financial losses resulting from the costs of fixing the problem and lost business, the victim may face lawsuits, regulatory fines, lower share price, loss of customer confidence, and tarnished brand. Some businesses comfort themselves with the belief that a cyber insurance policy will fully protect them from a major attack. Anyone who has such a policy is well advised to check it carefully for the exclusions.

The growing severity of cyber attacks, combined with the relative dearth of historical data on indicative losses, has led some insurers to tread with caution. When a single attack can bring losses of hundreds of millions of dollars, cyber insurance begins to resemble terrorism insurance—an unbounded and uncertain risk that requires pooled effort and government backing.

Uncertainty about the scale of potential losses has stimulated a market in cyber risk assessment tools, many of which claim to use artificial intelligence to divine the true underlying risk. For reasons discussed in Rule 9, buyers of such services should be sceptical.

A further benefit of resilience—the attribute that just keeps on giving—is that it can also act as a deterrent and hence reduce the threat. It does this by increasing the cost to the threat actors and reducing the benefit. Actively resilient targets are less vulnerable to attack and a successful attack has less impact. The discerning threat actor should therefore prefer to go after a less resilient victim.

Dealing with Crises

To quote the astronaut Chris Hadfield, no matter how bad a situation is, you can always make it worse. An essential strategy for reducing the impact of a disruptive incident is optimizing the ability to make good decisions quickly—or, at the very least, limiting the scope for making *bad* decisions. Every organization should have an *incident management plan* and exercise it regularly.

If a security incident is unusually bad, then incident management becomes *crisis management*. The dividing lines between business-as-usual, an incident, a crisis, and a disaster are not universally defined. Different organizations apply different thresholds beyond which an everyday event becomes an incident or a crisis becomes a disaster. A simple formula is to regard a *crisis* as an acute period of serious risk and a *disaster* as what happens if that risk materializes. You might be able to paddle your way out of a crisis, but if the boat sinks, you have a disaster.

An organization's ability to manage a security incident or crisis may determine whether it survives. Despite that, some organizations are poorly prepared even to deal with easily foreseeable problems. For example, a UK government survey of more than 1,500 UK businesses found that only one in nine (11 per cent) had a cyber security incident management plan.[17]

Three vital ingredients of effective crisis management are *governance, communication, and teamwork*. Good governance, which boils down to being crystal clear about who is in charge of what, forms the subject of Rule 10. It is even more vital in a crisis than in peacetime. Numerous public relations disasters have demonstrated the ease with which a lack of clarity about governance, combined with poor communication, can convert a crisis into a disaster.

During a live security incident, the communication between the various participants needs to be especially clear and disciplined. This is second nature for the military and emergency services, who have developed robust doctrines for *command, control, and communication* based on accumulated experience of what does and does not work. Good crisis management is not rigidly hierarchical and top-down. Rather, it involves a significant amount of delegated leadership, with local commanders given authority to decide, within certain parameters, how best to achieve the overall mission—hence the term *mission leadership*. The people on the ground are usually best placed to make local decisions and should be trusted to act appropriately, within defined limits. Micromanagement from the top is rarely the best way to manage a crisis.

One of the psychological pitfalls to guard against in a crisis is a universal tendency to overestimate the extent to which other people know the same things as you. We are all inclined to leave too much unsaid, believe that we have communicated more clearly than we actually have, and assume that other people understand the situation better than they actually do. *If in doubt, spell it out.*

Teamwork is another vital ingredient of crisis management. Psychological research has highlighted the distinction between professional task-related skills ('task work') and the interpersonal skills needed to work effectively in a team.[18] The soft skills of teamwork are just as important as knowing how to perform technical tasks. No matter how much expertise each individual may have, they will not perform optimally in a crisis if they cannot work together in a team. The best-performing teams share a common understanding of what to do, enabling them to anticipate each other's actions and cooperate implicitly. Arguably the most important ingredient of teamwork is *team cohesion*, which is the extent to which each individual feels bonded to the team and identifies with its mission.[19] Research has shown that the performance of teams is strongly correlated with their level of team cohesion, and the two appear to be mutually reinforcing. However, too much cohesion can cause trouble if it leads to a collective tunnel vision known as *groupthink*, in which everyone converges around the same plan regardless of its flaws. (More on this in Rule 7.) Some degree of creative tension is desirable.

One phenomenon to expect in any security crisis is the *fog of war*. When something bad happens out of the blue, the full facts often do not emerge for some time, leaving the responders and decision-makers to act before they know for certain what is going on. For example, when the 7/7 suicide bombers struck London on the morning of 7 July 2005, some initial reports were of a power surge on the Underground. More than an hour elapsed before it became clear that the UK had experienced its first ever suicide bombings. A former head of MI5 recalled that morning as a classic example of the fog of war.[20] In such situations, it is important to recognize the uncertainty, while not allowing it to become a reason for dithering.

Confusion, lack of firm information, and multiple versions of the truth are standard features of most crises. Therefore, it pays to have robust procedures for collating what information *is* available, sifting out the dross, and deriving the best single version of the truth, which is known as the *common operating picture* (COP). Another valuable tool in a crisis is a *playbook*, which presents decision-makers with a pre-scripted menu of possible responses to various types of foreseeable situation. Playbooks are best developed through testing, exercising, red teaming, and simulation.

Another unhelpful phenomenon to expect in a crisis is the psychological tendency to discount evidence that what is happening is in fact a crisis. People under acute stress are often inclined to believe that things are not as bad as they seem. They persist with what they were doing before the crisis erupted because their mind is telling them that this cannot really be happening. The tendency to deny the reality of a crisis is less evident among individuals who have personal experience of genuine crises and those who have practised dealing with simulated crises. Those managing a crisis should be prepared for the fog of war and irrational optimism. They should also be mindful of how excessive cognitive loads—having too much information to process—can impair people's ability to absorb new information and make sound judgements. In Rule 7 we will explore various psychological predispositions that can impair our ability to respond appropriately.

Like buses, security crises do not always arrive one at a time at neatly spaced intervals. Even if crises were entirely independent of one another, they would still exhibit some clustering for purely statistical reasons. In reality, crises tend to be causally interrelated to some extent, making clustering even more likely. One example is the homogeneity of the cyber domain, where the vast majority of computer systems run on one of three software platforms (Windows, Mac, or Linux). If a major security problem affects one of these platforms, the consequences can be global and systemic, affecting many organizations and individuals in interdependent ways. A basic precautionary principle is that you should be prepared to cope with two or more crises at the same time (otherwise known as a cluster****).

Managing the immediate crisis is just the beginning. Then comes the business of dealing with the consequences and restoring normal functioning as quickly and painlessly as possible. The purpose of *business continuity planning* is to do the detailed thinking before a risk materializes, not when it happens. The plan should include *disaster recovery* arrangements that allow the victim to fall back on alternative facilities if the usual ones are out of action. For instance, a high-risk building might have emergency generators, an alternative security control room, and off-site facilities where critical business functions can continue if the building is rendered unusable. Business continuity plans should acknowledge the reality that it may not be possible to recover fully to the pre-incident state. Following a major crisis or disaster, normality may have to be redefined.

Business continuity plans and disaster recovery arrangements should be tested regularly to ensure that they work as intended. A real disaster is not the time to discover gaps in the planning or find that no one has the key to the fall-back facility. Plans are rarely perfect. As the boxer Mike Tyson put it: 'Everyone has a plan, until they get punched in the mouth.' The best way of finding and fixing the flaws is through regular live exercising under realistic conditions. Another, less intrusive way of honing crisis management is through computer simulation. Practising responses in an immersive virtual environment has the additional advantage of allowing a larger range of scenarios to be explored than would be practicable with live exercises.[21]

Building Active Resilience

An organization that implements the impact-reduction measures outlined above should be much more resilient than one that relies only on perimeter security. If an attack does get through, the damage should be less severe and normal functioning restored more rapidly. But there would still be *some* damage and more attacks to come in the future. So, what more can be done to reduce the risk? The answer lies in building active resilience.

An actively resilient person or organization is one that learns from experience and applies the lessons to make itself progressively tougher. Each time it manages an incident, it adapts by improving its ability to prevent or manage the next one. Like a muscle growing stronger through vigorous exercise, it grows stronger through adversity.

Building active resilience is a cyclical process in which the organization or individual *detects* a disruptive incident, *responds* to it, *recovers* its critical functionality, and *learns* from the experience. The virtuous cycle incrementally strengthens its ability to resist the next attack and reduces the impact if the attack succeeds.

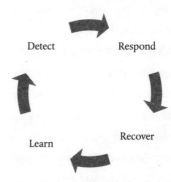

Many organizations can do the *detect, respond*, and *recover* parts but neglect the *learn* bit, leaving them no stronger than they were before. They are passively resilient but lack the active resilience born of learning from experience.

Fortunately, there is no need to suffer an actual attack in order to learn from experience. Active resilience can be developed through simulated experience acquired through testing, exercising, and red teaming. Another relatively painless way of building active resilience is by *learning from others* through mechanisms such as information-sharing forums. As a wise person once observed, smart people learn from their own mistakes, but wise people learn from the mistakes of others.

Learning does not happen automatically and it should not be taken for granted. As every teacher knows, effective learning depends on clear and rapid feedback about the consequences of behaviour. Learning is reinforced when the right responses are rewarded in some way, if only by being acknowledged or praised. Psychology also tells us that we tend to learn better from being rewarded for doing the right thing than from being punished for making mistakes. Unless these basic conditions for learning are in place, it is quite possible to keep having bad experiences without learning the right lessons.

One of the problems with many security systems is that 'good' security behaviour results in nothing happening, no rapid feedback, and no reward. Moreover, the consequences of 'bad' security behaviour, such as clicking on a dubious email attachment or allowing someone to tailgate through a locked door, often do not become apparent for a long time, if at all. The lack of rapid feedback can impede learning.

The value of learning from others means that building active resilience works better as a cooperative process. Resilience is not a zero-sum game, in which my gain is your loss and vice versa. Everyone (apart from the threat actors) stands to benefit from cooperating. Each organization will benefit directly from becoming more resilient. It will gain even more if others do the same. In a highly interdependent world, organizations are safer if their suppliers, partners, customers, and perhaps even their competitors are also resilient. Furthermore, collective resilience can create a sort of herd immunity that makes it harder for threat actors to shop around for the most vulnerable, particularly in the cyber domain.

Resilience depends as much on *people and relationships* as it does on plans or infrastructure. An organization is much better able to weather a storm if it has trusted leaders, a motivated workforce, loyal partners, and crisis managers who understand how people behave in stressful situations.

A well-run organization will take extra care to nurture its people during a crisis, knowing that their ingenuity and persistence will be crucial. The effects of a major crisis and its aftermath may extend over weeks or months. The wise thing to do at the outset may be to resist the urge for heroic endeavour and send some people home to rest. The critical phase of a crisis may come after days of intense activity, by which time the sleepless heroes are too exhausted to think straight. Lack of sleep has crippling effects on mental ability. As we shall see in Rule 7, very tired people behave rather like drunk people. In a crisis, it is safer to be well rested and sober.

Personal and professional relationships are another crucial component of resilience. We all need help from others, especially when the going gets tough. During a crisis we are critically dependent on our existing relationships and networks. It is too late by then to start developing new ones. Therefore, another good way of building resilience is to *invest in relationships*. Regrettably, the short-term imperatives of cost-saving and efficiency sometimes get in the way. Frequent reorganizations and so-called transformation programmes can have the unintended effect of breaking up informal networks and reducing organizational resilience. Economic pressures can result in whole cities or nations becoming less resilient. For example, the high cost of living in some large cities makes it hard for public service workers on low wages to afford to live there. A 2016 study found that more than half of police officers, firefighters, and ambulance paramedics serving London live outside the capital, where rents and property prices are lower. In a crisis, particularly one affecting public transport, it is harder, and takes longer, for them to get to work helping others.[22]

Personal Resilience

The concept of resilience is as relevant to people as it is to organizations. The American Psychological Association defines personal resilience as 'the process of adapting well in the face of adversity, trauma, tragedy, threats, or significant sources of stress [and] "bouncing back" from difficult experiences'.[23] This definition encompasses passive resilience ('bouncing back') and hints at active resilience ('adapting well'). Personal resilience is in turn relevant to organizational resilience because the resilience of key individuals will have a critical bearing on the successful handling of any crisis. An organization that aspires to be more resilient should think about the resilience of its people, not just its infrastructure.

What does psychological research tell us about the nature of personal resilience and how it can be strengthened? The evidence shows, not surprisingly, that highly resilient people tend to be happier, healthier, and more successful, other things being equal. It also shows that humans are surprisingly resilient. Each of us will endure many stressful experiences during our lifetime and most of us will cope reasonably well. Individuals differ in their ability to cope with stress and we all have an upper limit beyond which we may suffer lasting psychological harm. In cases of extreme stress, the harm may be manifested in debilitating disorders such as burnout, depression, or post-traumatic stress disorder (PTSD). Even so, only a minority of people (generally fewer than one in ten) who have been exposed to highly stressful situations go on to develop full-blown PTSD.[24] The majority cope pretty well, even in the face of extreme stress. Resilience is the norm, not the exception.

Why are some people more resilient than others and how can we strengthen our own resilience? There is no single magic ingredient. Rather, the research shows that resilient people tend to display an array of characteristics in varying combinations. Among the most common psychological attributes of resilient individuals are self-confidence, realistic optimism (as distinct from delusional optimism), a sense of humour, the ability to stay focused under pressure, persistence, and finding meaning even in negative experiences. To take just one of these ingredients, humour helps to bolster resilience in various ways. It can soften the debilitating effects of anxiety, anger, and other negative emotions. Humour can also act as a social lubricant by reinforcing relationships and breaking down barriers. The right kind of humour can strengthen team cohesion. There is even evidence that humour increases our tolerance of pain.

Other factors that are known to contribute to personal resilience are expertise, supportive relationships, and adequate sleep. You are more likely to cope well in stressful situations if you know what you are doing, have friends and colleagues to support you, and are not debilitated by sleep deprivation.[25] No surprises there. Genetic differences also play a role, including influencing susceptibility to PTSD. But the most significant factors relate to our experience and are therefore amenable to change. There are multiple pathways to resilience and individuals can be resilient in different ways. The same is true for organizations.

One of the strongest themes to emerge from research on personal resilience is that overcoming adversity often has positive consequences. Individuals who repeatedly cope with moderately stressful events tend to become psychologically more robust and better able to cope with future stress. To put it another way, the experience of coping with challenging situations helps to build active resilience.[26] Highly resilient people typically have a track record of dealing successfully with stressful situations. The 'good' forms of stress that help to strengthen personal resilience are generally acute (i.e. relatively short in duration), controllable (i.e. you can do something to alleviate the problem), and moderate in intensity. In contrast, stress that is chronic (enduring), uncontrollable, and severe is more likely to cause psychological and physical harm and weaken the individual's capacity to cope with further stress. 'Good stress' makes us more resilient whereas 'bad stress' does the reverse.[27]

Findings like these provide useful pointers to ways of building resilience in the workplace. When selecting and developing people, an organization should value personal resilience. Being clever, ambitious, and hardworking is not enough. Personal resilience has more bearing on ultimate success or failure than most other personal characteristics.[28] An organization that wants to become more resilient should try to create an environment in which its people can become more resilient. Among other things, this could involve regular testing and exercising, to give people the experience of coping successfully with demanding situations, and training to equip them with the relevant expertise. A resilient organization will also respect people's need for adequate sleep, foster supportive interpersonal relationships, and value humour.

Finally, is it possible for individuals or organizations to be *too* resilient? Well, yes. Excessive resilience of the wrong kind can be an obstacle to necessary change and consequently destructive.

An unhealthy passive resilience built on delusional optimism, unfounded overconfidence, and unbending persistence can keep people plugging away in hopeless situations, pursuing unattainable goals, when a better course of action would be to stop and change tack. Seemingly resilient superheroes sometimes self-destruct. In a milder form, unhealthy passive resilience can make people too tolerant of adverse conditions that would be amenable to improvement, such as tolerating a boring job for longer than is necessary.[29] The findings of psychology are in pleasing harmony with those of complex systems theory (as outlined in Rule 2), which show that systems that are too strongly anchored in a stable equilibrium can be resistant to evolutionary change and consequently more vulnerable to big shocks.[30] For similar reasons, unhealthy passive resilience can prevent individuals and organizations from recognizing that they need to change. Those that resist change for too long can end up breaking.

RULE 6

IT'S ALL ABOUT PEOPLE

The human dimension is the most important and least well-understood
aspect of security. People are central to both the problems and the solutions.

———

It used to be said that security is only as strong as its weakest link and the
weakest link is people. That saying has become less popular among security
practitioners, largely because it is untrue. People are the most complex and
least well-understood aspect of any security system, but they are not the
weakest. On the contrary, people are the glue that holds everything together.
The misleading view of people as the weak link in security often reflects a lack
of understanding, compounded by badly designed policies and technologies
that fail to take account of how people think and behave.

The human dimension is central to security, and any organization that
neglects it is asking for trouble. Unfortunately, many organizations do just
that, preferring instead to concentrate on hardware and procedures. People
are the ultimate source of all security risks. Threat actors are only human,
after all; so too are the victims and the security practitioners trying to
protect them. Even the best technology cannot stop a skilful con artist,
social engineer, or spy. The Director of the US National Security Agency
(NSA), whose remit is all things cyber, put it like this: 'Don't forget that at
the end, you're dealing with a choice that some humans made on a
keyboard somewhere ... Never, ever forget the human dynamic.'[1]

People are central to defence as well as offence. An organization's biggest
security asset is its people, both individually and collectively. Despite that,
the protective security world continues to suffer from something of a blind
spot. The cyber security industry, in particular, has been justifiably

criticized for its tendency to portray cyber security as essentially a technology problem with technology solutions. The more mature defence industry does at least acknowledge the human dimension, but its habitual use of the term 'human factors' evokes a limited perspective in which the human is regarded as an awkward component to be fitted into the engineering solution, rather than the other way around. For protective security to work well, it must be designed with people in mind. Usability is crucial.[2]

Security is all about people. The difficulty is that people are far more complex and apparently harder to fathom than locks, bombs, or malware. Getting to grips with the human dimension means contending with abstruse psychological attributes like trustworthiness, integrity, reliability, loyalty, discretion, gullibility, deception, malice, betrayal, recklessness, and vengefulness. These attributes are hard enough to define, let alone measure in a way that would satisfy an auditor. But that is no excuse for glossing over them. One of the main reasons why so many security systems remain vulnerable is that threat actors pay more attention to the psychology of their victims than do most security designers and practitioners.[3]

This chapter is about the human dimension of security risks and countermeasures—or to put it another way, protecting *against* people and protecting *with* people. First, we will look at the risk from insiders and how to mitigate it through personnel security. Then we will consider how the security culture of an organization makes a crucial difference to the effectiveness of protective security.

The Insider Risk

Potentially the most serious source of security risk for any organization is the people who work for it and have legitimate access to its assets. A well-placed insider can damage any business or institution by stealing its money or intellectual property, committing fraud, leaking sensitive information, physically damaging property, assaulting people, perpetrating a terrorist attack, sabotaging infrastructure, or helping a third party to do any of the above. Insiders can do this more easily than external threat actors because they have legitimate access, more understanding of how things work, and more opportunity to circumvent security. For the same reasons, insider attacks tend to be more sophisticated, harder to detect, and more likely to succeed.

The biggest insider risks stem from malicious and determined insiders with free access to the most valuable assets—the archetypal saboteur, thief, or spy at the heart of the organization. But not all insiders are malicious or intend to cause harm. Some insiders unwittingly cause harm by doing the wrong thing, such as misplacing sensitive data or leaving doors unlocked; others are duped into doing the wrong thing by external threat actors. They inflict damage without meaning to because they are overworked, distracted, unaware, impatient, lazy, gullible, or complacent. A British government minister once quipped that his department was full of officials working to bring about his downfall, and the really frightening thing was that most of them had no idea they were doing it.

Whether or not someone is regarded as an insider should depend on their behaviour, not their presumed motivation. With that in mind, a good working definition of an insider is *a person who exploits, or intends to exploit, their authorized access for unauthorized purposes.*[4] This definition does not require the insider to harbour malicious intentions, but merely to act in an unauthorized manner or set out to do so.

Another important point is that insiders need not be permanent employees: they could be contractors, suppliers, or other third parties. All that matters is having authorized access. Most organizations have an inadequate understanding of the insider risk from their own employees and an even weaker grasp of the risk from third parties. They generally know less about their contractors or suppliers than they do about their own employees, making it even harder to assess the risk. This is despite the fact that some third parties have authorized access to the crown jewels, such as the IT contractor with systems administration access to the corporate system.

Malicious insiders are responsible for huge amounts of financial crime and fraud in the workplace. For instance, a junior UK government official was found guilty in 2018 of conspiring with criminals to defraud the national immigration system. The fraud was estimated to have cost UK taxpayers £56 million in false benefit claims.[5] Malicious insiders have also been responsible for stealing sensitive information that has helped hostile governments and terrorist organizations to harm their adversaries. Aldrich Ames, a CIA officer, and Robert Hanssen, an FBI officer, spied for the Russians for many years before being uncovered and arrested. The damage they caused to US national security is unfathomable. In 2011, a former British Airways software engineer was jailed for plotting to destroy a passenger plane on behalf of Al Qaeda. He exploited his insider access to search for ways of smuggling a bomb onto a plane and investigated how he might sabotage the airline's computer systems.[6]

Insiders have sometimes exploited their trusted status to deadly effect by assassinating people to whom they have privileged access. The victims have included King Faisal of Saudi Arabia, who was shot at point-blank range by his nephew in 1975, and the Indian Prime Minister Indira Gandhi, who was assassinated by her own bodyguards in 1984. In 2009, a US Army psychiatrist, Major Nidal Hassan, opened fire on his compatriots in Fort Hood, Texas, killing thirteen people.

Unwitting insiders are often exploited by external threat actors. Criminals, terrorists, hackers, spies, and ideological activists use deception to penetrate the protective security of target organizations by manipulating well-meaning employees—in effect, turning them into insiders. A standard manipulation technique is *social engineering*, in which the threat actor poses as a customer, colleague, or authority figure, and tricks the hapless employee into revealing information or providing material assistance. The employee thinks they are being helpful. In fact, they are helping to harm their employer.

Many cyber attacks are facilitated through social engineering. For instance, in 2016 Iranian hackers used social engineering to penetrate the accounting firm Deloitte. An attractive but fictitious woman called Mia Ash used her fake Facebook account to develop an online relationship with an employee who worked in cyber security, before eventually tricking him into opening a document spiked with malware. This case illustrates another general point, which is that people who work in cyber security are among the tastiest targets for social engineering because they have such good access.

Most cyber security breaches have an insider element involving current or former employees. In 2000, for example, a disgruntled insider conducted a cyber sabotage attack on an industrial control system in Australia, causing 800,000 litres of raw sewage to be released into parks and rivers.[7] Various studies have found that more than half of all cyber security incidents involve people inside the organization rather than external attackers, and of these insider-related incidents, more than half are unintentional acts like inadvertently sending sensitive information to the wrong recipient. A large survey of mostly US businesses and institutions found that 40 per cent of organizations judged the risk from malicious insiders to be the most damaging type of cyber security risk they faced, while almost the same proportion (36 per cent) judged unwitting insiders to be the most damaging. Despite this, more than a quarter of the organizations surveyed had no budget for insider security work.[8]

Just as most cyber attacks have an insider element, so, conversely, do many malicious insider attacks have a cyber element, in which the insider exploits their organization's own technology to cause harm. The insider Edward Snowden stole 1.7 million classified documents from the US government using its own IT systems. An insider theft on that grand scale would have been almost impossible in the days of paper records.

Hostile foreign states routinely collect secret intelligence by recruiting covert human sources within target businesses and governments. The agencies that conduct these so-called humint operations are experts in the business of creating insiders within target organizations. They also use cyber methods to enhance the effectiveness of their humint operations. If your aim is to recruit someone to be a covert source—which is a big ask—then it helps to know what makes that person tick, what turns them on, what turns them off, and how you can get to know them. That knowledge can be acquired relatively easily by collecting and analysing personal data lifted from open sources and stolen through cyber attacks. Once a covert human source has been recruited, he or she may then be used to facilitate further cyber attacks by providing the threat actors with inside access to systems and data.

Despite the obvious potential for serious harm, many organizations are less well equipped to tackle the insider risk than they are other forms of security risk. It is not uncommon for an organization to spend substantial sums on its physical and cyber security, and discuss cyber risk at board level, but do little about its insider risk. One reason may be that it is easier to think about material things like the paraphernalia of physical and cyber security. An intruder alarm system or cyber security device is comfortingly tangible, whereas the complex motivations of people seem dauntingly intractable. Furthermore, in marked contrast to the burgeoning cyber security industry, there is no army of marketers selling personnel security solutions.

The human dimension of protective security remains something of a Cinderella subject, in the sense of being a neglected drudge. However, the Cinderella story has a happy ending in which the neglected drudge is eventually recognized for her true worth and rises to a position of prominence. A parallel happy ending is much needed for the human dimension of protective security.

Personnel Security

The defensive measures that organizations use to protect themselves against insider risks are conventionally referred to as *personnel security*. The core purpose of personnel security is to confirm the identity of individuals and provide sufficient assurance about their trustworthiness.[9]

The best-known element of personnel security is the pre-employment screening of potential employees. Another is the use of passes to control physical or cyber access. A less obvious but important element is good management. As noted earlier, an insider risk can arise from anyone with authorized access, regardless of whether they are direct employees or intend to cause harm. Personnel security should therefore encompass everyone with authorized access, including third parties.

The terminology in this area can be confusing, so it is worth pointing out the main trip hazards before moving on. Personnel security is sometimes mistaken for *personal security*, which means something different. Personal security refers to the protection of individuals against mostly physical threats in their private and professional lives. Personal security is about protecting people, whereas personnel security is about protecting organizations. To add to the confusion, some authorities use the term *people security*, which means something different again. *People* security refers to any way in which an understanding of human behaviour can improve protective security—for example, by promoting vigilance among staff or deterring threat actors. For the avoidance of further confusion, I will avoid the term.

A good place to start is the nature of the threat. What is known about the intentions and capabilities of insiders? Some of the best research in this area has been commissioned by the Centre for the Protection of National Infrastructure (CPNI), the UK national authority for protective security. Their analysis of hundreds of known cases has revealed various things about insiders. One is that most malicious insiders do not join an organization with a pre-existing intention of causing harm; rather, they develop malicious intentions sometime after joining. A second conclusion is that, although insiders have different motivations, a frequent theme is feeling undervalued or insufficiently rewarded. Thus, an archetypal malicious insider would be a middle-ranking employee who has worked in the organization for several years and feels resentful that their talents have not been properly recognized. In some cases, such people are manipulated or coerced by external threat actors who want to exploit their inside access. The ways in which threat actors go about cultivating insiders are in some respects analogous to the radicalization of vulnerable individuals by terrorist groups or the grooming of children by paedophiles.

This sort of empirical evidence about the insider threat should inform the design of personnel security. For a start, it tells us that *pre-employment screening* (also known as 'vetting' or 'clearance') will not solve the problem by itself, because the insider risk often develops after the individual has joined. Good personnel security requires continuous assurance, known as *aftercare*, throughout the individual's relationship with the organization. Indeed, personnel security should concern itself with what happens after someone leaves the organization, because disgruntled former employees or contractors, otherwise known as *bad leavers*, could still cause harm.

A second reason for not relying too much on pre-employment screening is that it cannot provide a high level of assurance that someone does not, and will not, present a security risk. Most pre-employment screening is fairly crude and does two basic things: it verifies the individual's identity and checks whether they have a criminal record. Confirming that applicants are who they say they are, and then checking whether they are known to be serious criminals or terrorists, is obviously prudent. However, record checks are only as good as the quality of the records and they are only valid on the day the check is made. An applicant might have done bad things that are not logged in official records and they might go on to do bad things after the records have been checked. Therefore, failing to find significant adverse traces, which is what happens in the great majority of cases, provides only limited assurance. It certainly does not prove that the individual is eternally trustworthy.

Even something as apparently simple as verifying a person's *identity* is not straightforward in an era of mass identity fraud and cyber crime. How can you be certain that people are who they say they are, given the prevalence of cloned identities and forged records? Come to that, how would you prove your *own* identity if cyber criminals had stolen it and used it to create a new you? The degree of assurance required about someone's identity should depend on the impact of getting it wrong. A name and postcode might be sufficient for a trivial marketing transaction, but more substantial evidence should be sought before giving someone access to treasure.

There is no perfect solution for verifying identity. Documents can be forged and passwords are frequently compromised. The safest strategy is to cross-match several credentials of different types. The larger the number of unrelated credentials, the less plausible it becomes that the entire set has been stolen or forged.

A basic precaution in cyber security is the use of *two-factor authentication* (2FA) to establish a user's credentials before allowing them to log on. The first identifying factor is something the individual *knows*—typically a password. The second factor is something the individual *has*, such as a special token or a registered mobile phone to which a one-time passcode is sent. A common manifestation of 2FA is the chip-and-PIN credit card. (You *know* the PIN and you *have* the chip in your card.)

Even though 2FA improves security, many people do not use it on their personal devices and rely on just a password. Passwords are notoriously fragile defences: threat actors guess them and steal them in vast quantities. In 2018 a cyber security company reported finding on the dark web a single trove of stolen data containing 1.4 billion sets of personal credentials, comprising pairs of usernames and passwords in unencrypted plain text.[10] To make matters worse, many people reuse the same password for several accounts, which means that losing one password will compromise all of them.

Having verified an applicant's identity, what happens next? The central purpose of pre-employment screening is to reduce the chances of inadvertently recruiting someone who presents a risk, which is where record checking comes in. In the absence of other solid evidence about an individual's trustworthiness, *the best guide to future behaviour is past behaviour.* A serious criminal record is an obvious warning sign that requires attention. Which is not to say that everyone with a criminal record presents an unacceptable risk: it depends on the nature, severity, and frequency of the offences, and the type of job. The decision whether to employ someone with adverse traces boils down to a judgement about risk. Pragmatically, that judgement needs to take account of the fact that criminality is remarkably common. In England and Wales, for example, approximately one in four males has had at least one criminal conviction.[11]

Pre-employment screening can be far more sophisticated than verifying identity and checking criminal records. Personnel security gatekeepers have a rich menu of options for sharpening their risk judgements about individuals, ranging from the simple interview to psychometric testing, physiological monitoring, and data analysis. The drawback with many of these options is that they are time-consuming and intrusive, so the temptation is to omit them and hope for the best. More importantly, some methods work poorly, if at all. Before subjecting applicants to a battery of tedious tests, an employer should examine the evidence that the tests are actually effective in identifying risk. In other words, they should be *validated*. The evidence often turns out to be limited or absent.

The commonest method of assessing potential recruits is to *interview* them. The value attached to the common-or-garden interview is greater than it deserves, given its unimpressive track record in predicting people's behaviour. Interviewing certainly has its place in personnel security, but it can be a blunt instrument. One weakness is the inherent tendency for interviewers to place too much confidence in their immediate subjective impressions and pay insufficient attention to contradictory information—a psychological bias known as the *halo effect*.[12] Another weakness is our inherent bias towards people who are similar to us.

An informal, unstructured interview is generally a poor way of assessing an individual's trustworthiness—or indeed anything else for that matter, including future job performance.[13] (To use the language of psychology, it has low predictive validity.) The unstructured interview is an especially poor way of judging whether someone is telling the truth.

A wealth of empirical evidence shows that whereas most people believe they can tell when someone is lying, their objective performance in detecting lies is actually little better than chance. The average accuracy found in psychological studies of deception is just over 50 per cent.[14] People's confident judgements about lying are in fact little better than random guesswork. This uncomfortable truth applies to security professionals and police officers as well as the general public. Many popular beliefs about supposed tell-tale signs of lying, such as hesitation, rapid blinking, avoidance of eye contact, and shifts in body posture, have no solid basis in evidence. Decades of research have failed to uncover a reliable nonverbal signal of lying. Inconveniently, the behavioural equivalent of Pinocchio's nose does not exist.

Structured interviews are generally better than unstructured interviews at making predictions about trustworthiness, future behaviour, or perform-ance.[15] Even so, they are still subject to many common forms of psychological bias (the most relevant of which are described in Rule 7). If the purpose of an interview is to judge whether someone is telling the truth, a more fruitful approach is to concentrate on eliciting factual information that can be independently verified and checked for internal consistency. The same information is repeatedly requested in different ways, to see if the story changes. That way, the interviewer has a better chance of catching out someone who is being evasive or untruthful about their past behaviour. Untruthful accounts tend to contain more discrepancies, less complicated background detail, and fewer admissions of imperfect memory.[16]

The effectiveness of lie detection can be further improved with a struc-tured approach known as the *cognitive interview*, which is designed to flush out discrepancies.[17] The cognitive interview uses three main psychological tactics. First, it imposes a high cognitive load (i.e. a large demand on thinking capacity)—for example, by making the interviewee relate their account in reverse chronological order. Telling lies uses a lot of thinking capacity and is harder to sustain under high cognitive load. A second tactic is asking for a lot of detailed information, because liars find it harder to provide details. A third tactic is asking quirky, unexpected questions that a liar with a pre-cooked story would find hard to answer quickly, such as where people were sitting or the colour of the walls. Studies have shown that cognitive interviews are better than standard methods at detecting truth and lies. But even cognitive interviews only get it right around 70 per cent of the time.[18]

Another set of tools are *psychometric tests*, which are designed to assess particular aspects of cognitive ability, personality, or attitudes. There are many thousands of tests to choose from and some are much better than others. Buyers should sniff the air carefully for the whiff of snake oil; they should also be wary of using respectable psychological tests that have little relevance to the problem in hand. A test might be good at assessing some aspect of personality, but that does not make it a reliable indicator of trustworthiness.

Certain psychometric tests have been designed specifically to uncover warning indicators relevant to personnel security. They include the *dark side* tests, which look for aspects of personality that are known to be associated with problematic behaviour. Psychological research has highlighted three characteristics in particular, known as the *dark triad*. They are *narcissism* (excessive self-love and grandiosity), subclinical *psychopathy* (characterized by impulsivity and lack of empathy), and *Machiavellianism* (cynical manipulation of others).[19] All three characteristics are marked by callousness and manipulation. Individuals who display dark triad characteristics are often hard to manage in the workplace. They are charming and persuasive but see nothing wrong with their bad behaviour.[20] The narcissistic trait, in particular, is a noteworthy indicator of insider risk.[21]

No matter how good the pre-employment screening, new insider risks could emerge after an individual has come on board. Any organization that is even half-serious about managing the insider risk should therefore devote much of its personnel security effort to what happens *after* recruitment. The term *aftercare* is used to describe these post-recruitment elements of personnel security. As with pre-employment screening, aftercare should apply to everyone with authorized access, including third parties.

A crucial, if unglamorous, element of personnel security aftercare is *competent management*. This is important both for preventing people from becoming insiders and for detecting those who do. No amount of cognitive interviewing, psychometric testing, polygraphing, or automated data monitoring can substitute for managers doing their jobs properly.

An individual who is on the path to becoming a malicious insider may display behavioural signs of distress or disaffection, such as declining performance, repeated grievances, hostile language, or symptoms of mental health problems or substance abuse. The people who are best placed to notice these warning signs at an early enough stage are the individual's managers and colleagues. Good personnel security aftercare includes mechanisms for enabling such concerns to be reported discreetly and appropriate action taken. The appropriate action will usually be to find out what is troubling the individual and, where possible, help to resolve it. The problem may turn out to be related to their private life rather than work. Aftercare becomes more difficult if employees are working remotely, cut off from regular contact with colleagues and managers.

A simple process that can contribute to aftercare is requiring each employee and their line manager to complete a security questionnaire once or twice a year. The employee is asked if their personal circumstances have changed, if anything is troubling them, and if they have anything to declare. They may be asked specific questions about financial difficulties, mental health problems, and tangles with the law. The manager is separately asked if the individual's behaviour has changed significantly and if they have any reasons for concern. The manager's questionnaire may also cover known indicators of risk, including poor relationships with colleagues. A questionnaire cannot provide much assurance, but it does at least compel the main players to think about the issue from time to time.

Competent management is not only vital for detecting problems; it is also central to preventing problems from developing in the first place. Bad or indifferent management can stoke up the insider risk by eroding trust, alienating employees, and failing to recognize the warning signs of impending problems. Disaffected employees are often found in clusters, with an incompetent or bullying manager as the common factor. Poor treatment by managers is a significant factor behind theft, absenteeism, and other undesirable workplace behaviours. The toxic environment created by a bad manager can ferment an insider risk. As two experts in this area memorably put it, *rotten barrels make rotten apples.*[22] The clear implication is that personnel security should not just be about hunting for insiders (rotten apples): it should also concern itself with the toxic working environments that breed insiders (rotten barrels).

A common but mistaken belief is that personnel security is a specialist function performed by the security department or HR. When a serious insider case is discovered, it often transpires that the perpetrator's colleagues had long suspected that something was wrong but were reluctant to report their suspicions or assumed that HR or security were dealing with it. The history of personnel security is littered with instances of everyone being wise after the event. An example from the Cold War is the case of Michael Bettaney, a rogue MI5 officer who in 1983 attempted to spy for the Soviet Union. Before Bettaney could do much damage, MI5 received a secret warning from an agent working for British intelligence within the Soviet Embassy in London. Bettaney was arrested, tried, and sent to prison.[23] In the ensuing official inquiry, it emerged that Bettaney had been well known among his colleagues as a troubled individual who drank heavily and behaved erratically. The Bettaney affair led to major organizational reforms within MI5, which included modernizing its system of personnel management and making managers and colleagues responsible for significant aspects of aftercare.

As an aside, the Bettaney case is also a delicious example of the need-to-know principle at work. At the time he volunteered to spy for the Soviets, Bettaney was working in the counter-espionage section of MI5, which was responsible for investigating Soviet intelligence activity in the UK. He therefore had extensive access to secret intelligence about Soviet intelligence officers based in the London embassy. Fortunately, Bettaney was not privy to the tightly held secret that one of those Soviet intelligence officers was also a British agent, Oleg Gordievsky, who was supplying crucial secret intelligence during a particularly dangerous phase in the Cold War. It was Gordievsky who alerted his case officer to the existence of a traitor within MI5. A covert investigation then established that the traitor was Michael Bettaney. Gordievsky was able to do this without compromising his own delicate cover because Bettaney did not know he was a British agent.[24]

The Bettaney case featured another important component of personnel security, which is the capability to *investigate* leads to potential insiders or individuals about whom there are security concerns. This is a sensitive area, in terms of both employment law and the maintenance of trust between employers and employees.

Technology has a growing role to play in personnel security, though it is not the panacea it is sometimes cracked up to be. Technology can be brought to bear in two main forms: automatic *protective monitoring* systems that search for warning signs of potential insider activity; and technical tools that aid the *detection of deception* by helping investigators to judge whether someone is lying.

The concept of protective monitoring is well established in cyber security, where it refers to automated systems that continually search within digital networks for signs of unusual activity that might be symptomatic of a cyber attack. The same basic concept applies in the personnel security domain. Protective monitoring systems are designed to sift through huge quantities of data on corporate networks looking for indicators of potential insider activity such as individuals working unusual hours, accessing information they do not need for their role, illicitly copying data, or emailing sensitive information to an unknown external address. Such systems often work by comparing the individual's behaviour against their previous behaviour or a behavioural profile that would be expected for someone with their job role. Others search for 'tripwire' behaviour patterns that are deemed to be indicators of potential insider activity.[25]

The technology is the easy bit. The hard part is deciding which behavioural indicators to monitor, how much risk they indicate, and what to do next. Some products incorporate the latest technology, with AI-enabled systems to crunch the data and impressive dashboards to display the resulting measurements of insider risk. However, the marketing claims are not always borne out by solid evidence that the indicators reliably reflect the actual security risk. Even the *presumed* relationships between indicators and underlying risk are less obvious than they may seem. The fact that, say, an employee has been entering and leaving a building at unusual times clearly does not constitute evidence of malicious intent, although it may warrant further investigation.

Some technology vendors have made bracing claims about the ability of AI to detect insiders by analysing language patterns in email traffic or other streams of data. However, it is not that easy to draw reliable deductions about a person's state of mind or covert intentions from their emails or movement patterns alone. Smart systems learn by comparing the incoming data against real-world data about known insider activity, which is in short supply. Furthermore, malicious insiders are covert and intelligent adversaries. They try hard to stay below the radar, and if they suspect they are being monitored, they will adapt their behaviour and game the system. The technology is seductive because it dangles the alluring prospect of cheap, automated personnel security. But it is not magic and it does not negate the need for human judgement.

Protective monitoring systems, like all detection systems, are imperfect. They inevitably generate false positives (innocent people flagged as suspicious) and false negatives (real insiders not detected). The false positives may upset those who wrongly fall under suspicion. The certainty of false negatives should unsettle the security team. Furthermore, the act of monitoring a workforce can make employees feel they are not trusted, leading potentially to disaffection and a consequential *increase* in insider risk unless it is sensitively managed. Research has shown that excessive monitoring of employees can erode trust and increase the incidence of depression, anxiety, and fatigue.

Detecting an indicator of insider activity is one thing. Acting on that information is another. Even the best technology can only take things so far. The information must at some point be passed to humans for assessment and action. If the risk looks credible and serious, the usual next step would be to mount an investigation (though many organizations lack the capability to do that).

Automated monitoring of employees raises significant privacy issues. If an employer can use corporate data to make judgements about people's trustworthiness and insider risk profiles, they might also be able to use the data to make judgements (whether accurate or not) about their employees' sexual orientation, religious beliefs, and political views. Big social media platforms can already do this and more. The legal and regulatory controls on intrusive surveillance by the state are quite tightly drawn in liberal democracies. Fewer restrictions are placed on big tech companies whose business model relies on farming us all for our personal data. Electronic surveillance is ubiquitous on the internet and most of it is done by the private sector. Few people fully appreciate the awesome power of Big Data, by which I mean the aggregation and automated analysis of very large and diverse data sets.[26] Big Data literally enables organizations to know more about you than you know about yourself.

If you think electronic surveillance is of no consequence unless you have done something wrong, think again. Setting aside the inevitability of false positives, the mere fact of surveillance affects us all. We change our behaviour when we think we are being watched. We tend to behave a little more virtuously when we are not alone, even if we are not always conscious of doing so. Ubiquitous online surveillance induces people to self-censor, somewhat like medieval peasants fearing that their sins would consign them to Hell. The Russian government has harnessed this psychological effect. Many Russians have been convinced by state-controlled media that Russia's enemies are using the internet to weaken their nation, leading them to avoid websites and social media channels that are critical of the regime. Researchers who have studied internet use in Russia refer to a 'psychological firewall' which keeps people away from troublesome sources without the government having to block those sources. A similarly insidious form of censorship is going on in Turkey.[27]

Back in the realm of personnel security, technology can support aftercare investigations by aiding the detection of deception. Various technologies are capable, to limited and varying degrees, of detecting signs that an individual is telling a lie, feels guilty about something they have done, or intends to behave badly in the future. The best-known example is the *polygraph*, which measures fluctuations in heart rate, blood pressure, breathing, and skin conductivity as proxy indicators of psychological stress and deception. The effectiveness of the polygraph in detecting deception remains controversial. Most psychologists who have reviewed the empirical evidence have concluded that although the polygraph has value, it is nowhere near as reliable as some of its more ardent proponents have claimed. Moreover, the polygraph is susceptible to being subverted because all of the physiological variables it captures can be skewed by mental or physical actions.[28] Newer technologies such as facial thermal imaging, laser Doppler vibrometry, and voice stress analysis are designed to measure similar physiological variables at a distance, without the subject necessarily being aware. At the other extreme of invasiveness lies brain imaging, which requires the subject to lie motionless inside a brain scanner.

These and other technological tools have considerable potential to support personnel security. Nonetheless, the evidence for their effectiveness is often far from conclusive and they should be approached with healthy scepticism. As always, the buyer should beware of being seduced by technologies that seem to offer quick and objective diagnoses of complex security risks. The need for human judgement cannot be avoided. Furthermore, no single method can reveal the whole picture on its own. As far as possible, screening and aftercare should combine and cross-compare a wide variety of methods.

Psychology and technology are not the only weapons in the personnel security armoury. The humble organizational structure can also make a contribution. A useful tactic for inhibiting insider risk is to artificially increase the number of people required to form a successful conspiracy. Other things being equal, *the more people it takes to conduct an insider attack, the less likely the conspiracy is to succeed.* The archetypal example is the dual-key safeguard against the unauthorized launch of nuclear weapons, whereby at least two key-holders must independently authorize a firing. A similar method has evolved in the civil nuclear industry, where security systems have been designed to ensure that the malicious compromise of hazardous radiological material would require the willing participation of two or more individuals. It should be physically impossible for one person acting alone to remove dangerous nuclear fuel or radioactive waste from a secure store. This approach works even better if the individuals do not know each other well, making it less likely that a covert conspiracy could be sustained.

An analogous principle of requiring a large conspiracy lies behind the blockchain technology that underpins cryptocurrencies like Bitcoin. The technology is arguably more interesting than the currency. A blockchain stores data about transactions in a huge distributed digital ledger which is replicated among all users, making it theoretically impossible for one user to make unauthorized changes. Blockchains are inherently more secure because they would require a very big conspiracy, involving large numbers of anonymous users, to alter the data. However, that does not make cryptocurrencies immune from crime. In 2018, for example, hackers stole £380 million of cryptocurrency from a Japanese digital currency exchange.[29] Cryptocurrencies appeal to criminals and enthusiasts because they do not involve a central authority such as a bank or a government. But this can come at a cost in terms of speed and computational demand. One sceptic has described them as a computationally burdensome way to hate the government.

A small but growing number of organizations are applying the discipline of programme management methodology to personnel security. The result is an *insider programme*, in which the various elements of personnel security, such as pre-employment screening, aftercare, investigation, and education, are managed in a coordinated way to achieve explicit objectives.

Security Culture

A critical component in the security of any organization is its *security culture*, which affects not only the insider risk but also the physical and cyber security risks. What is meant by 'security culture'? The culture of an organization is analogous to the personality of an individual. In essence, it means a consistent tendency to behave in certain ways. An organization's *security* culture may be thought of as its personality with regard to security. To put it another way, culture is 'the way we do things around here' and security culture is 'the way we do security around here'. Security culture has a big influence on individuals' behaviour and hence on the risks to an organization.

A good security culture is one in which everyone wants to do the right thing because they understand the risks and support the need for security. This sort of security culture is sometimes referred to as a *concordance* culture. It is a relatively rare beast. The more conventional type is a *compliance* culture, in which the organization seeks to enforce compliance with security rules through a regime of checking and auditing. Employees are told the rules, threatened with sanctions for disobeying them, and checked for their compliance. Relying too much on compliance creates a false sense of being in control and hence a false sense of security.[30]

A concordance culture is a more conducive environment for developing and sustaining good security behaviour. It equips people with an understanding of the risks and provides rapid positive feedback when they do the right things. The emphasis is on behavioural nudging and reward rather than punishment. And, as any psychologist or parent will attest, rewarding good actions is generally more effective at changing behaviour than punishing wrongdoing. Which is not to say that wrongdoing should go unremarked. However, a high likelihood of being detected is a better deterrent than the severity of punishment.[31]

A crucial ingredient of a good security culture is good *leadership* (which is discussed at greater length in Rule 10). If leaders set a bad example by ignoring security policies or tolerating unethical behaviour, then the rest of the organization is likely to follow suit.

Another characteristic of a good security culture is a willingness to *speak truth to power*. An organization is courting trouble if its employees are afraid to be open and honest about their security concerns, or if they are simply indifferent. One of the worst things that anyone involved with security can do is give *false assurance*, by saying that all is well when they know that all is *not* well. Bad managers unintentionally invite false assurance by creating an atmosphere of deference or fear in which their subordinates only ever want to give good news. The managers of an organization must in turn be willing to speak truthfully to their masters, such as shareholders, regulators, or government ministers. The historian Christopher Andrew commented that there are few more remarkable examples of an intelligence agency

THE RULES OF SECURITY

telling truth to power than when the head of MI5 informed the then Prime Minister Neville Chamberlain, during the build-up to World War Two, that Hitler privately considered Chamberlain to be an 'arsehole'.[32]

Security risks and safety risks are different, as noted in Rule 1. Security cultures and safety cultures are also different, although they can be mutually supportive. The aviation and civil nuclear industries have understandably been dominated by strong safety cultures for many decades, whereas their security cultures were more recent developments. Safety cultures are reinforced by regulations and policed by inspectors. However, prescriptive rules can be slow to change, especially when enshrined in national or international regulations. The resulting lack of agility is problematic when confronted with dynamic and adaptive security risks that evolve far faster than most regulatory regimes.

Building and maintaining a good security culture requires effective *communication*. The purpose of communication is to change attitudes and behaviour, not simply to convey information. Merely presenting people with factual information about security risks and rules is not an effective way of bringing about a sustained change in security behaviour. *Telling is not the same as persuading.* Effective communication means engaging hearts (emotions) as well as heads (rational thought). Telling stories is a proven technique: we learn best from our own and other people's experiences. Communication is more likely to work if there is an existing relationship of trust between the parties—which brings us to trust.

The Currency Is Trust

How can we tell if personnel security is working? A crude outcome measure would be the number of known insider cases. However, their incidence could fluctuate for other reasons, such as changes in business practice or economic conditions. More importantly, an absence of known insider cases might simply signify that none of the insiders has been spotted.

A more fundamental yardstick is *trust*. The ultimate gauge of effective personnel security is a high level of trust, both between individuals and between the organization and its workforce. If an organization has good reason to trust its people, and the people have good reason to trust the organization and each other, then the insider risk is well on its way to being managed. But what is meant by 'trust'?

At its simplest, trust is the willingness to put oneself at risk by accepting the positive intentions of another. Trust and risk go together. If you trust someone, you believe there is a low risk of your relationship resulting in harm to you. Famously, trust is slow to build, quick to destroy, and even slower to restore after it is broken.

A more granular definition of trust distinguishes between four essential aspects: benign intentions towards the other person; the competence to do what is expected; integrity; and reliability. To trust a person or organization, you must believe they are benevolent in their attitude towards you, capable of doing what you expect of them, honest and fair in their approach to others, and consistent in doing what they say they will do.[33] Trust requires competence as well as good intentions. It is therefore conditional and depends on context. You might trust a colleague to perform an administrative task without necessarily trusting them to remove your appendix or mend your car. Trust is based on an assessment of the evidence, which can change. It is not like faith. (Incidentally, trust is a more profound entity than 'engagement', a widely used concept in management and HR. 'Engagement' is a measure of how much discretionary effort an organization can elicit from its employees.[34])

A core aim of personnel security is to assess the *trustworthiness* of the people who have authorized access—in other words, the extent to which potential insiders should be trusted. Assessing trustworthiness is not easy, even supposing the warning signs are detected. For a start, we must aim off for our inherent psychological biases, which predispose us to trust individuals according to characteristics that have no objective relationship with trustworthiness, such as physical features, clothing, and facial expressions. (More about psychological biases in Rule 7.) Fraudsters know how to exploit these empty *trust signals* to dupe their victims. Intruders do the same when blagging their way into a secure area by wearing the right uniform and striding confidently ahead. Smart suits and high-vis jackets work wonders in creating a false sense of trustworthiness.

Reputation is a proxy measure of trustworthiness, insofar as it reflects a collective view of an individual or organization. However, reputation is vulnerable to manipulation by the unscrupulous. Organizations that suffer a major security breach usually suffer some damage to their reputation with customers and other stakeholders. Reputational damage is hard to quantify, but no less important for that. Indeed, some organizations appear to place more weight on reputational damage than other, more tangible forms of harm.

A more systematic approach to assessing trustworthiness would involve breaking it down into its four main elements—namely, benign intentions, competence, integrity, and reliability. Pre-employment screening and after-care are intended to assess these elements—most crucially, whether someone has lied or behaved in ways that suggest they lack integrity. Well-structured interviews and the right psychometric tests can cast light on an individual's intentions, competence, and reliability.

The Chinese government is taking a highly structured approach to judging the trustworthiness of each of its 1.3 billion citizens. It is doing this by harnessing Big Data in a national scheme called the Social Credit System.[35] Each individual is continually judged by analysing data generated by their online activity and mobile devices. The data sources include social media activity, official records, and locational data from personal devices. These rich streams of data about where each person is, what they are doing, who they are with, and what others are saying about them online are automatically collated and analysed. The output is an overall trustworthiness score for each person which everyone can see—somewhat like a star rating for online commercial services. The personal trustworthiness scores will increasingly have significant real-world consequences. The government plans to use them to determine such things as the individual's creditworthiness, employability, freedom to travel, and children's education.

The theory is that everyone will be incentivized by this extreme form of transparency to behave well in order to avoid a life-blighting low score. According to the official policy, the Social Credit System 'will allow the trustworthy to roam everywhere under heaven while making it hard for the discredited to take a single step'. It will certainly put everyone under pressure to conform to standards of behaviour set by the Chinese government, which decides how the score is calculated. Enrolment will be mandatory by 2020. It seems unlikely that citizens will be rewarded for scepticism or dissent.

EVERYONE IS BIASED

*Judgements about risk, security, and crises are prone to
systematic distortion by psychological predispositions. It is
better to understand these biases and aim off for them.*

———

In the protective security arms race between threat actors and defenders, the two sides continually vie with each other to cause or prevent harm. The outcomes depend on human judgements shaped by psychological influences that extend far beyond any simple calculus of costs and benefits. These influences encompass the beliefs, perceptions, experience, personalities, and emotional states of the protagonists. They underline once again the centrality of the human dimension in protective security. We humans are not rational calculating machines in possession of all the facts (a reality that economists eventually came to recognize). Rather, we are emotional and social animals. Our feelings, relationships, and experiences have pervasive influences on our judgement and decision-making, even more so under conditions of stress and uncertainty.

Each of us is equipped with a suite of psychological predispositions that systematically influence how we think and behave in different situations. These predispositions may be regarded as *unconscious heuristics* or rules of thumb. Evolution has equipped us with these predispositions because they help in making potentially life-saving decisions when there is insufficient information and not enough time to think. They work remarkably well in a wide range of situations. In some circumstances, however, they can lead us to make systematic errors in how we perceive risks and how we respond to those risks. Our unconscious heuristics do not always cope perfectly with complex and protracted challenges of the sort that twenty-first-century security risks present. However, a modicum of psychology can improve our chances of making better judgements.

Reacting to Danger

Let us start with our immediate reaction to an acute threat. The starkest security threat that most of us are ever likely to encounter is that of sudden and unexpected physical violence from an assailant. If you have ever found yourself on the receiving end of a violent confrontation, you will have experienced at first-hand how the biological fight-or-flight response alters perception and thinking. Your attention narrows and the subjective passage of time slows down. Long after the event, you retain a vivid memory of what happens in those few seconds or minutes. In the small minority of cases where extreme trauma leads to PTSD, those memories may repeatedly recur in the form of intrusive flashbacks.

When we are confronted with immediate danger, a cocktail of stress hormones floods the body, rapidly preparing us to fight or take flight. Among other things, the hormones mobilize energy in the form of glucose for the muscles. The physiological reactions include sharp increases in heart rate and breathing, the diversion of peripheral blood flow into the body core, and a rapid shutdown of digestion, reproduction, and other non-essential processes. These rapid physiological changes are 'designed' (by biological evolution) to protect us in a fight. They produce the symptoms that are famously associated with acute fear, including rapid breathing, bloodless extremities (pale face and 'cold feet'), churning guts ('getting the wind up'), and loss of libido.[1] On a really bad day they cause involuntary emptying of the bladder and bowels.

The flight-or-fight stress response includes significant changes in perception and thinking, which again are predominantly helpful. Your field of attention narrows down to a razor-sharp focus on the immediate threat. You unthinkingly pay close attention to the source of danger and lose interest in the scenery. This focusing-down of attention enables you to

121

devote your full mental capacity to the immediate threat. But it can be a mixed blessing in more complex and slower-burning incidents. If you remain too tightly focused on the apparent task in hand, you may fail to notice other salient information. In other words, you miss the wood for the trees. Worse still, you might attend to the wrong problem and fail to notice a bigger one emerging from the undergrowth. This form of cognitive narrowing, or tunnel vision, is referred to as *inattentional blindness* and it happens in stressful and non-stressful situations. When we are concentrating intently on one thing, we may become blind to everything else.

The effect was illustrated by a famous experiment in which volunteers were asked to watch a video of a basketball game and count the number of times the ball was passed between the players of one team, while ignoring the other team. The task was sufficiently absorbing that more than half the observers failed to notice an actor in a full gorilla suit walking into the middle of the game and thumping its hairy chest at the camera for several seconds before walking off.[2] Experts are not immune to inattentional blindness. In another experiment, radiologists were asked to search for signs of a lung abnormality in a series of scans. A large image of a gorilla was embedded in one of the scans. Of the twenty-four radiologists tested, twenty failed to spot the gorilla, even though eye-tracking proved that most of them had gazed directly at it.[3] They looked but did not see.

Inattentional blindness can lead to poor decisions when important aspects of a situation are inadvertently ignored. In times of crisis, it is not unknown for people to dive under the comfort blanket of minutiae instead of confronting the metaphorical gorilla-suited actor in the room. Tunnel vision can equally be a problem for day-to-day security. The security personnel who carry out search and screening procedures at airports and other high-security environments are looking for concealed objects that might cause harm. If they are instructed to search for too many other types of item, such as liquids, drugs, alcohol, pornography, and protest banners, they become less effective at finding the objects that really matter—the guns, bombs, and knives. The distraction is made worse because the low-risk items occur much more frequently than high-risk items. Casting the net too widely impairs their ability to perform their most crucial security function because they end up fixating on the wrong things.

The changes in brain function that accompany acute stress enable us to react faster, but at the expense of a reduced ability to process complex information. Parts of the brain responsible for processing new information and managing working memory are inhibited when we are stressed. The need for speed takes priority over the capacity for careful analysis, as our pattern of thinking switches into short-term survival mode. We consider fewer options and revert to familiar responses. At worst, the changes in brain function can produce a form of paralysis in which we dither and wait for others to act. We feel under pressure to make quick decisions but do nothing. This response can be fatal, as demonstrated in aviation disasters in which conscious passengers have remained in their seats and died rather than climbing out of a burning plane.

A notable feature of our reaction to acute threat is falling back on semi-automatic, intuitive responses. (*Semi*-automatic because they can be over-ridden by training or conscious effort.[4]) In life-threatening situations we act without thinking. A car pulls out in front and you unthinkingly slam on the brakes; an assailant throws a punch and you unthinkingly parry the blow. Our intuitive, semi-automatic responses may be based on expertise that we have acquired through experience and training. Failing that, they are guided by unconscious heuristics which have evolved to point us in the right direction in the absence of specific expertise or instructions.

Responding intuitively is obviously beneficial when there is no time to review all the options and devise an optimal plan. It is doubly beneficial because acute stress impairs our ability to remember procedures. During the long history of our species, our ability to react unthinkingly has made the difference between surviving and dying for countless of our ancestors. However, intuitive responses can be problematic in novel situations where a different and counter-intuitive response is required. The problem was illustrated by a series of experiments in which inexperienced trainees were tested on their ability to escape from a simulated helicopter crash into water—a frightening situation for anyone encountering it for the first time. The first time that people experience this, some freeze but most try to escape. However, their impaired thinking gets in the way. As the test rig plunges into the water and the cabin rapidly fills, the trainees try frantically to release their safety harness from the side, as they would a car seatbelt. In the acute stress of the moment, they revert to a habitual response learned from travelling in vehicles with seatbelts. In aircraft, however, the harness release buckle is situated centrally, not to the side. Their semi-automatic response was the wrong one in these circumstances and they might have drowned had it been a real accident. Experienced aircrew reach immediately for the central release buckle because their experience, acquired through training and exercising, has taught them the correct response. The trainees soon learn, however, and after five or six plunges into the water they unthinkingly do the right thing.[5]

The best way to avoid doing the wrong thing in a dangerous situation is to keep practising the correct response until it becomes semi-automatic. Military operators refer to this as developing *muscle memory*. A well-trained soldier can clear a jammed weapon without thinking, even in the heat of battle. For the same reason, people who are going to work in dangerous places are given hostile environment awareness training (HEAT). The training familiarizes them with acutely stressful situations they have not experienced before and allows them to practise the right responses in a safe setting. HEAT creates a muscle memory that might save their lives if their thinking is impaired by a real crisis.

Another way to stop people doing the wrong thing in an emergency is to design the technology so that their untrained intuitive response is also the correct response—in other words, *fitting technology around people* rather than the reverse. This principle lies behind the design of the panic bars (or crash bars) which are fitted as standard to fire exit doors. People do not have to be trained to use them because their intuitive behaviour in an emergency is also the right way to open the door. By the way, the notion that emergencies invariably cause people to panic, in the sense of thrashing around in a self-destructive frenzy, is a myth. Most people behave quite rationally in emergencies and many surprise themselves with their cool self-possession. Being trapped in a fire with no escape route is an extreme exception.

A tragic example of bad technology design was a battlefield friendly-fire incident in Afghanistan in 2001, in which eight soldiers were killed. A US Special Forces team was relaying the coordinates of a Taliban position to a US bomber when the battery on their GPS satellite navigation device ran low. They replaced the battery and transmitted the location. Sadly, the machine was designed to automatically reset the coordinates to its own location when restarted. The bomb therefore landed on the soldiers, not the Taliban.[6]

A legitimate criticism of some cyber security technology is that it falls short on intuitive user-friendliness. Users unwittingly do the wrong things and are then blamed for causing security problems. The conventional response from the authorities is to try cajoling the pesky humans into using the technology correctly by insisting on more training and stricter compliance. Sometimes, however, the best solution lies in fixing the technology, not trying to fix the people. (We return to cyber in Rule 8.)

A pervasive example of poor technology is the use of passwords to authenticate identity. Passwords are cheap to implement but place excessive demands on users. In the interests of security we are exhorted to use unique and complex passwords for each of our different accounts, where 'complex' means a string of a dozen or more characters including letters, numbers, and symbols. Then we are forced to change the passwords regularly and told never to write them down. Few normal humans can reliably remember dozens of complex passwords that change every few months. Consequently, many users recycle the same weak passwords across multiple accounts, making them vulnerable to hacking. The core problem here is not stupid or unwilling people—it is inadequate technology. In a better world, passwords would have died out long ago and we could authenticate our identity securely without requiring superhuman memory. Things are moving in that direction: technology is improving, with the growing adoption of biometric identifiers such as fingerprints and facial recognition.

While we are waiting for technology to make passwords extinct, the expert advice has been catching up with the human reality. The UK and US authorities have in recent years advocated a simpler approach to passwords that imposes a less unreasonable burden on users. In particular, they now advise that it is perfectly acceptable to base a password on an easily memorable (but long and obscure) phrase, and that passwords should be changed only if there is some suspicion they might have been compromised, not as a matter of routine. The sensible advice also recommends, among other things, that the operators of IT systems should only require passwords to be used when they are really needed and that they should provide users with secure means of recording their passwords.[7] Many businesses and institutions have yet to adopt this more human-compatible approach.

An example of well-designed technology working to support imperfect humans is security software that automatically prevents users from unwittingly sending sensitive data outside their organization or to the wrong recipient, which is one of the commonest causes of data compromise. Relatively simple software can enforce security policies that determine, for example, the types of files that can be downloaded onto USB sticks or sent to external email addresses. The financial services sector has adopted a systematic approach to what they call data loss prevention (DLP). The software will also make life harder for a malevolent insider who is deliberately trying to break the rules.

Misreading Risk

Psychological research over many decades has uncovered an assortment of inherent predispositions that can lead us astray when confronted with the sorts of novel, complex, and protracted challenges presented by contemporary security risks. These predispositions, which psychologists refer to as *cognitive biases*, have systematic effects on the way we think. They influence our judgement in a wide range of situations, not just those associated with risk and security. We will look at the most relevant ones, starting with our perception of risk.

As the products of evolution, we are built to be fearful or anxious in situations that could present an immediate threat to our wellbeing.[8] In the natural environment of our ancient ancestors, the cues that elicited fear were usually reliable indicators of genuine dangers, particularly those emanating from other humans, predators, or natural hazards. However, fear and anxiety are no longer reliable indicators of objective risk in the complex world of the twenty-first century. We are prone to be excessively alarmed by some types of risk and excessively relaxed about other risks that are in fact worse.

We are systematically inclined to overestimate the likelihood of exotic, attention-grabbing risks and underestimate the likelihood of mundane risks, even when the mundane risks are objectively more likely to materialize. A well-known example is the belief that sharks are more dangerous than stairs, even though the opposite is true by a wide margin. This distortion in our perception of risk is fuelled by a phenomenon called *availability bias*, whereby we find it easier to believe that something might happen if it comes easily to mind. The more easily we can picture an event, the higher our intuitive estimate of its likelihood. Events come more easily to mind if we have seen memorable accounts of them in the media, causing us to overestimate their likelihood. Shark attacks receive more media attention than domestic accidents, fostering a perception that they are more common than is actually the case. For similar reasons, we are inclined to overestimate the likelihood of bad events that we can easily imagine happening and underestimate risks that we find hard to imagine. A *failure of imagination* can therefore distort our perception of risk by leading us to discount the possibility of something that might actually happen.

Availability bias can distort our perception of security risks by skewing our anxieties towards risks that have attention-grabbing effects, such as mass-casualty terrorism, and away from risks that are less shocking but more likely to occur, such as cyber crime. Biological and radiological weapons have featured in films, books, and media stories, and the availability bias reinforces the 'dread factor' that makes these risks seem more likely to materialize. That said, it is still rational to be concerned about these methods of attack because of their potentially catastrophic impact. The likelihood of major terrorist attacks in western countries is low, but only because of strenuous efforts to stop them, and the impact of a successful attack would be far too grievous to discount.

Our perception of the effectiveness of protective security can also be distorted by availability bias. The public and senior managers of organizations tend to hear about security only when it has failed, leading them to believe it may be less effective than it really is. Security practitioners know from their daily experience that most of the time the security works well, and there would be far more incidents if it were badly flawed.

The availability bias also lies behind the recurring cycle of attack, anxious reaction, and complacent inaction that typifies the management of security risks. Following a major incident, we act to strengthen security because the event is still clear in our minds and we are anxious to avoid a repeat. But as time passes, the anxiety fades, and so too does our sense of how likely another attack will be. This false sense of security persists until the next attack dispels it. And so on.

Another source of distortion is *optimism bias*, which is a tendency to regard the world as a kindlier place than it really is, and ourselves as better and more capable than we really are. Optimism bias helps to explain why big projects overrun, why some people are dangerously overconfident about taking big risks, and why we all think we are better-than-average drivers.

Our tendency to delude ourselves about being better than average was first highlighted in the 1960s by two psychologists. They gave a questionnaire to fifty drivers who had ended up in hospital as a consequence of crashing their cars. All fifty disaster-prone drivers judged themselves to be above average in driving ability. So too did all fifty drivers in the control group, who differed only in not having crashed their cars.[9] The optimistic tendency to regard oneself as better than most other people is sometimes given its own label—*illusory superiority bias*. A majority of people believe they are above average on most skills and desirable personality traits, even though obviously this cannot be true. Research has shown that doctors, university professors, and other subject-matter experts are similarly prone to illusory superiority bias when judging their own professional prowess, and it is safe to assume that the same is true for security practitioners.[10]

Optimism bias has pervasive effects on our judgements about risk. Indeed, the pre-eminent psychologist in this field, Daniel Kahneman, believes that it may well be the most significant of all the cognitive biases. The movers and shakers in life tend to be the most confident and optimistic individuals. Bullet-proof confidence and optimism are attributes that society rewards.[11] Optimism bias can distort our perception of risk because it predisposes us to be over-optimistic about the risk of something bad happening, and overconfident about our ability to manage the risks. At worst, this can result in outright denial.

The Norwegian authorities appear to have displayed optimism bias in their attitude towards protective security before the terrorist attacks by Anders Breivik in 2011, as described in Rule 2. They were slow to take action when faced with clear expert advice about the scale of the risk. The government building that Breivik bombed housed the offices of the Norwegian Prime Minister and the Ministry of Justice and Police, making it a prime target. The 9/11 attacks had taken place a decade before and the high terrorist threat was evident to all, though Norway had thus far escaped. In 2003, the Norwegian Prime Minister's Office commissioned a review of government security, which made numerous recommendations for improving the protective security for government buildings. The recommendations included closing the street where Breivik's target was located, which would have prevented him parking his vehicle bomb outside it. As is so often the case, however, complacency and inertia stood in the way. A newspaper described the risk as 'hypothetical' and ridiculed the planned road closure as 'hysterical'.[12] Nothing was done. Attitudes changed dramatically after Breivik's bomb exploded.

A recurring feature of protective security is the need to experience a major attack before converting thought into action. In the cyber security industry, the tendency of clients to deny that anything bad might be happening to them, even in the face of clear evidence to the contrary, is known as 'ostriching'.

A moderating influence on optimism bias is personal experience. Research studies of people who engage in parachuting, paragliding, BASE jumping,[13] and other extreme sports have found that experienced practitioners tend to be more realistic—which is to say more pessimistic—about the risks. Individuals with extensive experience are more likely to have had personal exposure to bad outcomes, making them more respectful of the dangers. Coming within sniffing distance of disaster can be a powerful incentive to think about the risks and plan carefully to mitigate them.[14]

Optimism is not all bad, of course. Apart from making us feel good, one of its great benefits is helping us to be more persistent in the face of difficulties. If we blithely assume that everything will work out fine, we are less likely to give up. In that sense, a healthy degree of optimism can strengthen personal resilience (as discussed in Rule 5).

Another reason why our perception of risk may drift out of kilter is that we *habituate* to risky situations, so that bad becomes the new normal. The greater tolerance of risk that comes with habituation may be counteracted by greater knowledge and experience. Most of the time, however, we become blasé because nothing terrible has happened yet.

A further source of distortion is our predisposition to worry less about risks that are likely to materialize in the more distant future, compared to more immediate risks. This form of cognitive bias, known as *present bias* or *future discounting*, can make it harder to form sound judgements about how much effort to invest in preventing very low-likelihood/very high-impact risks such as catastrophic terrorist attacks. A related issue is our inability to understand intuitively how risk accumulates over time as we repeatedly expose ourselves to the same relatively small risk. The risk of dying in a single car journey or from smoking a single cigarette is tiny. But the *cumulative risk* from a lifetime of car journeys or smoking is surprisingly large. The likelihood of dying in a single car journey in the US is about one in 10 million, but the lifetime likelihood of dying in a car accident is more like one in 200.[15] (For comparison, the average 60-year-old man in the UK has a roughly 1 in 100 chance of dying in the next year.)

An important and pervasive influence on our perception of risk is a universal form of bias known as *loss aversion*. We humans are inherently more sensitive to potential losses than we are to potential gains of equivalent size.[16] When making decisions that might lead to gains or losses, our judgements are consistently biased towards the avoidance of losses. The biological explanation is simple: along with other animals, we have evolved to be more sensitive to situations that might threaten our wellbeing (potential losses) than we are to situations that might improve our situation (potential gains). Threats are more cogent than opportunities, and bad news takes priority over good news, because it is better to live to fight another day.

Loss aversion can be illustrated by a simple thought experiment. Imagine you are offered a gamble on a single toss of a coin. Heads, you win £11; tails, you lose £10. Rational analysis says you stand to gain more than you might lose. Nonetheless, most people choose not to take the gamble, because the unpleasant prospect of losing £10 weighs more heavily in their mind than the equally likely prospect of winning £11. Losses weigh more than gains. In fact, psychological experiments have established that *loss weighs roughly twice as much as gain.*[17] In other words, most people would have to be offered a win of at least £20 (double the potential loss) to make the coin toss an attractive gamble.

One consequence of loss aversion is that we will take bigger risks in order to avoid a loss than we would to acquire an equivalent gain.[18] Another consequence is that we need bigger perceived security gains to offset small perceived losses in time or effort. In cyber security, the users of computer systems immediately perceive the loss associated with having to perform an irksome security task such as updating software, whereas the gains are intangible. Not only that, but loss aversion means the perceived gain must be considerably bigger in order to win out over the loss.

Psychology also tells us that our evaluation of losses and gains is relative rather than absolute—that is, we judge a loss or a gain by comparing it against some reference point, such as our current situation or our expectations, rather than in absolute terms. That is why a 5 per cent pay rise seems good when compared against your current wage but feels like a loss if everyone else is getting 10 per cent. When evaluating security risks, it means that we pay more attention to small changes in risk than we do to the underlying baseline level of risk. We might feel excessively relieved to reduce a huge risk by a small amount, or excessively worried by a rise in a tiny risk.

Our asymmetric response to loss and gain is another reason why security receives less attention during periods of peaceful stability when everyone feels safe but immediately becomes the overriding priority when something bad happens. If we feel personally threatened, our normal desire to improve our situation by acquiring new benefits is overridden by a stronger desire to preserve what we already have. Threats are more cogent than opportunities. To put it more crudely, *fear trumps greed*. This makes good biological sense. For similar reasons, we humans are equipped with many more types of negative emotion than positive emotion. Moreover, the negative emotions, including fear, sadness, anxiety, guilt, disgust, anger, embarrassment, and jealousy, are more cogent than positive emotions like joy or gratitude. A feeling of pleasurable contentment can be overturned in an instant by sudden fear or anger. The negative emotions are there to protect us from threats to our wellbeing, so it is unsurprising that they take precedence.[19] Terrorists, criminals, and other threat actors are also subject to the asymmetric pressures of fear and greed, making it possible to influence their behaviour. Deterrence benefits from the fear of failure (and worse) weighing more heavily in the minds of threat actors than their countervailing desire to achieve their goals.

Another consequence of loss aversion is a tendency to stick with the status quo rather than making changes, even when those changes are known to be beneficial. A significant change, such as improving security, creates some losers, even when most people are winners and the net effect is overwhelmingly beneficial. Thanks to loss aversion, those who stand to lose are more highly motivated to avoid their loss than the winners are to acquire their benefit. The net result is resistance to change, including resistance to improving security.

Forming a realistic assessment of security risk depends on understanding the intentions and capabilities of threat actors (as discussed in Rule 3). Our ability to do this can be impaired by a cognitive bias known as the *fundamental attribution error*, which is a tendency to attribute the actions of other people to inherent characteristics of the person or group, rather than their particular circumstances or history, while doing the opposite for ourselves. When we see someone stumble, we judge them to be clumsy, whereas when we stumble, we blame the uneven floor. Attribution error is an obstacle to thinking seriously about the factors affecting other people's behaviour and hence how their behaviour might be changed. If the other side is simply judged to be irredeemably stupid or evil, then less effort is made to analyse their motivation and influence their behaviour.

Once a security risk has been assessed, we must decide whether it is tolerable, which is where another bias comes into play. There is reasonably good evidence that we are inclined to take bigger risks when we are feeling safe—a phenomenon known as *risk compensation* (or risk homeostasis). Cyclists tend to ride faster when they are wearing a helmet and drivers are more likely to speed when wearing a seat belt.[20] With tongue only slightly in cheek, an experienced skydiver remarked that the safer skydiving gear becomes, the more chances skydivers will take, in order to keep the fatality rate constant.[21] In similar vein, a road safety expert quipped that the most effective automotive safety device would be a large spike projecting from the steering wheel. A possible consequence of risk compensation is that some protective security measures do not reduce the risk by as much as expected because users take more risks. One example is the tendency of computer users to behave less securely online if they believe their system is protected by technical defences. They take bigger risks because they believe they are safe, even though the technology is rarely as effective as they think.

In addition to these universal cognitive biases, some individuals have personality traits that make them more than averagely inclined to take excessive risks. The personality traits that have the biggest bearing on risk-taking include *sensation-seeking* and *impulsivity*. Individuals who score highly on these traits are statistically more likely to smoke, abuse drugs, drink too much, gamble, drive too fast, not wear a seat belt, and engage in risky sex (though not necessarily all at the same time). In common with other personality characteristics, they are influenced to varying extents by genetic make-up. A number of specific gene variants are associated with individual differences in sensation-seeking and impulsivity, along with associated behaviours like gambling, financial risk-taking, and illicit drug use.[22] However, these traits are also heavily dependent on the individual's background, experience, and environment. Genes alone do not cause risk-taking behaviour. Psychological experiments have shown that even something as ephemeral as the presence of an attractive member of the opposite sex can have a measurable effect on people's propensity to take risks.[23]

The influence of personality traits and situational factors should be borne in mind when choosing people for security roles and designing the environments in which they operate. A reckless individual who enjoys behaving dangerously may not be ideally suited to taking responsibility for the security of others.

Mishandling Risk

The psychological predispositions and traits described above affect our perception of risk and reaction to immediate threats. Our subsequent ability to manage those risks and deal effectively with crises is influenced by a range of other cognitive biases. Five examples are worth singling out because of their relevance to protective security.

Confirmation bias is the universal tendency to pay attention to information that supports our existing beliefs while ignoring information that contradicts them, thereby entrenching our preconceptions. Obviously, this can be hazardous in major security incidents, where the situation is rarely clear-cut and existing beliefs sometimes turn out to be wrong. The ability to heed contradictory information and modify our beliefs in the light of new information is vital.

Our ability to work effectively with other people in a crisis can fall foul of the illusory superiority bias described earlier. Team dynamics are seldom improved when everyone in the team believes they are above average in ability. Then there is *groupthink*—the inclination to follow the pack and conform to the majority view, even when we privately suspect that the majority view is wrong. During security incidents or crises, the people trying to manage the situation rarely have a full understanding of what is going on and how best to deal with it. Groupthink can increase the risk of uniting around the wrong course of action and failing to consider better options.

Next on the list is *sunk-cost bias*, which inclines us to persist with a course of action because we have already invested heavily in it, even if objective evidence suggests it would be better to cut our losses and desist. The sunk-cost bias is a manifestation of the loss aversion described earlier. We continue to throw good money after bad to avoid the pain of accepting the loss. The investment need not be financial, of course. Sunk costs include time and emotional investment, and hence the bias keeps people plugging away at failing projects or persisting with the wrong policies or defences.

Finally, when things have gone badly wrong and the inquiries are underway, we are inclined to exhibit *hindsight bias*—the unattractive propensity to be wise after the event.[24] When we retrospectively blame people for making the wrong decision, we assume that the error lay in their poor judgement or folly. A more likely explanation is that they did not know then what we know now. Many well-made decisions turn out to be wrong for reasons that were unforeseeable at the time, and many of those who cast blame from the lofty position of hindsight would probably have made the same decision had they been in the same situation. We apply hindsight bias to our own judgements as well, with the result that we react to a surprising event as though we had been expecting it all along. We unconsciously revise our beliefs in the light of what we have just experienced and forget what we previously believed.

Hindsight bias is an obstacle to learning from adverse experience and therefore a barrier to developing active resilience. If we knew all along that something bad was going to happen, then what more is there to learn? Hindsight bias also fosters an unhealthy culture of risk aversion. Decision-makers soon come to realize that if something bad happens, they will be judged by the outcome, not the quality of their prior decisions. This encourages them to avoid risks and adopt standard procedures that would be harder to criticize after the event, regardless of whether they are the best procedures. A similar effect is apparent in the world of medicine, where litigation has incentivized doctors to act defensively rather than purely in the best interests of the patient.

The mirror image of hindsight bias is *outcome bias*, in which we assume that good outcomes result from good decisions by clever people rather than chance and circumstance. Good outcomes sometimes arise despite bad decisions by incompetent people, but they often get the credit nonetheless. Outcome bias is what fuels the reputations of some economists and financiers, whose lucky guesses we ascribe to their skill, and reckless risk-takers whose irresponsible gambles happen to pay off. Outcome bias similarly inclines us to remember the accurate predictions of security pundits and forget the many instances of events that were predicted but never happened.

Cognitive biases and personality traits are not the only factors that inflate our willingness to take inappropriate risks or impair our ability to make good decisions. One big influence, which is widely neglected in the realm of security, is *bad sleep*, by which I mean sleep that is inadequate in quantity or quality. Security crises deprive people of sleep. Business-as-usual can also be detrimental to sleep. Guards, control room operators, and other security personnel are often required to work shifts, and there is clear evidence that shift-working is associated with sleep disturbances.

Bad sleep has an array of corrosive effects on physical and mental health and performance. Entire books have been written about the damaging consequences of bad sleep, and here is not the place to rehearse the extensive evidence.[25] However, some findings are particularly relevant to protective security. Bad sleep has psychological effects that are remarkably similar in many respects to those of alcohol. Tired people behave rather like drunk people. Some of the similarities are obvious, including the impairments in physical coordination, attention, reaction time, memory, and problem-solving ability. Bad sleep also has detrimental effects on our response to risk. In common with people affected by alcohol, sleep-deprived people are less able to assimilate complex information or update their judgements in the light of new information, making them less able to assess dynamic risks. They become more reckless, more willing to take big risks, less aware of how impaired their judgement has become, and more confident in their own (bad) decisions. And despite being more inclined to take risks, they perceive themselves as *less* inclined. As people become progressively more sleep-deprived, they become more inclined to take risks that might produce large gains and less inclined to take risks that require effort. They also become more impulsive and less able to withhold inappropriate responses. One study, for example, monitored military pilots taking part in a maritime counter-terrorism exercise involving twenty-four hours of difficult flying. The pilots became more impulsive and more inclined to take risks as their tiredness grew.[26] Tired people have caused many road traffic crashes and industrial disasters.

You do not have to be without sleep for very long to start suffering the malign effects. Experiments have shown that measurable impairments in cognitive performance appear after only sixteen hours of continuous wakefulness. After twenty-one hours without sleep, the impairment in driving ability is similar to that caused by a blood alcohol level equal to the UK legal limit.[27] As if that were not enough, bad sleep disrupts our ability to work effectively in teams, by impairing communication skills and fraying tempers. In short, bad sleep is unpleasant, dangerous, and potentially a major obstacle to good security.

Aiming Off

This baleful catalogue of psychological snares and delusions should not be read as a counsel of despair. After all, most of us cope reasonably well with most problems most of the time, despite our predispositions and biases (and in many cases *because* of them). Moreover, there is much we can do to counteract their less helpful effects. Simply being aware of their existence is a start, and consciously bringing them to mind is a good practice. It is always advisable to be mindful of one's own psychological foibles, especially during stressful situations.

We can further enhance our ability to make better judgements by listening attentively to people with relevant experience and running a *lessons-learned* exercise after every significant incident. Beyond that lies a menu of tactics and methods for countering our cognitive biases. A simple technique for confronting confirmation bias and groupthink is *devil's advocacy*. This entails making someone explicitly responsible for challenging the consensus and advocating an alternative view. Devil's advocacy serves as a check against a dominant opinion being accepted too readily. It also helps to build confidence that an eventual conclusion will withstand robust scrutiny.

A more elaborate technique that counteracts groupthink is the *Delphi method*—a structured process for distilling the views of experts.[28] The wicked problems of security require input from as many experts as possible. However, the problem with putting experts around a table is the inevitable intrusion of group dynamics, which can result in the conclusion being less than the sum of its parts. The Delphi method provides an antidote. It works by eliciting the experts' views individually, anonymously, and iteratively. Each expert gives their opinion, usually by means of an online questionnaire. The various opinions are collated and the participants receive moderated feedback, which summarizes the emerging views without revealing whose views they are. The process is repeated, usually for three rounds. The aim is normally to reach a consensus, although the exposure of dissent can be equally valuable. A practical benefit of the Delphi method is that the experts do not have to meet physically, making the process quicker and cheaper than organizing a large international gathering. Its main benefit, however, is diluting the powerful interpersonal dynamics that often play out when a roomful of opinionated experts convene to wrangle over their pet subject.

The distorting effects of optimism bias and groupthink can be resisted with a technique known as the *premortem*.[29] The premortem is held just before an organization commits itself to an important decision to proceed with a plan. The individuals most closely associated with the decision are gathered together and told to imagine a future in which they went ahead with their plan, which turned out to be a disaster. Each of them is then asked to write their own brief history of the disaster, describing what went wrong. The premortem gives the decision-makers licence to express doubts and forces them to contemplate, if only briefly, the possibility that they might be wrong.

Other techniques for countering biases and improving the quality of analysis include checking key assumptions, reviewing the quality of the evidence on which the conclusions are based, analysing alternative hypotheses, and 'What If?' analysis.[30] When trying to assess complex situations, it is a good idea to make a list of all the *key assumptions* on which the final judgement will rest and check that they are valid. If we rush to a conclusion based on flawed assumptions, the answer is likely to be wrong. Another good discipline is scrutinizing the *quality of evidence* from which the conclusions are derived. Some strands of evidence will be stronger than others, and it is all too easy to forget caveats about their reliability. We can improve our confidence in a judgement by systematically identifying and evaluating *alternative hypotheses* (a more elaborate version of devil's advocacy). This helps to avoid becoming too firmly wedded to the first solution we thought of—a tendency that is reinforced by confirmation bias.

Probably the single most effective defence against making bad decisions is *expertise*—the combination of relevant knowledge, skills, and wisdom needed to cope with demanding situations. Experts pay attention to the right things, whereas novices focus on irrelevant details and become overwhelmed with information. Experts also cope better with ambiguity. They ask the right questions and know what to do.[31]

Expertise forms the bedrock of sound intuitive judgement. In a stressful and uncertain situation, the ability to make quick, intuitive judgements is crucial. Intuition is often portrayed as a semi-mystical property born of age and wisdom. However, psychological research has shown it to be something more mundane. In simple terms, intuition is a form of pattern recognition—the ability to spot patterns or signals in uncertain situations, based on past experience. That is why individuals who are highly experienced in a particular field, whether it be mountaineering or cyber security, tend to have more accurate intuitions. Their experience has equipped them with a richer set of reference points against which they can recognize patterns and quickly judge how a situation is likely to develop. They spot a cue in their environment and can link this to relevant information in their memory. Intuition is not magical: it is largely a matter of relevant experience. One practical implication is that we should pay more heed to people's intuition (including our own) if they have more relevant experience. In the context of protective security, the surest way of acquiring relevant experience is through regular practice, training, testing, and exercising.

Our ability to think clearly under pressure can be enhanced by mindfulness techniques, which have a proven capacity to help regulate emotions and improve the ability to focus attention. Decisions taken in a state of intense emotion tend to underestimate high-probability outcomes and overestimate low-probability outcomes. One way of countering this intrinsic bias is by managing our emotions, and mindfulness can help. The simplest technique for focusing more calmly on the problem in hand is consciously slowing one's breathing and silently counting to five before making the next move. Some threat actors use similar techniques for managing their emotions. The Norwegian terrorist Anders Breivik, who brutally murdered seventy-seven people in one day, most of them face-to-face, claimed to have used meditation to quell his emotions.[32] However, it does not pay to be *too* relaxed when managing dangerous situations. Our cognitive performance varies according to the level of stress in an inverse U-shaped manner: too much or too little stress impairs performance, whereas an intermediate level is associated with peak performance. Moderate stress keeps us sharp.

For the more numerate, there is *Bayes' Rule*—a mathematical formula for helping us to change our opinion in the light of new information. Bayes' Rule, which dates from the eighteenth century, is an objective method for determining how one's subjective belief in the probability of something happening should be modified when new evidence emerges. It helps its users do something that politicians are often accused of avoiding—namely, changing their opinion when the facts change. Dogged consistency may be seen as a positive trait in the political world, but it is dangerous when dealing with dynamic and adaptive security risks. As new evidence becomes available, the confidence we have in our prior judgements should change. Bayes' Rule provides a quantitative method for reassessing that confidence and modifying our views accordingly.[33]

Technology can also help by providing automated *decision-support tools* that guide the thinking processes of decision-makers when they are under pressure. However, there is a world of difference between automated decision-support tools and automated *decisions*. Automated systems cannot be expected to make optimal, unbiased decisions in complex and uncertain situations, not least because the algorithms that underpin them are the products of imperfect human judgements. If anything, the application of huge datasets and AI to security runs the risk of creating *more* opportunities for unconscious bias, not fewer. The prospect of fully automated security decision-making, free from the foibles of human psychology, is mightily seductive. But it remains illusory, at least for the foreseeable future.

RULE 8

CYBER IS NEW WAYS OF
DOING OLD THINGS

*The cyber domain brings distinctive problems. Nonetheless, its security
is subject to the same fundamental principles as other forms of protective
security, including the pre-eminence of the human dimension.*

The C-Word

We turn now to cyber—currently the most anxiety-provoking and attention-grabbing domain of protective security. Cyber security has left its physical and personnel security cousins in the shadows, with a global expenditure of more than 90 billion dollars a year and rising.[1]

The C-word is alluring: almost anything can be made to sound more interesting by attaching the 'cyber' prefix. Even insurance. Thus we have cyber crime, cyber bullying, cyber threats, cyber espionage, cyber fraud, and so on. We even have cyber terrorism, which arguably does not exist (yet). To add to the allure, cyber security practitioners make liberal use of steely martial terms like 'attack surface', 'threat vector', 'kill chain', 'logic bomb', 'payload', 'beachhead', and 'DMZ' (as in de-militarized zone) to describe quintessentially intangible entities. The C-word also helps security vendors to prise open their clients' coffers. But what does it mean?

The term cyber simply denotes that the matter in question has something to do with digital systems. Cyber security is *the protection of digital systems, the data on them, and the services they provide from unauthorized access, harm, or misuse.*[2] We live in a world that depends on data and digital systems.

Many of the world's biggest companies are essentially traders in data. But as the definition makes clear, there is more to cyber security than protecting digital data, important though that is. In this era of smart devices, autonomous vehicles, and computerized industrial control systems, the risks are far wider in scope. The cyber domain is as much about physical devices as it is about the movement of electrons.

The *Internet of Things* (IoT) is thought to comprise in the region of 20 billion internet-connected devices of many kinds, including smart watches, televisions, domestic lighting, energy meters, fitness monitors, domestic heating systems, cameras, conference equipment, pacemakers, vehicles, digital assistants, toothbrushes, traffic lights, and fridges.[3] They are all at some degree of risk because any device that connects to the internet is potentially vulnerable to attack from threat actors anywhere in the world. The locations and electronic identities of IoT devices can be discovered with relative ease using Google-like online search engines such as Shodan, which have been designed specifically to catalogue them. One important characteristic of the IoT is that it is always on. The internet is no longer something we occasionally switch on and access through a browser.

Sex toys have joined the IoT too, in the form of internet-enabled vibrators that log where, when, and how they are used. Some models pinpoint the user's location, record usage, and enable the user's partner to control them remotely via the internet. Some even record the user's body temperature or have a camera in their tip to stream live images of the immediate operating environment (as it were). The users of these smart vibrators may have been disconcerted by revelations that their devices could easily be hacked, allowing access to live streaming from the camera and data linked to their personal identities.[4] Cyber wags have enjoyed pointing out that these insecure devices would fail a penetration test.

Even more unsettling is the vulnerability of internet-connected children's toys equipped with cameras and microphones. In common with many IoT devices, some are highly vulnerable.[5] When hacked, these internet-connected cuddly toys and dolls can be used to listen to children, watch them, and talk to them. Some toys also harvest personal information from hundreds of thousands of children, which in turn becomes vulnerable to hacking.[6]

Everyone's privacy is at stake. Using widely available malware, a hacker could surreptitiously take control of the camera and microphone on your phone, tablet, or computer, turning them into covert spying devices. No wonder a former director of the FBI habitually put tape across his webcam. The teleconference hubs that sit blinking on tables in many conference rooms are hackable, turning them into exquisitely located surveillance devices. And it is a reasonable bet that government agencies, organized criminals, and amateur hackers around the world have been investigating how to hijack the ubiquitous home digital assistant devices. If they succeed, they will have access to ever-listening ears in every home.

Cyber Is Different—But Not *That* Different

Cyber technology offers threat actors powerful new tools for engaging in age-old vices including theft, espionage, sabotage, subversion, extortion fraud, bullying, harassment, stalking, intimidation, and warfare. In almost every instance, the most interesting issue is the espionage, fraud, or whatever, rather than the technological means by which it is done. For that reason, it is useful to distinguish between *cyber-enabled* crime and *cyber-dependent* crime. The former refers to conventional crimes that use digital technology to help them along. The latter refers to more genuinely 'cyber' phenomena, in which cyber technology is both the tool and the target of the crime—for instance, the use of ransomware to extort money. Most forms of crime have migrated to some extent into the cyber domain and the majority of fraud cases are now cyber-enabled.

Cyber may be new ways of doing old things, but the cyber domain undeniably has features that can dramatically alter the shape and size of the risk. In particular, cyber tools are:

- massively scalable;
- cheap and easy to use;

- seemingly immune from risk to the threat actors;
- plausibly deniable; and
- transnational.

These features make the cyber domain an attractive operating environment for threat actors of all types.

The *massive scalability* of cyber methods means that it is generally as easy to steal a thousand documents as it is to steal one. Once threat actors have managed to plant the right malware on a target network, they can do more or less whatever they want with the data on that network, or with the network itself. In a successful cyber attack, the winner takes all.

A startling illustration of massive scalability was the revelation in 2017 that, four years earlier, hackers had gained access to the records of three billion users of Yahoo. Three billion users equates to fewer than three billion people, because some people would have had more than one account and some accounts would have had no people because they were generated automatically. Even so, the data loss affected a large proportion of the 3.2 billion people around the world who have regular access to the internet. The breach took place in 2013 and was not initially made known to the public. The compromised information included names, passwords, and in some cases dates of birth and phone numbers. Yahoo suffered a separate cyber attack in 2014, which affected 500 million accounts. The US Department of Justice subsequently indicted four men who were implicated in the 2014 breach, two of whom were Russian intelligence officers. Internet researchers later found stolen Yahoo records for sale online.

Other companies that have suffered well-publicized breaches in recent years include Target (70 million user accounts compromised), Anthem (80 million), Sony (100 million), LinkedIn (117 million), and Equifax (143 million). At one point it seemed as though cyber breaches were obeying a form of Moore's Law, in which the amount of data being stolen was doubling every few months.

The Equifax breach, which came to light in 2017, is thought to have compromised the personal data of at least 143 million people in the US, which is getting on for half the US population, and around 700,000 in the UK.[7] The data included credit card details, Social Security numbers, dates of birth, home addresses, phone numbers, and driving licence numbers. Victims of this and similar attacks will be haunted for years to come by the spectre of spam, scams, and identity fraud. As is often the case in cyber espionage attacks, the hackers penetrated Equifax's system several months before the breach was detected, giving them ample time to roam its networks and steal its data. The post-mortem suggested that the hackers had exploited a failure by Equifax to update a critical piece of software—an avoidable hostage to fortune.

A second striking feature of cyber attack methods is their *low cost and ease of use*. Powerful malware tools are available online at little or no cost. Malware is generated automatically, with thousands of new variants appearing every day. According to one estimate, some 45,000 different ransomware products were available for purchase online in 2017 from more than 6,000 dark web marketplaces for an average price of ten dollars.[8] Even nation states use off-the-shelf malware tools. Crucially, the would-be amateur hacker does not need to know anything about computers or coding in order to use these tools, just as we can happily drive our cars without knowing how to repair the engine. The old Hollywood image of the hacker as a youthful computer genius is a myth. Anyone can do it.

As if that were not easy enough, the would-be hacker can delegate the entire task to cyber criminals who offer hacking as an online service, complete with help desks and websites on which customers can rate the quality of service. Criminals will also produce tailored malware to order. In another creepy parallel with the physical domain, cyber mercenaries will fight other people's cyber wars for a price. Thanks to the low cost and ready availability of cyber sabotage tools, the ability to inflict large-scale damage is no longer restricted to nation states. The weapons are democratically available to everyone, regardless of means.

A third reason why threat actors are drawn to the cyber domain is the *perceived lack of personal risk to the attackers*. Many hackers feel, with some justification, that they are able to act with little or no risk to themselves. The personal risks to the perpetrator are certainly lower than those associated with terrorism or burglary. Many victims of cyber attacks do not even know they have been attacked, and those who do know are often reluctant to report it. Most estimates place the proportion of all cyber crimes that are reported at less than one in five. And even when they are reported, the police often lack the resources and skilled investigators to pursue the perpetrators. For the cyber criminal, the risk of being detected, caught, and punished is minuscule.

In the relatively few cases where a cyber attack has been detected, reported, and investigated, it is often difficult or borderline impossible for investigators to attribute the attack to an identified person in a way that would meet the evidential standards of a court of law. Thus, another attraction of cyber attacks is their *plausible deniability*.

Hostile foreign states add to the difficulty of attribution by deliberately making attacks look as though another state or organization was responsible. They do this by issuing false claims or sprinkling the malware with subtle clues that point investigators in the wrong direction. This tactic, which is known as *false flagging*, is another age-old phenomenon that existed long before the advent of cyber. A Russian state cyber sabotage attack on the French TV station TV 5 Monde was accompanied by bogus social media postings claiming responsibility on behalf of the 'Cyber Caliphate', and the TV 5 Monde website was defaced with the slogan 'Je suis ISIS'. Nevertheless, government and industry experts concluded that the saboteur was in fact a group of Kremlin-affiliated Russian hackers operating under a false flag. In similar vein, the 2016 Russian cyber attack on the US Democratic National Committee was claimed publicly by a hacker calling himself Guccifer 2.0, who purported to be Romanian. Again, it was a false flag planted by the Russian GRU military intelligence service.[9]

Some cyber security practitioners argue that there is no point in even trying to attribute cyber attacks to particular threat actors because all that really matters is dealing with the consequences and fixing the vulnerabilities that allowed the attack to succeed. Many others would disagree. Knowing or suspecting who was responsible for an attack is useful because it enables the victim to prepare for what might happen next. Different threat actors have different motivations, intentions, and capabilities. When a victim discovers that their system has been penetrated, the implications will depend in part on who did it. If the threat actors were criminals, they will probably have stolen data for financial gain. If they were hacktivists or hostile foreign state actors, there is a bigger risk that the victim's emails or sensitive records will end up being published online, or that the system itself will be sabotaged. Attribution may be hard but it is helpful.

The ability to make confident judgements about attribution is improving, thanks to advances in data analytics and cyber forensic techniques. If threat actors have to worry more about their digital fingerprints being recovered from the scene of crime, they might be more cautious about attacking in the first place. Better attribution should have a welcome deterrent effect.[10]

Another significant feature of cyber attack methods is their *transnational* nature. Thanks to the internet, a threat actor can attack a victim from almost anywhere in the world. The hacker does not have to be on the same continent, let alone in the same building. Even if a cyber attack can be confidently attributed to an identified person or organization, there is a distinct possibility that the perpetrator will be in another country, which may be beyond the legal jurisdiction of the victim's country. Much of the worst cyber crime is committed by organized crime groups in Eastern Europe.[11] For all these reasons, only a tiny minority of cyber attacks culminate in successful law enforcement action.

Finally, it used to be said that *people behave differently* in the online and physical worlds. Insofar as there is such a difference, it seems to be diminishing, as more of our lives are conducted online and we become increasingly aware that there is no anonymity on the internet. The more we live online, the harder it is to project a false image of who we are. The proof of the pudding is that the big tech companies profit handsomely from making accurate deductions about our personalities based solely on our online behaviour. Our personal data would not be worth so much money if it did not reveal so much about how we think and behave in the physical world. That said, there is reasonably good evidence that many people are less inhibited online, particularly when interacting with strangers. This so-called online disinhibition can manifest itself in anti-social behaviour, aggression ('flaming'), or self-disclosure.[12]

Cyber Risk

Judgements about protective security should rest on an understanding of the risks. What are we to make of cyber risks? Alarming headlines abound, leaving an impression that cyber attacks are growing unremittingly in frequency and severity. Many successful attacks go unnoticed or unre-ported by their victims, which implies that published statistics may under-estimate the true scale of the problem. Companies spend huge amounts of money on cyber security and still end up being turned over—sometimes publicly, sometimes out of sight. On the other hand, the cyber security industry has been accused, not without reason, of trying to boost sales by sowing fear, uncertainty, and doubt—and this being the cyber world, it has an acronym: FUD. The Fear in FUD is fuelled by a torrent of stories about devastating cyber attacks, while obscure technical language helps to deepen the Uncertainty and Doubt. Many cyber practitioners recognize the need for the subject to be demystified.

Dubious factoids are in plentiful supply and identifying reliable evidence requires some judgement. Most of the dubious factoids emanate from the cyber security industry, which obviously stands to benefit from not know-ingly understating the problem. However, a sample of relatively recent headlines from reputable sources may help to give a flavour. More than 90 per cent of large businesses reported suffering a cyber security breach within the previous five years. Half of all Britons who used the internet had been victims of cyber crime. The number of cyber crimes in England and Wales could be as high as 20.5 million a year, after taking account of massive under-reporting. And the estimated global cost of cyber crime was between 445 and 600 billion dollars a year.[13]

Cyber security risks come in many different forms, ranging from ineffectual tinkering to devastating cyber warfare. However, the diverse risks can be sorted into three broad categories—namely, cyber espionage, cyber sabotage, and cyber subversion. *Cyber espionage* means gaining illicit access to someone's data over a digital network—for example, when criminals or foreign states secretly lift copies of personal data or intellectual property from a victim's system. Cyber espionage is conducted covertly, with the aim of not alerting the victim. *Cyber sabotage* is the overt disruption of digital systems—for example, when politically motivated hacktivists deface a company's website, or when one nation state disables the IT systems or infrastructure of another. *Cyber subversion* is the use of the internet, social media, or other digital systems to undermine established democratic processes—for example, when a hostile nation state conducts information warfare to undermine its opponents.[14]

You will notice that the terms espionage, sabotage, and subversion refer to age-old activities that were widely practised long before the advent of computers (espionage famously being the second-oldest profession). In all three cases, the 'cyber' element is a new set of tools for doing things that people have always done. Let us consider each of them in more detail.

Cyber Espionage

Cyber espionage is the means by which nation states, organized crime syndicates, and other threat actors steal personal data, money, and intellectual property in vast quantities every year. Criminals use cyber espionage to steal valuable data including passwords, credit card details, financial information, and healthcare records. Vast amounts of personal and corporate data are available for sale on the dark web. Why steal one wallet when you can steal a million credit card details? Why spend your own money on developing weapons systems when you can steal someone else's finished designs? The head of the NSA described cyber espionage as the greatest transfer of wealth in history.[15]

The aim of cyber espionage is essentially the same as traditional espionage, which is stealing information without being detected. Cyber espionage has the advantage of being much safer for those doing it than old-fashioned spying. It is also capable of capturing much larger hauls of intelligence. For instance, in 2015 hackers stole the sensitive personnel records of 20.5 million US government employees from the Federal Office of Personnel Management, causing unquantifiable long-term harm to US national security.[16] On the other hand, a well-placed human spy can intervene physically in ways that computers cannot yet replicate.

An unnamed head of cyber at MI5 once said: 'There are now three certainties in life—there's death, there's taxes, and there's a foreign intelligence service on your system.'[17] The most capable state actors include Russia, China, the US, UK, and Israel. A US government report in 2018 concluded that for more than a decade the Chinese government had 'conducted and supported cyber intrusions into US commercial networks', giving them access to a wide range of valuable information, including 'trade secrets, technical data, negotiating positions, and sensitive and proprietary internal communications'.[18] Many other states are also active, including Iran, which was reportedly responsible for a covert attack on the UK Parliament's IT network in 2017.[19] It is not unknown for two or more nation states to attack the same target; a cyber security company once reported finding a computer in the Middle East that had been penetrated by at least six different nations including the Americans, Russians, and Israelis.

Cyber espionage is occasionally conducted for supposedly nobler reasons than making money or undermining enemies. Political activists and whistle-blowers have used cyber methods to uncover evidence of alleged wrongdoing. In 2015 an insider within the Panamanian law firm Mossack Fonseca covertly copied forty years' worth of its private client records and passed them to a consortium of journalists who were investigating international tax evasion by some of the world's wealthiest individuals. At the time, it was thought to be the largest known breach in the history of hacking, although that record has since been repeatedly broken.

In 2017, hackers leaked the Paradise Papers—a haul of 13.4 million confidential documents about offshore investments by ultra-rich individuals.

The malware used in many cyber espionage attacks is planted on the victim's system by means of *phishing*, once again illustrating the importance of the human dimension. The innocent recipient of a phishing email clicks on a seemingly innocuous attachment that, unbeknown to them, contains malware and, bingo, their system is infected. Some phishing emails are crude to the point where it is hard to imagine why any sentient being would click on them. But the hackers send out millions of automatically generated phishing emails in a strategy of 'spray and pray'. It only takes one recipient to click for an attack to succeed. Some hackers deliberately exploit the crudeness, spelling mistakes, and grammatical errors as a means of identifying the most gullible victims, who are worthy of closer attention. The dark web offers lists of repeat victims who have previously fallen prey to cyber crime. The lists are worth money because the hackers' experience shows that a victim who has been duped before is more likely to be duped again.

For more targeted attacks, hackers use phishing emails that are carefully tailored to look indistinguishable from the genuine article. These emails incorporate details that make them appear authentic, including the correct in-house format, names of employees, and content that relates to real job roles. This made-to-measure product of the phishing industry is known as *spear phishing*. When hackers are constructing spear phishing emails, they harvest the convincing details from company websites and employee social media postings. Many organizations are surprisingly relaxed about publishing names, job titles, corporate email formats, internal phone numbers, and other details. These seemingly innocuous nuggets can be helpful to spear phishers and social engineers.

The prevalence of phishing as an attack method has encouraged the notion that people are the weakest link in cyber security, because it takes a person to click on the infected attachment. However, studies have shown that a deftly tailored spear phishing email is capable of fooling almost anyone, including a security professional.[20] Busy people who are multitasking while receiving an unceasing deluge of look-alike emails cannot consistently make optimal judgements about every email. Everyone makes mistakes, and it only takes one person to click on an infected link for a whole system to be infected. An organization with thousands of employees, each receiving hundreds of emails a day, cannot expect to prevent phishing attacks simply by instructing everyone not to click on suspicious links.

Another flaw in the 'weakest link' notion is that phishing emails are not the only means of attack. Hackers also make extensive use of fake software updates, infected adverts (*malvertising*), and infected websites (*watering hole attacks*). These attack methods leave the victim little chance of identifying or avoiding the threat. For example, watering hole attacks work by embedding malware within legitimate websites that victims are likely to visit. Neither the website owner nor the victim knows what is happening, and all the victim has to do to become infected is visit a respectable website.

Despite all of that, a standard response to the threat is an awareness campaign. In its most basic form, it involves telling employees about the perils of phishing and possibly sending them some simulated phishing emails to see how they respond. The communication methods used for awareness-raising campaigns are often lacklustre, amounting to nothing more sophisticated than what marketers call SPLAT (Some Posters, Leaflets, Ads 'n' Things).[21] The underlying assumption is that simply telling people about the threat will stop them clicking on infected attachments. However, the approach is based on faulty psychology. Merely presenting people with factual information is not an effective way of bringing about enduring changes in their behaviour—hence the continuing prevalence of smoking and obesity. One-off awareness campaigns have little lasting effect on click rates. The organizations that rely on such methods often appear to be more interested in demonstrating compliance than actually changing behaviour.

Studies have also revealed that employees' attitudes to the phishing threat are not always straightforward. When asked confidentially why they persist in clicking on suspicious links, many say they see no disadvantage in doing so. They assume (incorrectly) that the corporate IT provides robust protection, and know they can get their machine fixed or replaced in the event that it is infected. Therefore, why agonize over every email?

Another factor is *security fatigue*—a weary indifference produced by a relentless stream of hectoring security instructions and tedious awareness campaigns. Those on the receiving end of endless demands to do irksome things in the name of cyber security often end up feeling resigned and fatalistic. They stop trying, with the result that the security gets worse, not better.[22] Sometimes the rule-breaking is deliberate, as overworked or disgruntled employees prioritize getting their work done regardless of security, or indulge in small acts of rebellion. The net result is that despite all the efforts to educate, the rules are regularly broken and a significant proportion of malicious emails are opened.

Building and maintaining a good security culture requires persistent effort (as discussed in Rule 6). It cannot be achieved by short bursts of awareness-raising once or twice a year. A tick-box compliance approach might reassure regulators and shareholders that something is being done, but it is unlikely to solve the problem. Advice and instructions should be measured and helpful, not strident and finger-pointing. Policies should make sense and be easy to follow without having to make lots of complex judgements. Ultimately, though, the only robust way of protecting against phishing and more sophisticated methods of attack is with intelligent automated software tools. Meanwhile, the best practical advice is to *pause, take a breath, and think* before clicking. In the second or two it takes to do that, you may realize that you were about to click on a dubious link.

Cyber espionage is usually initiated by gaining remote access to the victim's system through methods like phishing. However, a system can also be attacked by *direct access* to the hardware. One method is to insert a USB stick loaded with malware into one of the unsecured ports that can be found on many computers. An action taking less than a minute could potentially compromise an entire network. The security response to this cyber risk requires a holistic combination of physical security (preventing unauthorized physical access to devices); personnel security (reducing the risk of malicious insider action); and cyber security (securing or disabling USB ports). The holistic approach, which is one of the hallmarks of good protective security, is discussed in Rule 9.

A tactic that hackers have used with some success is to scatter infected USB sticks on the ground outside the target's building. Quite often, someone finds one and plugs it in to see what it contains. Business travellers to high-threat countries are sometimes presented with gifts of USB sticks or other plug-in devices that come pre-loaded with malware.

Direct-access attacks can also be used to conduct cyber sabotage, which is discussed next. One nasty little item that illustrates the dangers of untrusted USB sticks is the 'kill stick'—a cheap and readily available device disguised as a USB stick. The kill stick charges itself from the victim's USB port and then releases a high-voltage pulse into the computer, disabling its circuits—which brings us to sabotage.

Cyber Sabotage

Cyber sabotage was once less prevalent but its incidence and severity have been growing in recent years. The consequences of a really big attack, such as taking down critical energy infrastructure or a large cloud service provider, could be colossal. The World Economic Forum estimated that a major cyber attack could cause economic damage comparable in cost to Hurricane Katrina which devastated New Orleans in 2005.[23] In the Forum's global risk matrix, cyber attacks appeared in the dreaded top-right corner along with extreme weather events, natural disasters, and failure to cope with climate change.

The classic form of cyber sabotage is the *denial of service* attack, which involves trying to overwhelm a website with huge volumes of electronic requests. When they succeed, such attacks can be disruptive for the organization concerned, although no one is likely to die because of a disabled commercial website. Many organizations have invested in ways of resisting denial of service attacks, making success costlier for the attackers.

In response to improved defences, threat actors have found ways of increasing their firepower by harnessing vast numbers of IoT devices to form *botnets*—swarms of internet-connected IoT devices or computers that are hijacked by malware. Botnets are used to conduct large-scale denial of service attacks and for other nefarious purposes. A striking example was the massive Mirai botnet attack in 2016, which used infected IoT devices to conduct a damaging attack on the infrastructure of the internet itself, causing significant disruption to online services including Twitter and Netflix.[24]

Denial of service attacks have also been used as a distraction for cyber espionage. While the victim is preoccupied with fending off the overt attack, the threat actors surreptitiously penetrate the victim's network and steal data. However, for threat actors who want to cause really serious harm, the basic denial of service attack is no longer the weapon of choice. In recent years there has been a steady growth in more damaging forms of cyber sabotage, where the consequences can be far worse than the temporary disruption of a website.

Cyber sabotage has the potential to cause harm on an enormous scale when aimed at *industrial control systems* that run vital infrastructure such as electricity grids, telecommunications systems, or industrial plants. Many of these systems are decades-old and were designed in an era when the risk from external attack was not so apparent. In 2017, the US National Infra-structure Advisory Committee (NIAC) warned that the US was in a 'pre-9/11 moment' before a catastrophic cyber attack on its critical national infra-structure. In similar vein, the British Defence Secretary warned in 2018 that possible Russian cyber attacks on UK infrastructure could kill thousands. One of the many types of malware that have been designed specifically to attack national infrastructure is disconcertingly called Industroyer.

An iconic example of cyber sabotage was the *Stuxnet* attack on the Iranian nuclear proliferation programme, which first came to public attention in 2010.[25] The Stuxnet attack employed highly sophisticated malware to subvert industrial control systems running thousands of high-speed centrifuges, which the Iranians were using to refine uranium for nuclear bombs. The attack, which was conducted over a long period, physically damaged the precision-engineered machines by covertly altering the rate at which they spun. The malware misled the control system, causing it to increase the rate beyond safe limits, while reassuring the human operators that it was functioning normally.[26] Stuxnet set back Iran's production of nuclear weapons by years. It demonstrated how a cyber attack could be used to achieve militarily significant physical effects that would once have required the use of large bombs or nuclear weapons. Cyber sabotage is becoming the weapon of choice for states that cannot afford large conventional military forces.[27]

The Stuxnet attack succeeded even though the secret Iranian systems were not connected to external networks or the internet. In cyber parlance, the systems were air-gapped. It is thought that a human agent was used to infect them with malware. Either way, the elaborately tailored malware could not have been designed successfully without knowledge of the Iranian systems.[28]

Iranian hackers struck back in 2012, with a cyber sabotage attack that disabled the corporate IT system of the giant oil company Saudi Aramco, destroying more than 30,000 of its computers. (In cyber parlance, the computers were bricked.) Hidden within the malware was an image of a burning American flag.[29] In a separate incident, seven Iranian hackers were indicted in 2016 by a US federal grand jury for trying to sabotage the operation of a dam in New York state.

The Stuxnet case nicely illustrates three general points about cyber security. The first is that *the human dimension is central*. The attack needed inside knowledge and, very probably, insider action. The second point is that *air gaps cannot be relied upon* to provide complete protection from external attacks. There are many ways of bridging air gaps and the easiest way is usually through people. In the absence of a human agent, there are ingenious technical methods for extracting useful information from a system's electromagnetic emissions, flashing LEDs, heat emissions, and even the noise made by its cooling fans. However, a human agent (witting or unwitting) is faster and better.

The third point is that *cyber weapons escape and breed*. The Stuxnet attack was originally conducted in great secrecy, in what is thought to have been a joint operation by the US and Israel. It came to notice when a revised version of the malware started spreading to computers in other countries.[30] Once the malware had escaped into the wild, software engineers were able to analyse the code and deduce how it worked. They could then produce improved versions to attack their own enemies. And so it goes. If you drop a conventional bomb on an enemy, the bomb explodes and that is the end of it. If, however, you drop a malware weapon on an enemy, the enemy might reverse-engineer it and then fire it back at you and lots of other people. A striking example of cyber weapons escaping and breeding came to light in 2016, when a hacking group calling itself Shadow Brokers dumped onto a public website a collection of extremely potent malware tools that had been purloined from the NSA. Some of these tools were later used in cyber attacks by criminals and hostile foreign states.

Stuxnet has come to be regarded as the grandmother of cyber sabotage attacks. However, the history books show that it was not the first sabotage attack on an electronic communication system. That honour probably goes to an attack carried out more than a century ago, on the first day of World War One. On 5 August 1914, the first day of armed conflict between Britain and Germany, the British ship *Alert* sailed into the North Sea and cut Germany's main undersea communication cables. The attack was the first offensive act of the war and succeeded in severing almost all of Germany's communications with the rest of the world.[31] It was a prime example of a direct-access attack involving physical intervention. Of course, you do not need a ship to sabotage computer systems. A screwdriver will often do.

Two states that have become conspicuous, if not downright flagrant, in their use of cyber sabotage are Russia and North Korea. Russian state hackers were responsible for a series of attacks that disrupted the electricity distribution system in Ukraine, causing widespread blackouts. The two biggest attacks took place in 2015 and 2016, cutting off the electricity supply to hundreds of thousands of people for several hours. In 2015 the same Russian state hacking group took a French TV station, TV5 Monde, off the air for eighteen hours. These were by no means the first cyber sabotage attacks attributed to Russia. As far back as 2007 and 2008, Russian hackers were attacking government and media systems in Estonia and Georgia. The 2007 attack on Estonia caused widespread disruption to banking and government services for weeks, prompting the Estonian government to develop an ambitious strategy to strengthen its cyber resilience.

The NotPetya malware that disrupted computers around the world in 2017 started as a targeted attack on businesses in Ukraine that were working with the Ukrainian government. The malware was almost certainly built by the Russian government and targeted at Ukraine.[32] It was originally spread through an infected software update for an accounting package specific to Ukraine. However, the malware escaped into the wild and infected vulnerable systems in many countries. The outbreak is estimated to have cost businesses billions of dollars.

North Korean cyber saboteurs first hit the headlines in 2014, when they penetrated the corporate network of Sony Pictures and dumped large volumes of embarrassing emails, documents, and unreleased movies into the public domain, causing financial and reputational damage to the company. The Sony corporate network was also taken down, forcing the company to communicate by phone and pay their staff with paper cheques. The attack is thought to have been in retaliation for a Sony-produced film that mocked the North Korean leader Kim Jong-un.[33]

Unlike most other state actors, the North Koreans also use cyber attacks to steal money, which is unsurprising in view of their broken economy and international sanctions. North Korean state hackers have been behind a spate of cyber thefts and ransomware attacks. One example was the Bangladesh Bank heist of 2016, in which they subverted the SWIFT inter-bank payment system and transferred funds to accounts in the Philippines.[34] The hackers had intended to move almost a billion dollars in this way, although they eventually netted only $81 million. Most of the payments were blocked after a vigilant employee noticed a spelling mistake in one of the spoof messages. (The human dimension again.) The carefully planned attack was preceded by a period of hostile surveillance using covert malware to gather intelligence on Bangladesh Bank's procedures for moving funds.

Criminals have widely adopted the use of cyber sabotage for financial gain by deploying a form of malware known as *ransomware*. The FBI estimated that there were about 4,000 ransomware attacks a day in 2016.[35] Ransomware encrypts the victim's data, rendering it unusable. The criminals offer to unlock the data in return for a ransom payment in the form of a supposedly untraceable cryptocurrency such as Bitcoin. The ransom demands are often relatively modest when compared to the cost of losing the data, prompting many victims to pay up. Predictably, the criminals do not always honour their commitment to decrypt the data. In fact, the psychology works the other way around, as victims who pay a ransom are more likely to be attacked again.

A more insidious variant of cyber sabotage is the tactic of altering—as opposed to stealing, encrypting, or erasing—the victim's data. It takes little imagination to think of the harm that could be caused by manipulating the financial and legal records of large institutions, let alone the medical records of millions of patients. This form of cyber sabotage presents a threat to the *integrity* of data, as distinct from its confidentiality. One possible means of protecting the integrity of data is blockchain technology, which makes it harder to alter data surreptitiously. Blockchain technology can also strengthen the trustworthiness of data by providing proof of existence and proof of signature (non-repudiation).

When one nation state conducts a damaging cyber sabotage attack on another nation state, we enter the uncharted territory of *cyber warfare*. The pursuit of warfare by cyber weapons is not yet the subject of established international laws or conventions, which makes it a dangerously ambiguous phenomenon. Many nations are known to have developed a substantial cyber warfare capability, including the US, UK, Russia, China, Iran, South Korea, and North Korea. Cyber weapons are cheap compared to planes and ships, making them popular with less wealthy nations. They are probably increasing the risk of old-fashioned physical conflict by creating endless new ways of causing harm that stop just short of spilling blood.

We seem to be in a phase at present when nations are experimenting with their offensive cyber capabilities, while aiming to fall just short of provoking a full-blown retaliation. Several nations, including the US and UK, have publicly warned that they would regard a serious cyber attack as an act of war and would retaliate by all appropriate means, including conventional weapons. NATO's rules of engagement permit the alliance to trigger its collective defence clause if one of its member states is subjected to a serious cyber attack. It seems likely that some covert cyber attacks have already provoked unpublicized responses, but at the time of writing none has yet crossed the threshold for triggering an old-fashioned shooting war.

Hostile foreign states employ cyber espionage as a precursor to cyber sabotage. They do this by covertly penetrating a target network, inspecting it from the inside, and leaving behind malware that could sabotage the network when instructed to do so. This form of pre-attack activity, known as *preparing the battlefield*, can come perilously close to cyber warfare in its own right. The attacker has the potential to destroy the target network at a time of their choosing, as though they had planted a remotely controlled bomb inside it. If a victim finds such malware in one of their critical systems, they face a dilemma about how to respond, not least because they may not want to reveal their cyber forensic capability. Moreover, it is hard to be certain about attribution and the perpetrator will deny responsibility.

Cyber Subversion

Subversion is another age-old activity that is now routinely conducted by nation states using cyber tools. Its ultimate aim is to gain political, economic, and military advantage over the threat actor's opponents by undermining and weakening their governmental and social systems.[36] One way of doing this is by causing confusion and undermining belief in objective truth. When people no longer know what to believe, they no longer know whom to trust, with damaging consequences for the integrity of society.

The methods of cyber subversion include the use of automated *troll armies* to spread false news, conspiracy theories, and other divisive information. The threat actors aim to create an impression that a story or opinion is more widely believed than is actually the case. In doing this, they exploit an inherent psychological tendency for people to suspend disbelief when everyone around them is behaving in the same way.[37] Much of the disinformation is delivered through social media platforms such as Twitter, Facebook, and YouTube, which judge the value of information by whether it is popular, not whether it is true. Their business model has been hugely successful. However, the increasingly pernicious social consequences have prompted a public debate about whether it is acceptable for the companies running the platforms to have no liability for their contents.[38]

The Russian state and its Soviet predecessor were conducting subversion and information warfare operations long before cyber technology joined its armoury. The Russian intelligence agencies have been doing it since the birth of the Soviet Union in 1917, employing a spectrum of methods including human agents and traditional media. During the Cold War, the Soviet KGB intelligence service used propaganda, agent operations, and 'useful idiots' in western nations to manipulate public opinion. The Russian government is still doing it.

The problem eventually erupted into the public domain. In 2017 the British Prime Minister stated publicly that Russia was acting against the UK's national interest in cyberspace. International relations with Russia soured even more following the Salisbury nerve agent attack in 2018, prompting the head of MI5 to talk publicly about the Russian government's 'flagrant breaches of international rules' and 'bare-faced lying', and the director of GCHQ to talk of the Russian government 'blurring the boundaries between criminal and state activity'.[39]

One of the earlier instances of Russian state cyber subversion to grab public attention was the interference with the 2016 US presidential election. Among other things, Russian hackers stole US Democratic Party emails and released them into the public domain through helpful channels like

Wikileaks, causing political fallout and prompting the US Defence Secretary to warn Russia against interfering with democratic processes. The hackers also used fake accounts to pay for adverts on Facebook that dealt with socially divisive issues like immigration, race, and guns. In 2017 the US intelligence community published a declassified version of their assessment of Russian interference. Among its judgements were that 'Russian efforts to influence the 2016 US presidential election represent the most recent expression of Moscow's longstanding desire to undermine the US-led liberal democratic order' and that Russia's goals had been 'to undermine public faith in the US democratic process, denigrate Secretary Clinton, and harm her electability and potential presidency'.[40] In 2018, following an FBI investigation, the US authorities charged thirteen Russians with interfering with the election. The indictment also named Russian companies, including the Internet Research Agency in St Petersburg, which ran a 'troll factory' pumping out fake news and disinformation. According to the indictment, the strategic goal of the Internet Research Agency was 'to sow discord in the US political system'.[41]

The US was not the only country to receive such attention. The fingerprints of Russian hackers were found on attempts to interfere with political parties in France and Germany, for example, and in 2015 the German federal parliament was the victim of a prolonged cyber espionage attack that was attributed to the Russian government.[42]

Cyber subversion is able to push against an open door, thanks to human psychology. Untrue stories travel faster and spread more widely than true stories on social media. Scientists at MIT discovered that fake news stories and false rumours of all kinds were 70 per cent more likely to be shared on Twitter and spread six times faster than true stories.[43] Fake news and false rumours were more likely to contain novel or shocking information and more likely to be accompanied by expressions of surprise or disgust—and therein lies their psychological appeal. The truth is often less riveting than lies and less likely to grab our attention. There are good biological reasons why we are predisposed to follow the herd and pay more attention to novel information that might signal a threat to our wellbeing. Ironically, our inherent preference for novel falsehoods means that humans are better at selectively spreading lies than botnets, which indiscriminately pass on whatever they are given.

The spread of fake news, propaganda, conspiracy theories, and personal abuse through social media has been likened to a disease epidemic. The analogy is more than superficial, because mathematical models that predict the transmission of diseases through populations also work quite well in predicting the transmission of malicious information through digital networks. The models highlight the importance of highly connected individuals, or 'super-spreaders', who play a disproportionately large role in infecting others.

The Russian state is of course not the only source of cyber-enabled threats to the integrity of democratic and social processes in the UK, US, and other liberal democracies. A more diffuse threat stems from a diverse range of other threat actors, including fixated individuals and domestic political extremists. These disparate and largely unconnected threat actors differ hugely in their motivations, intentions, and capabilities. The threat is expressed mainly through social media, although it does sometimes erupt into physical violence. The combination of internet trolls intimidating individual politicians and hostile foreign states manipulating public opinion makes an unhealthy environment for democracy. As such, it poses a threat to national security.

In recent years there appears to have been a significant growth in the personal intimidation of public figures in the UK, largely through social media.[44] I say 'appears', because systematic long-term evidence about the scale of the problem has not been collected, perhaps because no single national authority unequivocally owns the problem. However, plenty of compelling anecdotal evidence shows that it has become normal for politicians, media figures, journalists, and other individuals in public life to face a barrage of abuse and intimidation, mostly through social media. In the UK, for example, there was widespread abuse and intimidation of parliamentary candidates who stood in the 2017 general election, including threats of violence and damage to property, most of it transmitted through social media. Intimidation of this sort deters people from standing for public office and has a chilling effect on those already in positions of authority. A committee of parliamentarians who reviewed the problem concluded that it 'presents a threat to the very nature of representative democracy in the UK'.[45]

The sources of this intimidation are many and varied: angry people venting their spleen; mentally ill and fixated individuals obsessing about their chosen victim; and political and ideological extremists of all sorts. Very few are terrorists in the accepted sense, but that could change. Some older people in the UK will have bad memories of the PIRA terrorist campaigns in the 1970s and 1980s, when individual politicians and officials were systematically targeted for assassination (see Rule 3). Many online abusers behave as though they lack any awareness of how much distress they are causing and believe they can act with impunity. In practice, their chances of being identified, prosecuted, and punished are small. Most of them would be more restrained if they had to administer the abuse face-to-face.

The great majority of online abuse of public figures does not signify a real underlying threat of physical violence, although the psychological impact on its victims and their families can be severe. In a few cases, however, hatred or fixation can turn into violence. A pivotal incident in the UK was the murder in June 2016 of the Member of Parliament Jo Cox on a street in northern England as she went about her constituency duties. Her murder by a lone right-wing extremist prompted much-needed improvements in the protective security provided to elected politicians. Meanwhile, the deluge of abuse and threats continues.

Politicians and other individuals in public life are of course not the only ones affected. Cyber-enabled bullying, harassment, intimidation, and stalking can affect anyone. Doctors, teachers, lawyers, and other professionals often find themselves in the firing line.[46] Social media companies have been widely criticized for not doing much to tackle these issues.

Cyber Threats, Vulnerabilities, and Impacts

As we saw in Rule 4, there are three ways to reduce security risk and the first of these is to reduce the threat. So, who are the cyber threat actors, what are their intentions, what sorts of capabilities do they possess, and what can be done about them?

At present, the main types of threat actor operating in the cyber domain are criminals, hostile foreign states, insiders, hacktivists, fixated individuals, political extremists, and 'script kiddies' (unsophisticated hackers motivated mainly by curiosity and entertainment). Their aims are many and varied. Hacktivists want to cause annoyance or embarrassment, criminals want to make money, hostile states want to gain advantage over their enemies, and so on. Between them, this highly disparate assortment of threat actors is trying—often successfully—to do the following things:

- steal valuable data or intellectual property;
- steal money;
- harm or disrupt their rivals or enemies;
- influence, coerce, or blackmail;
- damage reputations; or
- enhance their own reputation or self-esteem.

One notable absence from this list is terrorism. Terrorists make extensive use of digital technology to radicalize and recruit new followers, communicate privately, gather information, and conduct online reconnaissance of intended targets. So far, however, they have not used cyber methods to conduct actual terrorist attacks. At the time of writing, there have been no known instances of what might reasonably be called *cyber terrorism*, even though the prospect has been an intermittent source of anxiety since the era of 9/11.[47]

The explanation for this striking fact is a matter of conjecture. A simple but compelling argument is that terrorists have so far shunned cyber attacks because cyber attacks do not terrify. Terrorists, so the argument goes, set out to achieve their ideological goals by causing terror. The clue is in the name. We humans have a visceral reaction to the dismemberment and bloodletting caused by bombs or beheadings. We also have a deep-seated revulsion to the visible signs of deadly illness, which may be one reason why terrorists persistently hanker after biological, chemical, and radiological weapons. If an attack does not cause terror or revulsion, then arguably it is not terrorism, and the terrorists seem implicitly to understand that. Guns, bombs, and knives can cause terror. So too can aeroplanes and vehicles when used as kinetic weapons. Cyber attacks can be disruptive, expensive, and annoying, but they have not so far been terrifying. Terrorists might develop the capability to, say, hack into autonomous vehicles and use them to mow down people on the street, but they can already achieve the same effect more easily with a suicidal jihadi in the driving seat, as they have repeatedly demonstrated in Nice, Stockholm, London, and elsewhere.

Set against that, the rapidly evolving IoT is lowering the entry barrier for cyber terrorism by creating more opportunities to conduct life-threatening cyber sabotage attacks on infrastructure, public facilities, domestic properties, implanted medical devices, and transport systems. The current crop of terrorists may not yet have the capability to produce terrifying effects in the cyber domain, but that could change and change suddenly. Meanwhile, most counter-terrorism practitioners agree that physical rather than cyber methods of attack will remain the priority for terrorist groups for the immediate future.

Vulnerability is a major factor in cyber security risk. When organizations are hit by a big cyber security breach, they often take to the media and emphasize the highly sophisticated nature of the attack, as though there was nothing they could have done to stop it. That is seldom true. In fact, the evidence shows that basic security precautions—strong passwords, updating software, correctly configuring networks, and managing access credentials—would prevent most attacks. To put it another way, *most cyber security breaches are more a reflection of the victim's vulnerability than they are of the attacker's capability.*

One reason why patching and other basic security precautions are often neglected is that they are a bit dull. The people responsible for cyber security in large, well-funded organizations often prefer to spend money on eye-catching measures like AI-enabled protective monitoring systems and security operations centres (SOCs). Other organizations, including many in the charity and healthcare sectors, have substandard cyber security because they lack the resources to pay for specialist support. Many charities and healthcare organizations are also inclined to be so focused on their core mission that they neglect their own security.[48] However, some organizations just appear to be in denial. A UK government survey of more than 1,500 businesses found that one in three (33 per cent) had spent *no* money on cyber security in the previous year and four out of five (80 per cent) had provided no cyber security training to their staff in the previous year.[49]

The evidence that avoidable vulnerabilities cause most of the problems is not hard to find. For example, in 2018 a cyber intelligence company reported finding more than 1.5 billion files containing sensitive information that were easily accessible through the open internet. The files included payslips, credit card transactions, tax files, and medical records. The compromised information was not there because of hacking. It was there because sloppy security practices had unintentionally left the information open and unprotected. Contractors and other third parties were major offenders in exposing the data.[50] Another damning statistic emerged in 2016 from the NSA, which stated that of all the high-profile cyber security breaches in the US over the previous two years, not one had involved zero-day malware. (Zero-day malware exploits a previously unknown security vulnerability for which there is currently no fix.) In every case, the hackers had used widely available malware to defeat weak cyber security. Why waste precious zero-day malware when basic tools will do the job? North Korean cyber attacks have often relied on exploiting unpatched and outdated software. As a general rule, nation states, organized criminals, and other capable hackers will use the crudest available malware that is adequate for the job, otherwise known as the *principle of the least effective tool*.

Paradoxically, *cyber security itself can be a major vulnerability*. In order to do its job properly, cyber security technology must have deep access to the system it is meant to protect, in much the same way that security guards must have deep access to the buildings they are meant to protect. For example, anti-virus software must scan all incoming email and files, compare them against a blacklist of known malware signatures, and then quarantine or disable any material for which it detects a match. In order to keep their malware blacklists up to date, anti-virus providers collect and analyse information from the machines they are protecting. In this and other ways, security software is afforded extensive access to the protected systems. Consequently, if the security software itself is compromised, the risks are greater. The physical security analogue would be a rogue guard force equipped with keys to every door.

The risk of security software attacking its own clients is more than a theoretical possibility. In 2017 the US Department of Homeland Security announced it was banning US government departments and agencies from using security software or services provided by the cyber security company Kaspersky Lab. The US authorities stated that the Russian-owned company's anti-virus software had been exploited to gather classified information from computers on which it was installed and that some of this information had found its way to the Russian government.[51]

As digital systems and software grow ever more blindingly complex, it becomes exceedingly difficult to find every possible vulnerability—and there are many to find.[52] To give some sense of their pervasiveness, an analysis of 1,388 commercial software packages uncovered no fewer than 1.3 million weaknesses in their coding which could be exploited by hackers.[53] The problem of ubiquitous vulnerabilities becomes even more intractable when threat actors can exploit physical and behavioural methods such as social engineering to bypass the technical security. It is therefore hard to avoid the conclusion that *all digital systems should be assumed to carry unknown vulnerabilities that threat actors will eventually discover and may try to exploit.* Threat actors will not necessarily exploit every new vulnerability they discover, because they may already know of easier ways to achieve the same effect. But if a new vulnerability opens up attractive opportunities, it is a racing certainty that someone will have a crack at exploiting it.

The vast numbers of threat actors, the ubiquity of vulnerabilities, and the often substandard levels of cyber security combine to produce an environment in which no one is immune from cyber risk. Capable threat actors will get through because they can always find a victim with inadequate security or unknown vulnerabilities. This reality is reflected in a popular catchphrase of the cyber security industry: It's not a matter of *if* you are breached, but *when*.

The near certainty of intrusion implies that organizations should be well prepared to deal with a cyber security incident and should invest in building *cyber resilience*, in line with the strategy advocated in Rule 5. *Passive* cyber resilience is the capacity to resist attacks and recover from them quickly. *Active* cyber resilience includes the additional capacity to learn from experience, adapt, and become progressively stronger.

The systemic failure of cyber security to keep pace with dynamic and adaptive threats is nothing new. The journalist and author Gordon Corera discovered a prescient report on computer security that was produced in 1972 for the US Air Force and rings true to this day.[54] The Anderson Report described the principal features of what we would now call cyber security in terms that are easily recognizable, including patching known vulnerabilities, maintaining a perimeter firewall, encrypting data, and monitoring for intrusions. The report described such measures as useful to varying degrees but ultimately incapable of dealing with the fundamental problems. For all its innovation, today's cyber security industry still depends to a large extent on the same basic approaches that the Anderson Report decried nearly half a century ago as papering over the cracks. There have been some promising developments, however—notably the application of automated systems that improve the speed with which potential intrusions are detected and support human operators in making decisions about how to respond.

Let us turn finally to *impact*, the third element of risk. Most of the critical services on which we rely for normal life, including telecommunications, financial services, energy, and healthcare, depend on networked digital systems. The impact of a major cyber attack is therefore multi-dimensional, with an array of potential consequences ranging from loss of life to loss of money or business, regulatory action, litigation, and loss of confidence. The specific consequences will be different from those of physical terrorism or conventional crime, but the underlying risk principles are the same.

As concerns about cyber risks have grown, nations have been strengthening their regulations and legislation with the aim of improving security and privacy. The *General Data Protection Regulation* (GDPR), which came into effect across the European Union (including the UK) in 2018, includes the provision to levy a fine of up to 20 million euros or 4 per cent of an organization's annual global turnover, whichever is the greater, for a serious breach of the GDPR requirements. Fines on this scale mean that failing to provide adequate protection for personal data carries a substantial financial risk, leaving those responsible for cyber security with no grounds for complacency.

Various strategies for building cyber resilience by reducing the impact of attacks were discussed in Rule 5. They include data minimization, secure backup, and robust incident management procedures. Another strategy for building cyber resilience is *segmenting* assets and systems—in other words, dividing digital networks and the data they handle into separate compartments, or segments. That way, an attacker who breaches one compartment does not automatically gain access to everything on the network. Many older computer networks had a 'flat' architecture, meaning one large network inside a single perimeter. When it comes to resilience, segmented is better than flat. The same principle has been used for many decades to protect the most sensitive national security secrets, by dividing knowledge of those secrets into separate need-to-know groups, or compartments.

Two further strategies for reducing the impact of a successful cyber attack are encrypting and anonymizing data, so that less harm is done even if the data is stolen. *Encrypting* data, so that it becomes exceedingly difficult or impossible for a hacker to read without the key, should be relatively straightforward. Nonetheless, the effectiveness of encryption is sometimes undermined by procedural errors that enable threat actors to deduce the contents or get hold of the encryption key. The devil is in the detail.

Anonymization, which means completely separating the data from the identities of the persons to whom it applies, is harder to achieve. True anonymization would make it impossible (not just very difficult) to match the data to identifiable persons; for example, a truly anonymized database of medical records could never be linked back to named individuals. However, numerous studies have shown that by cross-matching different sorts of supposedly anonymized data, it is often possible to deduce the identities of the individuals to whom they refer. True anonymization requires something much more sophisticated than just deleting the names of the data subjects. There are measures that make life hard for hackers, while falling short of true anonymization. The GDPR legislation distinguishes between anonymization and *pseudonymization*, in which the data elements that could help to identify individuals are kept separate. Pseudonymization is easier to implement and provides additional protection, but it does not guarantee complete anonymity.

In sum, cyber security works on the same fundamental principles as other forms of security. However, the vast scale and diversity of the threat, combined with the ubiquity of vulnerabilities, make the business of protecting against all cyber attacks a noble but ultimately doomed quest. Sorting out the unglamorous basics like patching and access control will protect against most attacks, but even the shiniest of tech boxes will not guarantee immunity from everything. The only credible strategy is to build active cyber resilience.

RULE 9

KNOW WHAT GOOD
LOOKS LIKE

Good protective security has nine distinguishing characteristics:
it is risk-based, well governed, holistic, understandable, regularly
tested, well measured, layered, designed-in, and dynamic.

———

How can we distinguish good security from mediocre or bad security, other than by waiting for a breach to occur? Protective security can be impressively robust or dangerously weak, and it may not be obvious which of these you have until it is too late. This chapter outlines nine broad characteristics that indicate whether a protective security regime is likely to be effective. These diagnostic features can be used to make quick, qualitative judgements and they can also be refined into more granular metrics. They offer a useful rough guide to separating the sheep from the goats.

Most practitioners would, I hope, agree that protective security is unlikely to be highly effective and dependable unless it possesses five basic features. As a minimum, protective security should be:

- risk-based;
- well governed;
- holistic;
- understandable; and
- regularly tested.

In addition to these basic requirements, the best protective security is distinguished by four further characteristics. It is:

- well measured;
- layered;

- designed-in; and
- dynamic.

Other attributes are of course relevant. Cost is obviously an important factor. However, these nine hallmarks are fundamental to judging whether a system of security measures is likely to work effectively. And if it does not work effectively, then it cannot offer value for money.

The rationale for the first item on the list—a *risk-based* approach—was explored in Rule 2 and pervades every chapter, so I will say no more here. The second essential feature, being *well governed*, is so important that it forms the subject of Rule 10. Let us consider the other seven.

Holistic

Good protective security is said to be *holistic*, or integrated. What does that mean? As we have seen, protective security operates in three interdependent domains—the physical, personnel, and cyber. The three domains are distinct in terms of the skills needed to manage them, but they are inexorably intertwined and interact in important ways.

Physical security involves tangible devices such as locks, fences, vehicle security barriers, intruder alarms, and CCTV systems. It is intended to manage security risks that are primarily physical in manifestation, notably conventional crime and terrorism, and to protect the physical hardware elements of cyber systems. *Personnel* security, as described in Rule 6, comprises the systems and processes for protecting an organization against insider risks. It is all about people. *Cyber* security, the focus of Rule 8, is the means of protecting digital data and the electronic systems that handle it. Holistic security takes an integrated approach to all three domains; it considers them in the round rather than in isolation from one another. A holistic regime includes a combination of physical, personnel, and cyber elements and takes account of how they work together to reduce risk.

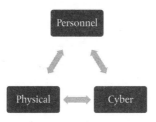

The reason for advocating a holistic approach to protective security is simple. Although the physical, personnel, and cyber domains are distinct and require specialist expertise, they are also highly interdependent. Dealing with any one of them in isolation is therefore liable to result in flawed security.

Consider just a few of the permutations. A well-placed insider can bypass most physical or cyber security defences. Expensive fences, locks, and digital firewalls will not protect an organization from a cyber criminal who can walk through the front door wearing a staff pass and log on to the IT system. Sophisticated cyber security technology will not protect valuable data if hackers can steal an authorized user's log-on credentials or gain physical access to the hardware in an unsecured server room. Physical security devices such as intruder alarms and CCTV systems rely on digital technology that is vulnerable to cyber attack. Digital technology can be sabotaged by physical means, using electromagnetic radiation or a big screwdriver. Personnel security depends on digital records and physical barriers to control authorized access. And so on. If you want good protective security, you must deal with all three domains in the round.

Another reason for favouring holistic security is that threat actors are holistic in their approach to conducting attacks. Always pragmatic, they will use whatever combination of physical, personnel, and cyber tools is best suited to the job. Threat actors increasingly conduct *blended attacks*, which exploit a combination of cyber, physical, and personnel vulnerabilities. Conventional criminals use cyber methods to gather information about their targets before using physical methods to steal from them, while cyber criminals exploit insiders to gather the information they need.

The commonest method for getting malware onto a target computer system is duping an insider into opening an infected attachment. The technique, known as *phishing*, was discussed in Rule 8. Phishing is easier than developing software tools to penetrate perimeter firewalls. As the computer security expert Bruce Schneier put it: 'Only amateurs attack machines; professionals target people.'[1] In similar vein, hostile foreign states use cyber espionage to facilitate traditional spying by covert human intelligence sources (humint). Conversely, human spies facilitate cyber espionage by providing access to target networks. Terrorists use cyber espionage to conduct surveillance on potential targets as a prelude to a physical attack. In conventional warfare, a 'kinetic' military assault is preceded and accompanied by cyber attacks to mislead and disable the adversary. And so on.

An often criticized characteristic of the cyber security industry is the lingering tendency to regard cyber security as a technology problem with technology solutions. However, the holistic perspective is gaining currency, along with a growing recognition of the personnel and physical security dimensions of cyber security. As cyber security defences become more sophisticated, hackers find it easier to target people. Why deploy complex malware to penetrate the target's network when a simple phone call or email can con a helpful employee into revealing the information?

Social engineering has become a standard tool of cyber crime, as it always was for conventional crime. A prevalent form of cyber-enabled social engineering is *business email compromise* or 'CEO fraud'. The criminals send an authentic-looking email to an employee who administers the target organization's bank accounts, instructing them to transfer money to an account belonging to the criminals. The email purports to come from the CEO, or someone suitably senior, and the obliging employee duly obliges. Success depends on making the spoof email appear authentic, which is achieved by harvesting details from open sources. The best defence against this type of social engineering is strengthening the business processes for authorizing payments. A simple precaution is phoning the senior person to verify the instruction before transferring the money. A variant on the theme is *whaling*, in which a social engineering attack is aimed directly at a senior individual or public figure with access to top-value information.

The holistic approach works for resilience too. As we saw in Rule 5, the best long-term strategy for reducing risk is to build active resilience. Achieving active resilience requires a holistic approach to the physical, personnel, and cyber dimensions.

Regrettably, holistic security is widely praised but less widely practised. No security practitioner worth their salt would argue against holistic security. Yet most security practitioners deal with only one domain and pay little more than lip service to the principle. Most organizations do not have holistic security, largely because of the way they are organized and managed. More on this in Rule 10.

Understandable

For security systems and procedures to work reliably, they must be easily understood by the people operating them. That means keeping it simple. We can only cope with a certain amount of new information and complexity. If too many variables are thrown at us, we tend to lose sight of the important ones, leading potentially to serious errors of judgement. During crises, when overstretched people must make critical decisions under pressure, *complexity can kill.*

When a security system or business process becomes too complicated, the people running it cannot fully understand what is going on and may fail to spot warning signs until it is too late. The Great Financial Crash of 2008 is an example of a disaster fuelled by excessive complexity, making it hard for the participants to comprehend the scale of the growing risk. (On top of that, risky behaviour was incentivized and the risk-takers had no skin in the game.) One of the responses to the Crash has been a desire to make financial systems easier to understand. Similarly, protective security systems will not work properly if their users cannot understand how to use them. Simplicity and user-centred design are crucial.

Excessive complexity is a significant issue in the cyber domain, where more and more essential functions, including security, depend on automated systems running on fabulously complicated software. The problem with fabulously complicated software is that no one can be certain how it will behave in every conceivable situation. Software packages with millions of lines of code are hard to test exhaustively. Automated systems are not unreliable in the traditional sense of components breaking, but they can be unreliable in the sense of occasionally behaving in ways the designers never intended. Intelligent, automated security systems can be prone to doing something surprising once in a while.

The personnel domain is also subject to excessive complexity. Most organizations have security policies and procedures that specify what people are expected to do. However, a common problem is having too many policies containing too much detail. The genuinely critical points become diluted in a sea of bureaucratic rules that are widely ignored. Policies, like paper clips, proliferate and become entangled when left unattended. It is good to weed them periodically. Doing the important things well is better than doing everything badly or not at all. As in so many other walks of life, *less is more*.

An effective tool for countering the mind-numbing effects of excessive complexity is a *checklist* of critical actions.[2] People can follow a well-constructed checklist even when they are overwhelmed by a pressurized situation and barely able to think clearly. The use of checklists started in aviation. In 1935 the US Army Air Corps was testing the prototype of an advanced bomber. The plane crashed because of a procedural error by the pilot, leading sceptics to conclude that the new machine was just too complicated to fly. However, a group of test pilots came up with a solution—a simple checklist which removed the need for the pilot to remember every critical task. The prototype plane that was thought to be too complicated to fly went on to become the hugely successful B-17 Flying Fortress of World War Two fame. Several decades later, the checklist method was adopted by medicine, where it has produced remarkable improvements in patient outcomes. An international study demonstrated that the use of a checklist for surgery led to a 36 per cent reduction in the rate of major post-operative complications and a whopping 47 per cent reduction in deaths.[3]

Security practitioners who manage complex risks are sometimes faced with problems that are analogous in certain respects to those faced by pilots and surgeons. Some tasks are too complicated to carry out reliably using only their memory. Checklists can deal with the crucial steps, leaving more mental bandwidth free for the subtler problems. Good checklists strike the right balance between effectiveness and brevity: they cover the essentials and no more. They are not a substitute for knowledge, but they do help to ensure that practitioners apply their knowledge correctly, even under acute pressure.

Regularly Tested

Another hallmark of good protective security is regular testing. It has three main purposes: to ensure that the security actually works; to provide the operators with practice; and to facilitate continual improvement.

In practice, testing often reveals security measures to be less effective than was believed. Organizations often derive too much comfort from the existence of security policies and standards that tick the boxes of compliance. But there is a world of difference between having a policy and having security defences that demonstrably work in anger. For example, most IT departments have a policy of regularly applying the latest security patches to their software. However, testing often reveals software that is in fact *un*patched. The only way to be truly confident that the commitments made in security policies have been fulfilled is by lifting the lid and taking a look.

Testing comes in many forms, some of which are more revealing but also more demanding than others. At the most revealing and demanding end of the spectrum is *penetration testing*. As its name suggests, this involves actively trying to penetrate the physical, cyber, or (much less commonly) personnel security defences. Specialist testers take on the role of threat actors and attempt to breach the security, albeit under controlled conditions. Penetration testing is most commonly applied to cyber security. Some organizations pay specialist providers to conduct regular tests in which friendly experts attempt to hack the customer's systems and expose vulnerabilities that could be exploited by genuine threat actors. The gold standard of cyber penetration testing is known as *STAR*, which stands for Simulated Target Attack and Reconnaissance. STAR makes use of threat assessments and prior reconnaissance to enhance the realism by mimicking the known intentions and capabilities of threat actors and identifying the most promising areas of vulnerability.

Penetration testing of physical security can be more demanding and is less commonly practised. It involves trying to circumvent the perimeter defences of a secure site and gain access to sensitive inner zones. At airports, for example, the search and screening procedures for preventing concealed weapons or bombs being brought onto aeroplanes are routinely tested to assess their effectiveness. The testers masquerade as passengers and attempt to smuggle inert guns, knives, or bombs past the security staff. In the most extreme version of physical penetration testing, Special Forces operators probe the physical security of the nation's most sensitive and secure sites. Razor wire fences are climbed and alarm systems disabled at dead of night. Penetration testing of personnel security is a rarity, once again reflecting its Cinderella status as the neglected drudge of protective security.

A penetration test provides only a snapshot of the risks at a point in time and cannot give lasting assurance. Tests must be repeated with sufficient frequency. The appropriate frequency is likely to be higher for cyber security, where the risks evolve more rapidly.

Penetration testing is expensive and carries some risk of unintended disruption. Organizations are understandably squeamish about allowing even the friendliest of hackers loose on their mission-critical IT systems, where one false step could bring their business to an abrupt halt. Physical penetration testing of sensitive sites must be carefully planned to ensure that the testers do not cause damage and, at worst, are not shot by armed guards.

Most of the testing of protective security is conducted in easier and cheaper ways that involve thinking rather than doing. The commonest method is the *table-top exercise*, in which the efficacy of security is tested by systematically working through one or more credible scenarios in a structured group discussion. *Red teaming* is a more rigorous type of virtual testing in which one group (the red team) plays the role of threat actors, while a second group (the blue team) plays the defenders.

Another good reason for regular testing is to identify ways of improving security. No security regime is perfect—the risks are always changing—and therefore it pays to invest in a process of continual improvement. Regular testing is also an efficient and relatively low-risk way of acquiring relevant experience from which broader lessons are learned. As such, it makes a useful contribution to building active resilience (as described in Rule 5). A further benefit of regular hands-on testing is that it slows the erosion of human skills. As security systems become increasingly automated, human operators have fewer opportunities to practise their skills during business-as-usual, rendering them less able to respond effectively in a crisis. The best way of learning is by doing, and the best time for doing is during a test, not a genuine crisis.

Well Measured

Good security is well measured, which means that the right *metrics*, or measurement tools, are used to judge its effectiveness. Bad measurement can give rise to bad security by distorting judgements. If a protective security regime is shaped by a set of *key performance indicators* (KPIs) that measure the wrong things, the security is unlikely to be optimal.

According to an old business school adage, you cannot manage what you cannot measure. Like many slogans, it is not entirely true. Problems can arise when this notion is applied simplistically to security (or anything else). A better slogan would be that *measuring the right things imperfectly is better than measuring the wrong things precisely*. It is an inconvenient truth that meaningful attributes are not always easy to measure, while attributes that are easy to measure are not always meaningful. This is true for security and many other walks of life, including science, politics, and economics. As we saw in Rule 2, some of the most important elements of security risk, including its social, psychological, and reputational consequences, are difficult to measure in the conventional sense, by which I mean assigning numerical values expressed in standard units. Ignoring these crucial aspects of security risk, just because they are hard to quantify, would be a mistake.

The desire for precise measurements can give rise to *spurious quantification*, in which subjective judgements are cloaked in a mantle of numerical respectability and multi-digit metrics convey a false sense of scientific precision. In reality, the seemingly 'scientific' measurements are based on ultimately subjective beliefs about values and relative weightings. First come the fuzzy estimates ('this feels like a 4 out of 5'; 'X is twice as important as Y'). The resulting numbers are fed into an arithmetical formula, which transforms the nebulous inputs into precise figures that look like readings from a scientific instrument. The results seem plausible, which is misconstrued as evidence of their accuracy. They are then used to make quantitative judgements about such things as risk appetites, cost–benefit ratios, or returns on investment. However, the whole edifice may be built on sand. Alter the starting assumptions a little, and the output numbers may shift markedly.

The pitfall with precise metrics is that the precision is sometimes more of an illusion than reality. Our judgements about risk, and our willingness to tolerate risk, depend ultimately on what we value in life. The judgements are inherently subjective, and there is nothing wrong with that. Problems only start to arise if we conceal the true nature of those judgements behind a veneer of spurious quantification.

So, how can we distinguish good metrics from bad? Once again, psychology lends a hand. There are certain parallels between measuring aspects of risk or security and measuring psychological characteristics or behaviour. In both cases, the attributes that are being assessed are complex and subtle; they must be clearly defined and measured using tools that have been devised for that purpose.

Behavioural scientists recognized a long time ago that a good metric must have certain essential features. The most important is *validity*, which means that it measures what it is supposed to measure. A valid metric provides information that genuinely reflects the phenomena being observed and produces verifiable answers to the question being asked. A good metric must also possess the characteristic of *reliability*, which means that you consistently get the same results if you repeatedly measure the same thing. Reliability reflects the extent to which the measurement is repeatable and consistent. A metric may be valid but unreliable, or reliable but lacking validity. A digital clock set to the wrong time would give readings that were reliable but not valid.[4]

For more than a century, psychologists have been devising metrics, or 'tools', for measuring specific aspects of behaviour, thought processes, or personality, often in the form of a structured questionnaire. No competent psychologist would take any such tool seriously unless it had been demonstrated empirically to be sufficiently valid and reliable. The same cannot be said of many of the metrics used in protective security and risk management, where acceptability often rests on little more than superficial plausibility. Cyber security, in particular, is rife with products that purport to use AI or sophisticated algorithms to generate precise measurements of risk, but where the evidence of validity and reliability is often lacking.

There are, of course, respectable reasons for wanting quantitative metrics of risk and security, including the need to reassure budget holders that their money is being wisely spent and to comply with the requirements of regulators. However, the reasonable desire for quantitative metrics is inflamed by the dubious belief that *qualitative* metrics are inherently inferior. There is nothing inherently wrong with qualitative measures, and the right qualitative measure is better than the wrong quantitative measure.

The crudest metric of how well protective security is working is that nothing bad happens. As a rough yardstick, an absence or low frequency of security breaches does convey useful information. After all, the purpose of protective security is to mitigate risk, and the ultimate measure of success is that the risk does not materialize. However, an apparent absence of security breaches may have other, less reassuring explanations. For example, the threat actors might not have attempted to attack yet, but plan to do so in the near future. Or, as is often the case with insiders and cyber espionage, the security has in fact been breached but the victim hasn't noticed. A popular saying in the cyber security industry is that there are only two types of client: those that have been breached and those that have been breached but don't know it yet. So, although an absence of known bad events is clearly a desirable state of affairs, it does not prove that the protective security is good.

Other simple metrics can provide a more granular and nuanced view. One such metric is the *time to detect*—that is, the time taken to detect a breach or attempted breach of security. Another good metric is the *time to respond* once an attempted attack has been detected. The faster you detect and respond to an incipient attack, the less opportunity the threat actors have to cause harm and the more opportunity you have to thwart them. Both metrics are applicable in the physical, cyber, and personnel domains. In the physical domain, the time to detect could be, say, the interval between an intruder attempting to get through a secure perimeter and the guards being alerted by an alarm. The time to respond could be the time taken for the guards to arrive at the scene or call the police. In both cases the times should amount to no more than a few minutes. The story is different in the cyber domain, where the time to detect a covert intrusion by hackers is often measured in months rather than minutes. As we saw in Rule 5, the median time to detect a network compromise is 101 days, which leaves the attackers plenty of time to do whatever they want. However, detection is becoming faster as technology improves. The time taken to detect a cyber intrusion tends to be significantly shorter when the victim detects the intrusion rather than having to be tipped off by a third party. Rapid detection would be crucial in some forms of CBRN attack, where the nature of the incident may not be immediately obvious, especially if biological or radiological agents were involved.

It is possible to devise reasonably respectable metrics for assessing the wider societal benefits of protective security (as discussed in Rule 1). For instance, the effectiveness of counter-terrorist security could be judged by proxy metrics such as changes in the number of foreign tourists visiting the country or the number of people willing to use public transport.[5]

Having obtained your valid and reliable measurements, the next steps are to interpret them and draw conclusions about what they mean. Are the results good, bad, or indifferent, and what do they say about your security? A simple way of assessing results is to *benchmark* them against comparable organizations. If you were assessing the cyber security of a large bank, for example, you could compare its test results against those of other large banks facing comparable risks (assuming they were willing to share the information). One obvious pitfall of benchmarking against others is that the comparisons are relative rather than absolute. Being average or above average in your sector does not prove that your security is good, but merely that it is no worse than other people's. The paradox of benchmarking is that the worse everyone else performs, the better you look in comparison.

A more solid approach is to compare your results against a recognized security *standard* or framework. There are many to choose from and it can be a bit of a lottery. The effectiveness of locks, alarms, cyber security systems, and the like can be judged against detailed standards published by authoritative bodies such as ISO (International Standards Organization), BSI (the UK's national standards body), CIS (Center for Internet Security), NIST (the US National Institute of Standards and Technology), CPNI (Centre for the Protection of National Infrastructure), and NCSC (National Cyber Security Centre).

A striking feature of security standards is that there are many—arguably *too* many—for cyber security but almost none for personnel security. A model of good practice for personnel security, known as the Personnel Security Maturity Model, has been developed by CPNI, but it is not yet widely adopted (and not strictly a standard).[6] In contrast, cyber security practitioners have numerous overlapping standards and frameworks to choose from, as a lucrative industry has generated a plethora of competing systems. The result is a complex landscape that even experts find hard to navigate. The multitude of standards also lends itself to cherry picking, which can undermine the objectivity of assessment. Physical security falls somewhere between these two extremes, with numerous technical standards for different types of equipment, such as locks, alarms, and vehicle security barriers, but no overarching standard that judges an organization's physical security in the round.

More striking still is the absence of any *holistic* standard for protective security. You can judge your organization's cyber security against one of many standards. You can judge individual items of physical security kit against the relevant technical standards for those devices. You can even judge your personnel security against the Personnel Security Maturity Model. But you cannot judge your organization's overall security regime against an integrated standard that considers all three domains. That must be wrong. One step in the right direction has been the development by CPNI of their standard for Cyber Assurance of Physical Security Systems (CAPSS), which at least straddles two of the three domains.[7]

Layered

The seventh of the nine hallmarks on our list is layering, which means the presence of two or more distinct layers of security defences, such that a threat actor would have to penetrate successive layers in order to carry out a successful attack. Layering is sometimes referred to as *defence in depth* (a concept that is also well established in the safety world). Each layer of protective security potentially provides opportunities to detect that an attack is underway, delay the attackers, and mount a response before the attackers have time to do more harm. Biological systems are also characterized by multiple layers of defence which provide the diversity and redundancy needed to deal with any surprises that life can throw at them. The immune system is an inspirational example of layered and adaptive defence in depth, but that is another story.

The concept of layered security works well in the physical, cyber, and personnel security domains. The outer layer of physical security would typically be a perimeter vehicle security barrier or fence; for cyber security it would be perimeter firewall software; and for personnel security it would be pre-employment screening. Deterrence communications and systems for detecting hostile surveillance could also be regarded as outer layers of security. Inner layers might include such things as locked doors, internal CCTV, intruder detection systems, protective monitoring of computer networks, restricted access to sensitive areas or systems, and personnel security aftercare.

Layered security is most evident in the physical protection of high-risk buildings against terrorism. Sites at significant risk from terrorism are defended against the most common methods of attack, which include vehicle-borne and person-borne explosive devices, marauding armed terrorists on foot, and vehicles used as kinetic weapons. During the PIRA era, another major threat was from standoff weapons in the form of sniper rifles and improvised mortars.

The outer perimeter layer is designed to prevent the unauthorized or forcible entry of any vehicle that might be carrying a bomb or used as a kinetic weapon. It does this with physical barriers capable of stopping a vehicle moving at speed, which is no mean feat of engineering. The best vehicle security barriers are intelligently designed and unobtrusive. They can even be aesthetically pleasing. For instance, the architectural balustrades along Whitehall and the visually striking 'ARSENAL' sign that graces the entrance to the Arsenal Emirates football stadium in London are cleverly engineered vehicle security barriers capable of stopping a large truck moving at high speed. The underlying purpose of the outer layers is to maximize the distance between the protected site and the nearest point at which a terrorist bomb could be detonated. This distance is known as *standoff*. It is a precious commodity. The physical destructive effects of explosive devices diminish in a rapid, non-linear manner with increasing distance from the seat of the explosion. Consequently, even a small increase in standoff brings a disproportionately large benefit.

Outer layers of counter-terrorist physical security are also designed to prevent the entry of intruders carrying explosive devices or weapons. The first perimeter layer for pedestrians would typically include detection equipment to scan visitors for concealed weapons or explosive devices before they are granted access.

One unavoidable risk associated with any perimeter entry point is that a terrorist might detonate their device there if they realize that they cannot penetrate the security. In 2015, for example, three IS suicide bombers attacked the crowded Stade de France stadium in Paris, where an international football match attended by the French President was underway. The first bomber detonated his suicide belt outside the stadium after being prevented from entering at a security checkpoint. The other two bombers then blew themselves up outside the stadium.[8] One passer-by was killed.

If a large queue of vehicles or pedestrians is allowed to build up at an entry point, it can become an attractive target in its own right, and one that is much easier to attack than anything inside the perimeter. Moving the perimeter further out does not eliminate this problem because it is still the perimeter.

If the outer layers of physical security fail to deter or stop an attacker, then inner layers are equipped with mechanisms for detecting the intrusion and triggering an alert. Internal and outward-facing CCTV, intruder alarms, and patrolling guards provide *situational awareness* of what is happening outside and inside the perimeter. The inner layers may also be designed to delay any attacker who gets through the perimeter, using barriers, locks, secure containers, lock-down areas, or defensive planting to slow them down. A suitably located thicket of thorny bushes should cramp the style of most intruders, as well as enhancing the environment. Plants are prettier than razor wire.

Similar principles apply in the cyber domain. If hackers manage to penetrate the outer perimeter firewall of a network, the intrusion should be detected by an automatic protective monitoring system, which protects the network by performing a function analogous to that of a burglar alarm or guard force. It metaphorically patrols the network looking for signs of an intrusion. Maintaining cyber situational awareness entails knowing what devices are connected to the network, so that the presence of unauthorized devices can be detected in real time. The situational awareness data generated by protective monitoring systems is brought together in a cyber *security operations centre*, or SOC, where security staff monitor the network and respond to alarms.

Cyber defences, like physical defences, can also be designed to delay an attack. During the 2017 French presidential election campaign, Emmanuel Macron's team used fake email accounts to slow down the Russian hackers who were attacking their systems. The delaying tactic, which Macron's team described as 'cyber blurring', reportedly had some success by forcing the hackers to stop and inspect each of the accounts they penetrated.[9]

Designed-In

The best way to achieve good protective security is by thinking about it from the beginning and weaving it into the overall design. When commissioning any new IT system, business process, building, or physical infrastructure, the protective security should be designed-in from the outset. When that happens, the result is known as *security by design*.

The worst way to achieve good security is to start thinking about it after the structure or system has been built. Once the basic architecture of a building or digital network has been determined, the only way to make it more secure is by bolting secondary security features onto the existing structure. *Security that is retrofitted to a finished structure or system is liable to be ugly, expensive, and less effective than security that is designed-in.* For example, it is easier to design and build a blast-resistant building than it is to improve the blast resistance of an old building to an equivalent standard. An ideal building, from a counter-terrorist security perspective, is a reinforced concrete structure with blast-resistant windows and plenty of standoff. If, however, you are handed an old brick-built construction with no internal structures strong enough to support blast-resistant glazing, in an exposed location with no standoff, you may struggle to protect it sufficiently without spending prodigious amounts of money. Brick buildings are inherently more vulnerable to blast because brick walls are strong in compression but weak against lateral forces. They crumble when hit from the side, the upper layers lose their support, and the falling masonry usually kills more occupants than the blast.

The same principle applies with equal force to cyber security. To quote two academic experts on the subject, designing bad behaviour out of systems at the start is much more attractive than trying to police it afterwards.[10] Arguably, one reason why the cyber domain is such an insecure environment is that the internet, on which it largely depends, has an inherently insecure architecture. The internet was originally conceived as a medium for the free and unfettered exchange of data, not as a way of keeping data safe. It was designed to be open, decentralized, and free from censorship.[11] Before long, the internet became so essential for normal life that any fundamental redesign needed to make it more secure became impossible.[12] The vulnerabilities became fossilized, and robust security has subsequently proved hard to achieve. The vast majority of digital systems are connected in some way to the internet, including many that are not meant to be connected, making it necessary to spend heavily on secondary security systems. Despite all the money, no digital system that touches the internet is completely safe.

Even though security by design has such compelling advantages, protective security often remains something of an afterthought. The main considerations in most projects are cost and convenience. In a highly competitive market like digital technology, the commercial pressures to put new products on sale quickly are intense. Instead of taking time to design and build inherently secure products, many technology and software companies sell insecure products and try to fix the vulnerabilities later, somewhat like selling a ship riddled with holes and distributing patches to stop it sinking.[13]

Risks change over time. One of the lessons from history is that designers of important facilities should *take the long view* by making the precautionary assumption that the future threat environment will be no better than the present one and possibly worse. That said, there is a limit to the prescience of planners. For instance, when Charles Barry and Augustus Pugin designed the Palace of Westminster as the new home of the British Parliament in the nineteenth century, they could not reasonably have foreseen the security threats it would face in the twentieth and twenty-first centuries from Irish republican terrorism and Islamist extremist terrorism. And even if they had foreseen such problems, Parliament showed little interest in the subject, which helps to explain why its security remained dangerously inadequate until the early twenty-first century.[14]

Security by design is highly desirable. *Security by default* is even better, if it can be achieved. Something may be described as secure by default if its core design or structure makes it inherently resistant to attack and the security risks are mitigated at the level of root cause rather than symptoms. North Korea's digital infrastructure is said to be secure by default because, unusually, very little of it connects to the internet and the North Korean government expends huge effort on maintaining that isolation (albeit mainly for other reasons). The relative lack of external connectivity would make it harder, though not impossible, to conduct cyber attacks on North Korea from outside the country.

The term 'secure by default' is most commonly encountered in cyber security, where it has a narrower meaning. A digital device or system that is 'secure by default' is one in which the security features are activated by default as factory settings. The user therefore automatically receives the maximum protection unless they deliberately deactivate the security features. In contrast, many conventional systems require users to opt *in* to security features, rather than opt out. Human nature is such that we naturally gravitate towards default settings because they are the path of least resistance. Therefore, it obviously makes sense for the default settings to be the secure ones.[15]

Dynamic

Finally, we come to an attribute that helps to distinguish the best security from the merely adequate. That attribute is being dynamic rather than static. As we saw in Rule 2, security risks are dynamic and adaptive, meaning they change over time and respond adaptively to defensive countermeasures. A static, unchanging security regime is therefore at an inherent disadvantage. Given time, threat actors will find ways of defeating it. They can analyse the defences at their leisure and devise ways of circumventing them. If, however, the security measures are also changing, the threat actors' job becomes harder. To put it another way, *a moving target is harder to hit.*

A simple example of dynamic security in the physical domain would be the variable deployment of security guards on a protected site. In a static regime, the guards would remain in fixed positions or patrol the same routes at the same times every day according to a fixed timetable. A threat actor who conducted hostile surveillance could establish where and when guards would be present, and hence how to bypass them. A better deployment pattern would be a dynamic one in which the guards moved around in unpredictable ways at unpredictable times, making it harder for any threat actor to avoid bumping into them. The dynamic principle can also be applied to access control systems, by requiring personnel to follow varying procedures or provide different combinations of credentials each time they enter or log on.

The advantages of dynamic security over static security are most apparent in the cyber domain, where the risk management cycle (as outlined in Rule 4) spins even faster than it does in the physical and personnel domains. Cyber security is more susceptible to becoming reactive, leaving the defenders perpetually struggling to catch up by patching the latest vulnerabilities. Static defences such as basic firewalls present easier targets. As soon as a previously unidentified weakness is discovered, they become vulnerable. The defender must then fix the vulnerability, restore the system, and wait for the next problem, in a never-ending cycle. Dynamic defences that present a moving target are harder to breach.[16]

Dynamic security can improve the verification of identity and hence access control. The old ways of verifying identity rely on static identifiers such as fixed passwords, dates of birth, or social security numbers. These identifiers present static targets that can be unpicked or stolen by hacking. Given the vast scale of cyber espionage, they are likely to be compromised eventually, and once they are gone, they are gone. To add to the problem, some static identifiers such as dates of birth are static in a more profound sense. Unlike credit card numbers or PINs, they cannot easily be changed when found to be compromised. Better technology is enabling the use of dynamic identifiers that automatically change each time they are used. They present a rapidly moving target that is harder for a threat actor to hit. A common example is the digital token that displays a continually changing number which the user must enter when logging on to a computer system. Other examples of dynamic cyber security include rotating encryption keys, randomized memory addresses, and dynamic network configurations. All being well, by the time a hacker has worked out the answer, the question has changed. In these and other examples, the underlying aim is to make life harder for threat actors by keeping them, rather than the defenders, permanently on the back foot.

Dynamic security systems are attractive in principle but not always easy to implement in practice. To work effectively, they must present an unpredictable target for the threat actors while also behaving in a predictable way for legitimate users.

RULE 10

KNOW WHO'S IN CHARGE

*Good security requires good governance, which means clear
lines of responsibility, an integrated structure, good leadership,
independent assurance, and sufficient bandwidth.*

———

Governance

Good governance is a vital ingredient of good protective security. What
does that mean? A simple definition of governance is *the way in which
an organization is structured, managed, and led.*[1] Governance is about people and
their behaviour: it determines who does what, how people know what to
do, and what happens when things go wrong.

For the avoidance of doubt, I am not referring here to corporate governance in the conventional sense, which is the subject of extensive analysis
by industry regulators, management consultants, and business schools.[2]
Rather, I am talking about the governance of *security*. As noted previously,
security risk differs in certain respects from corporate risk or project risk. It
involves adaptive and malicious adversaries; the risks are imposed upon us
rather than freely chosen; and we have little actuarial data about the nastiest
risks (those with very low likelihood and very high impact). Conventional
corporate governance frameworks do not always translate neatly across
into the security domain and applying them mechanistically to the management of security risk can be problematic.

Good governance is essential for effective security and its absence is a
sure sign of trouble. If ever you find yourself trying to judge whether an
organization has good protective security, then the first question to ask is

'*Who's in charge?*' If the answer is faltering or unclear, it is a safe bet that the security will turn out, on closer inspection, to be suboptimal.

Bad governance breeds bad security in several ways. Lack of clarity about lines of responsibility leads to indecision, buck-passing, and inertia, resulting in unnecessary exposure to risk. Fragmented organizational structures leave physical, personnel, and cyber security languishing in separate silos, making holistic security harder to achieve. Poor leadership results in under-investment in security and a weak security culture in which individuals are not motivated to do the right things (or perhaps even motivated to do the wrong things). Lack of independent assurance allows decision-makers to delude themselves that security is working well when it is not. Lack of bandwidth leaves managers unable to think through the problems.

Any well-run organization should have a clear *strategy* for managing its biggest risks over the longer term, together with robust arrangements for managing a crisis if one of those risks should materialize.[3] Strategic planning and crisis management are hard to achieve in the absence of good governance. You may have the best technology in the world, but if your governance is rotten, you will probably have underperforming security.

Of course, there is no perfect system of governance and no universal template for all organizations. The suitability of any particular governance arrangements will depend on various factors including the size and complexity of the organization, its culture and history, the sorts of risks it is trying to manage, its tolerance of risk, and how much money it can afford to spend. Governance arrangements that work well in one setting may not work in another. Nonetheless, certain basic principles apply anywhere. For security governance to be regarded as good, it should possess at least five essential attributes:

- clear lines of responsibility;
- an integrated structure;
- good leadership;
- independent assurance; and
- sufficient bandwidth.

Clear Lines of Responsibility

The first hallmark of good governance (whether for security or anything else) is having *clear lines of responsibility*. This is where the question 'Who's in charge?' gets answered. Confusion on this issue is likely to result in lack of action or duplication of effort.

To be more precise, there should be clarity about three distinct things: who has the *responsibility* for performing which security functions; who has the *authority* to do the work, together with the necessary resources; and who is *accountable* if it goes wrong.[4] These three terms are often confused, so it is worth spelling out what they mean in this context. Responsibility means having an obligation to perform a particular function; authority means having the decision-making rights and resources needed to perform that function; and accountability means being answerable for the results.[5] As a general principle, someone who is responsible for a function, such as guarding a gate or managing a company's cyber security, should also have the authority to make it happen and be held accountable for the results. In practice, however, the three are not always aligned. It is unfair, though by no means uncommon, to make someone responsible for a function without giving them the commensurate authority and resources.[6]

Accountability can be regarded as a mechanism by which one group of people—for example, a regulator, or the board or shareholders of a company—exerts control over the people responsible for doing the work. It is unwise to make someone responsible without also making them accountable for the outcome. Accountability tends to sharpen the will to behave properly and get the job done. The fear of being called to account and criticized can be a powerful influence on the behaviour of officials, especially in public life. You can delegate responsibility and authority to people below you in the hierarchy, but you cannot delegate accountability: if you are accountable for something, then the buck stops with you. That is the theory, at least. In practice, the heads of large companies regularly survive major cyber security breaches with relative impunity. At worst, they lose their bonus or bail out with a golden parachute. If you really need to depend on someone doing their job properly, they must have *skin in the game*.

Why does this theology matter for security? It matters because a lack of clarity about lines of responsibility can, and frequently does, result in a lack of action and consequent exposure to avoidable risk. At worst, everyone assumes it is someone else's responsibility to deal with the problem and consequently no one does. The bigger the organization, the greater the potential for ambiguity about who is responsible—a phenomenon that has been described as *the problem of many hands*.

One of the many ways in which blurred lines of responsibility cause trouble is by generating false assurance about the extent to which decisions have been properly scrutinized. This problem can arise in hierarchical organizations that insist on having decisions approved by multiple ascending layers of management. The theory is that the greater the number of people who sign off a decision, the greater the confidence that the decision is sound. In practice that may not be true if each link in the chain blithely assumes that someone else has scrutinized the judgements. It is also inefficient.

A systemic problem with cyber security is the tendency to regard it as a technology function and devolve it to the IT department. This leaves the technology providers marking their own homework. Depending on the organizational culture, they may feel inclined to present their achievements in a favourable light by underplaying the risk and assuring top management that everything is under control. Or it can work the other way, with ambitious IT folk talking up the risk to enhance their status and resources.

Devolving cyber security to the technology providers can also leave those at the top of the organization feeling somehow not accountable for the risk. Given the potentially enormous impact of a major breach, the accountability for cyber security risk should be held at the most senior level. The reality is often different; for example, a government survey of more than 1,500 British businesses in 2017 found that less than a third (29 per cent) had assigned ownership of security to identified board members.[7]

It usually takes a major incident to expose the underlying governance problem, as we shall see later with some real examples.

A recurring lesson from cyber security breaches is that senior leaders do not always understand the security risks they are sitting on or the technical advice they are receiving from specialists. If you do not understand the risks, you are unlikely to ask the right questions, get the right answers, or make the right decisions. When the people at the top of an organization do not feel accountable for security risks, they may be less inclined to assign sufficient resources to those responsible for providing the security. One large study found that more than a quarter of the worst breaches could be attributed to senior management giving insufficient priority to security.[8] An official survey of cyber governance in the UK's biggest companies found that only a third of them were making investment decisions about their own cyber security at board level, more than two-thirds of boards had received no training in how to respond to a cyber incident, and one in ten companies had no plan in place for responding to a cyber incident.[9] Basic good practice would be for named individuals at board level to be identified as the accountable owners of security risks, and for the board to be regularly briefed on those risks.

The human consequences of obscure governance can be serious, as the British National Health Service (NHS) discovered on Friday 12 May 2017, when many of its IT systems were seriously disrupted by a piece of malware called WannaCry.[10] The malware, which was a type of self-replicating ransomware, originated in North Korea. It spread rapidly around the world, affecting more than 300,000 computer systems in 150 countries. The WannaCry malware was highly infectious but relatively crude. It caused problems only when it happened to land on a vulnerable IT system running older Microsoft Windows software that had not been updated with the latest security patches.[11] WannaCry worked by encrypting files and demanding a ransom payment in Bitcoin for decrypting them. Microsoft had been aware of the vulnerability and had released a software security patch two months before the incident. As such, the risk should have been straightforward to mitigate, apart from certain bespoke systems that could not easily be patched for technical reasons. Organizations that had applied the security patches were not adversely affected.

In the UK, the biggest impact of WannaCry was felt in the NHS, which declared a major incident on the afternoon of 12 May and implemented its emergency plans to maintain patient care. More than a third of the main NHS organizations, including at least fifty hospitals, were directly affected and many more shut down their computer systems pre-emptively as a precautionary measure (in some cases unnecessarily). At least eighty-one NHS trusts in England and several hundred local GP practices were disrupted, leading to many thousands of treatments and operations being postponed or relocated. At least 139 potential cancer patients had their urgent appointments cancelled during the days following the outbreak and five acute-care trusts were unable to treat some patients at their accident and emergency departments.[12] More than 1,200 pieces of diagnostic equipment, such as MRI scanners and blood test analysis devices, were infected and many more were disconnected to prevent further infection. It is possible, though unproven, that some patients might have died or suffered serious consequences. There was certainly an adverse impact on healthcare from cancelled appointments, the unbudgeted costs of cleaning up the malware infections, and clearing the backlogs of treatments. The consequences could easily have been much worse, had it not been for two pieces of luck. The malware hit the NHS at the end of the week, when there was less activity to disrupt. More importantly, a lone cyber security researcher discovered a flaw in the malware that enabled him to stop it dead in its tracks on the evening of 12 May by activating a 'kill switch'.[13] This rapid intervention prevented the malware from spreading further. Future malware outbreaks of this type are likely to be harder to resist.

The NHS was not a deliberate target of WannaCry, which spread opportunistically across vulnerable systems. Why, then, was it so badly affected? The NHS was unusually vulnerable mainly because of its extraordinarily fragmented governance and the related chronic underinvestment in security.[14] The NHS is not a single organization with an identifiable person in charge of its cyber security. On the contrary, it consists of a very large number of quasi-independent entities, ranging from large regional health-care trusts to small local GP practices. The exact number of such entities is unknown, but it is thought to be in the region of 12,000. Between them, they treat more than a million patients every twenty-four hours. The wider UK health and social care sector comprises around 40,000 separate organizations employing a total of 1.6 million people.[15] Here we find the problem of many hands writ large.

The WannaCry outbreak was a security event of national significance. It highlighted the uncomfortable truth that no one was ultimately responsible for managing the cyber security of the public healthcare sector at national level, no one was truly accountable for the risk to patients caused by the inadequate security, and there was no enforcement of national standards for cyber security. The problem was primarily one of governance, not technology. In theory, accountability sat with the individual leaderships of the many thousands of NHS organizations. Government ministers did not rush forward to claim ownership of the problem at the time. The obscure governance had also allowed a chronic under-investment in cyber security. Many NHS organizations were still using an ancient version of the operating system (Windows XP) and many computers had not been updated with the readily available security patches before the attack. None of the NHS organizations infected by WannaCry had applied the Microsoft patch and some of them had previously been breached in other cyber attacks.

An investigation by the UK National Audit Office (NAO) concluded that the NHS WannaCry incident could, and should, have been prevented by following basic IT security best practice.[16] The NAO report commented that the NHS and its parent government department needed to get their act together to improve the security of vital systems on which the safety of millions of patients depended. It noted that the Department of Health had been warned about the risk of ransomware before the attack but had not taken decisive action and did not know whether local NHS organizations were prepared. Another national body, NHS Digital, had issued timely advice on cyber security but lacked the authority to implement or enforce that advice nationally. Before the WannaCry incident, NHS Digital had conducted on-site assessments of the cyber security of eighty-eight NHS trusts and none of them had passed.[17] The impact of WannaCry would have been much less if they had followed the NHS Digital advice. The NAO commented that the managers and boards of NHS organizations had failed to identify cyber security as a risk to patient outcomes and had tended to overestimate their readiness to manage an attack.

The net result of this governance morass was avoidable risk to the safety and wellbeing of patients. New regulations that were implemented following the WannaCry incident require every health and care organization to have a named senior executive, preferably at board level, responsible for data and cyber security.[18]

Another instance of dubious governance leading to avoidable trouble was the notorious cyber security breach that hit the UK telecommunications provider TalkTalk in 2015, when a teenage hacker gained access to the records of 157,000 of its customers, including names, addresses, dates of birth, and phone numbers. The hacker exploited a software vulnerability that had been known for years (it was older than he was) and the incident was widely judged to have been foreseeable and avoidable. The national regulator, the Information Commissioner, levied a then record fine of £400,000 on TalkTalk for security failings that had allowed a hacker to compromise customers' personal data 'with ease'. The Commissioner said the record fine was 'a warning to others that cyber security is not an IT issue, it is a boardroom issue'.[19] Had the current data protection legislation been in place at the time, the fine could have been tens of millions of pounds. Other losses arising from the breach are estimated to have cost the company around £60 million, as customers left and its reputation took a battering.[20]

When the TalkTalk chief executive later appeared before a committee of parliamentarians to be questioned on the breach, she conceded that responsibility for cyber security had been shared among multiple roles within the company and no one senior person was in charge of cyber security, apart from her. It later emerged that the company had been advertising for an information security officer just before the incident occurred.[21] The chief executive moved on from TalkTalk in 2017 and was appointed as Chair of NHS Improvement.

The terrorist attack on the Canadian Parliament in Ottawa in 2014 was arguably another example of convoluted governance getting in the way of good security. On 22 October 2014 a lone Islamist terrorist armed with a rifle shot dead a soldier on ceremonial duty not far from the Parliament building. The terrorist then hijacked a car and drove it towards Parliament, before abandoning the vehicle and running through the main entrance into the heart of the building. At one point, only an unlocked door separated the terrorist from the Canadian Prime Minister and a room full of politicians. Before he could kill again, the terrorist was shot (thirty-one times) by security staff and police officers in the central lobby.[22] Subsequent inquiries revealed that the parliamentary security authorities had been advised years before that the building was vulnerable to attack by marauding terrorists, but no decisive action had been taken to close this vulnerability.

The security governance structures in place at the time of the attack might have made good sense in terms of Canadian constitutional history, but they made less sense to anyone concerned about protective security. The Canadian Parliament has a two-house structure similar to that of the UK Parliament, with a House of Commons and a Senate. As in Westminster, the two Houses cohabit in a single building. Their security was separately presided over by the Sergeant-at-Arms in the Commons and Black Rod in the Senate, again mirroring the old UK roles. The Houses had their own internal security staff. The House of Commons Security Service personnel had no remit in the Senate, and the Senate Protective Service staff had no remit in the Commons. Outside the building, the all-important external and perimeter security was provided by various federal, provincial, and local police forces, none of which was permitted to operate inside the Parliament.

The attack ended with the death of the terrorist, but it might easily have ended in the deaths of parliamentarians in the heart of Canadian democracy. Soon after the attack, a decision was taken to rationalize the governance by assigning overall responsibility for the physical security to one senior police officer. As is so often the case, it took an actual attack to stimulate reform.

Integrated Structure

A second hallmark of good security governance is an *integrated structure*, by which I mean an organizational structure that facilitates an integrated, holistic approach to security (as advocated in Rule 9). Organizational structures by themselves cannot solve an organization's security problems but fragmented structures can make them worse. Holistic security is unlikely to flourish in an organization that separates the physical, personnel, and cyber security functions into disconnected silos under separate commands, or which neglects one of those domains (usually personnel) compared to the others.

Most organizations do not have integrated security structures and do not deal holistically with security risks. A common practice is for physical security ('guards and gates') and cyber security ('technical stuff') to sit in separate departmental silos, while the Cinderella function of personnel security belongs in HR or, more likely, nowhere at all. Some large organizations further subdivide the management of cyber-related risks into separate silos for information technology (IT), operational technology (OT), and information security. (By the way, what *is* the difference between information security and cyber security? And is the distinction, which some insist on making, still useful in an era when almost all information is generated, processed, communicated, and stored on digital systems? There are reasons why 'cyber' has made it into the dictionary.) If security is carved up in this way, then it is vital to have strong communication links between the different functions so that they can at least attempt to coordinate their actions.

Two job titles that are now commonplace in larger organizations are Chief Information Officer (CIO) and Chief Information Security Officer

(CISO). Some organizations have both. As the names suggest, one or both of these roles has responsibility for keeping the organization's information safe. The job titles signify a non-holistic approach: in their narrower manifestations, at least, CIOs and CISOs are denizens of the cyber domain only. There may also be some lack of clarity about who owns the risk at board level. A common structure has the CISO reporting to the CIO, who has a broader agenda beyond security. The CIO's primary role is to opti-mize the organization's use of information in support of its business—a function that could at times be in tension with security. Arguably, a better governance structure would have the CISO reporting to the CEO or Chair, who is (or should be) ultimately accountable for security risk, or to a Chief Security Officer or Chief Risk Officer whose remit also encompasses physical and personnel security. Some evidence suggests that governance structure is correlated with security performance. A two-year study of 1,200 organizations found that a large majority of lower-performing CISOs were in positions that reported to the CIO or a technology role, whereas the majority of high-performing CISOs reported to someone whose role was defined in terms of the wider business or risk.[23]

There are some honourable exceptions to be found among the frag-mented landscapes of security governance. For example, Barclays PLC announced in 2017 that it had restructured its security work in order to implement a holistic approach, by bringing together within a single div-ision its previously separate teams for cyber security, physical security, insider activity, and counter-fraud.[24] The bank's express aim was to create an integrated capability able to deal seamlessly with all aspects of security risk. This wise approach remains the exception rather than the rule.

An integrated security governance structure does not imply an absence of organizational boundaries. When dealing with complex fields like phys-ical, personnel, and cyber security, it is a practical necessity to recognize subject specialisms and distinct roles. In larger organizations, that entails making discrete teams or departments responsible for particular functions. No one is suggesting that the ideal structure would be an amorphous blob in which everyone dabbled in all aspects of security. The point is that specialist teams should be integrated within a unified management structure to achieve a holistic approach. The teams should work together to a common aim and their managers should be able to see the full picture of their composite effects.

Holistic security can be achieved even in highly complex organizations if a concerted effort is made to integrate the component parts. The planning and delivery of the physical, cyber, and personnel security for the London 2012 Olympics involved dozens of organizations from the public and private sectors, including numerous government departments, multiple police forces, the security and intelligence agencies, partner agencies in friendly foreign countries, the armed forces, public transport operators, private security companies, and commercial technology providers, as well as the organizations responsible for building the Games venues and running the events.[25] The potential for fragmentation was vast. However, the UK authorities recognized from the outset that coordinating the activities of the many different contributors would be crucial for success, as indeed it was.

The problems arising from fragmented structures are not unique to security, of course. They are endemic in other areas of corporate and public life, including government. In the UK, for example, the decentralization (some would say Balkanization) of public healthcare and public transport has made it difficult to pinpoint anyone at the top who can be held to account if the hospitals are full or the trains are delayed. Ministers blame the healthcare trusts or train operating companies, and vice versa. Who do you hold to account when bad things happen?

Most experts who pondered on the causes of the Great Financial Crash of 2008 concluded that the complexity and fragmentation of the financial system were important contributory factors in its downfall. Within the big banks, teams of traders operating in one silo often had little understanding of what traders in other silos were up to. Worse, the silos were sometimes competing with one another as individuals operated under incentive schemes that rewarded self-interest rather than the collective good. The banks' senior leaders and regulators were unable to piece together the fragments to form a picture of the overall financial risk. The journalist Gillian Tett described how one major bank had 3,000 'risk officers' on its payroll who were supposed to monitor the bank's exposure to financial risks. However, the 'risk officers' were divided among three separate departments that dealt with different types of financial risk and did not communicate much with one another. In institution after institution, senior managers failed to spot the enormous risks that were brewing in separate silos, because the silos did not communicate and the people at the top could not see the totality.[26]

Good Leadership

A third hallmark of good governance is *good leadership*. Of course it is. Here is not the place for another treatise on the nature of leadership, which has been the subject of countless books, websites, lectures, and social media outpourings. As long ago as 1974, an academic expert remarked balefully that there were almost as many definitions of leadership as there were persons who had attempted to define the concept. The number of leadership experts has grown enormously since then. That said, most experts seem to agree that the basic attributes of good leadership include integrity, strategic thinking, communication skills, and personal resilience.[27] Good leaders display grace under pressure.

Good leadership is crucial for creating a positive *security culture*—preferably a concordance culture in which everyone wants to do the right thing. As we saw in Rule 6, concordance cultures are generally better than box-ticking compliance cultures at achieving sustained improvements in security behaviour. Another component of a positive security culture is a willingness to raise concerns and speak truth to power. Many organizations have a formalized *whistleblowing* process that should allow any employee to report alleged wrongdoing in a way that protects them.

An important function of leaders is establishing the right tone and ethos within their organization. Strong *ethical standards* are integral to managing risk, as well as being virtuous in their own right. Organizations that lose sight of ethical principles are inviting serious trouble. Many organizations have been damaged by bad decisions arising from a deeper malaise in their leadership, ethos, and culture. Examples include Enron, Volkswagen's 'dieselgate', and the scandal that erupted in the UK Parliament in 2009 over MPs' expenses. The commission of inquiry into the Great Financial Crash concluded that one of its causes, in addition to greed, incompetence, and reckless risk-taking, was a systemic breakdown in ethics.[28]

Another reason why ethical standards are important for security is the subjective nature of the risks. As noted elsewhere, our judgements about security risks and our willingness to tolerate them depend on judgements about values. If those judgements are easy to manipulate with the lure of money or career advancement, then the effective management of security risks may be subverted. Strong ethical standards help to guard against manipulation by keeping everyone honest.

Leadership is not always good, of course. It may even be toxic. The adverse consequences of bad leadership are wide-ranging and dispiriting. For security in particular they can include disgruntlement, cynicism, and disengagement, which in turn breed bad behaviour ranging from lazy disregard for security to deliberate acts of malice. As noted before, rotten barrels make rotten apples.

Independent Assurance

A fourth essential ingredient of good security governance is *independent assurance*, which means independently verifying, to a reasonably high level of confidence, that all is as it should be. Writing rules and policies is not enough: you must satisfy yourself that the policies are being followed, the security risks are as you have been led to believe, and the protective security is working as intended. The guiding principle is *trust but verify*. Assurance is the process by which the verification is done.

The traditional approach to assuring security involves auditing the processes and people to check their compliance with the policies. A better way of gaining assurance is through active testing. The test results provide assurance (or not) that all is as it should be, with the added benefit of discovering opportunities for improvement.

A standard governance model for risk management in the corporate world is known as the *three lines of defence*. The first line of defence is the operational management—that is, the people managing the actual work. The second line comprises the specialist corporate functions that oversee risk management and compliance for the organization. The third line of defence is the independent assurance function, which is usually provided by internal audit. Its purpose is to furnish top managers and the board with objective and independent advice on how well the risks are being managed.[29] The three lines of defence model does not translate neatly into the management of protective security, especially for smaller organizations that do not have specialist risk management or internal audit functions. Nonetheless, the principle of *independent* assurance is sound. If you are accountable for security, you should be able to trust those responsible for performing the security functions. But you should also verify that their claims are true. The best way of doing that is not by asking them to fill in forms: it is by testing.

A rapidly developing challenge is how to obtain independent assurance about autonomous AI-based systems, which are capable of making complex decisions for reasons that may not be apparent to their human designers or operators.

Sufficient Bandwidth

An organization might have the right structures, processes, and leadership, but none of them will count for much if the decision-makers and those doing the work are too heavily preoccupied with other matters. For protective security to work well, the people who lead and deliver it must be able to devote enough time and thinking capacity to the issues. To put it another way, they need sufficient bandwidth.

Anyone who has worked in an organization, whether large or small, commercial or public sector, will know that the reality can sometimes be different. Their day job may be about one function, but another issue is absorbing much of their attention. The distraction may be self-imposed, such as a corporate restructuring or infrastructure project, in which case the organization still has choices about how best to use its available capacity. The trouble is that some organizations behave as though people had limitless bandwidth and continue to heap new tasks onto the pile. Bombarding overstretched people with further demands is a bit like mounting a denial of service attack on a computer network. It is unlikely to improve matters. Senior leaders must occasionally step back and consider the totality of what they and others are attempting to do. Sometimes, the key to better security may be doing less.

THE RULES IN SUM

Rule 1: Security Rules

Security is a basic human need. It enables individuals and organizations to go about their lives freely and without harm. Good security liberates us from the disruptive fear of harm and builds confidence to invest in the future.

- Protective security is the means of mitigating risks that arise directly from the potentially harmful actions of people such as criminals, terrorists, hostile states, and insiders.
- Security risks stem from the actions of purposeful adversaries. They evolve in response to defensive countermeasures. Unlike some other forms of risk, they are involuntary.
- There is more to security than stopping bad things from happening. It is a common good with wider benefits.
- Good protective security builds trust and confidence, freeing people and organizations from harm and the disruptive fear of harm.

Rule 2: Risk Is the Key

Risk is the universal currency by which security problems and solutions are judged. Security risk has three basic components: threat, vulnerability, and impact.

- Security risk is the amount of harm that is likely to arise if no further action is taken.
- Security risk has three components: threat, vulnerability, and impact.
- Threat is a product of the intentions and capabilities of threat actors; it is a measure of the probability that threat actors will make a credible attempt to attack.
- Vulnerability refers to the gaps or weaknesses in the potential victim's protective security defences. It is a measure of the probability that threat actors would succeed if they were to attempt an attack.
- Impact is a measure of the consequences of a successful attack. It is multi-dimensional.
- Security risks are dynamic and adaptive: they can change rapidly over time and arise from the actions of purposeful actors.
- Protective security is an enduring process, not a state.

- Security risks are emergent properties of complex adaptive systems. They are capable of undergoing very rapid, non-linear changes, the outcomes of which are impossible to predict.

Rule 3: Think Like an Attacker

Judgements about risk and security require an understanding of the current and likely future intentions and capabilities of threat actors.

- To manage security risk, we must first understand the threats we are facing, which means understanding the intentions and capabilities of the relevant threat actors.
- Mirror imaging can lead us to underestimate the extent to which some threat actors are ready, willing, and able to do truly terrible things.
- The most serious security threats are covert. Threat actors have secrets that must be uncovered in order to understand the threat. The defender's vulnerabilities should also be kept under wraps.
- Absence of evidence of a threat does not constitute evidence of an absence of threat.
- The defender's general protective security posture should be risk-based and intelligence-led.
- Security means staying safe now and preparing to stay safe in the future. It therefore pays to contemplate likely future threats, even though precise predictions are unattainable.
- We can think about possible future threats by extrapolating from current trends, learning from history, and considering how threat actors might exploit emerging technologies.

Rule 4: There Are Three Ways to Reduce Risk

The three ways to reduce security risk are to reduce the threat, reduce the vulnerability to attack, or reduce the impact of a successful attack.

- The process of managing security risk involves three basic steps, repeated cyclically: understanding the risks; deciding how much risk to tolerate; and acting to reduce the risks.
- Know what you are trying to protect. Understand your assets.
- Apply the principles of least access and asset minimization.
- Understand the risks arising from suppliers and other third parties, who may be the soft underbelly of security.
- Risk tolerance is ultimately a subjective judgement.
- Threat is hard to reduce, though deterrence, obscurity, and distraction can help.

- Most conventional protective security is intended to reduce vulnerability.
- Many potential victims could do more to reduce risk by reducing the impact of an attack.
- Attempts to manage security risk by avoiding it or transferring it to others are seldom fully successful.
- Avoiding one risk means accepting others. Doing nothing is doing something.

Rule 5: Build Resilience

Purely defensive security can never guarantee protection. The most enduring way to mitigate risk is by building resilience. Passive resilience comes from reducing the impact of disruptive events and returning quickly to normality. Active resilience goes beyond that and involves becoming progressively tougher by learning from adversity.

- Passive resilience is the ability to cope with disruption, recover quickly, and return to normality.
- Active resilience involves growing progressively tougher by learning from adversity and becoming better able to manage future stresses.
- Supply chains should be resilient too.
- Passive resilience is attained by reducing the impact element of risk. This can be achieved through early detection and rapid response; asset minimization; redundancy; secure backup; insurance; incident management and crisis management; business continuity planning; and disaster recovery.
- Asset minimization, including data minimization, is an underused strategy. Beware of digital hoarding.
- Apply the 3-2-1 rule to data backup.
- The crucial elements of crisis management are governance, communication, and teamwork. Expect the fog of war.
- Active resilience is built by learning from experience and applying the lessons to become tougher. This can be done by testing, exercising, and learning from others.
- Resilience depends on people and relationships. Invest in relationships.
- Individuals can strengthen their own personal resilience. Factors conducive to personal resilience include a successful track record of coping with moderate stress, focus, humour, supportive relationships, expertise, and adequate sleep.

Rule 6: It's All About People

The human dimension is the most important and least well-understood aspect of security. People are central to both the problems and the solutions.

- People are not the weakest link in security. They are central to defence.
- An insider is a person who exploits, or intends to exploit, their authorized access for unauthorized purposes.

- Insiders may be malicious or unwitting. Much of the harm caused by insiders is unintended.
- Many attacks are conducted through unwitting insiders by means of social engineering.
- The systems and processes for protecting an organization against insider risks are known as personnel security. The core purpose of personnel security is to confirm the identity of individuals and provide sufficient assurance about their trustworthiness.
- The basic elements of personnel security are pre-employment screening, good management, and aftercare.
- The best guide to future behaviour is past behaviour.
- Good management is a crucial part of personnel security. Rotten barrels make rotten apples.
- It is hard to tell when people are lying.
- The security culture of an organization is a crucial part of its defences. A concordance culture (wanting to do the right thing) is preferable to a tick-box compliance culture.
- The ultimate gauge of personnel security is the level of trust.

Rule 7: Everyone Is Biased

Judgements about risk, security, and crises are prone to systematic distortion by psychological predispositions. It is better to understand these biases and aim off for them.

- A range of psychological predispositions systematically influence how we think and behave, especially in complex, novel, or stressful situations.
- Our reaction to acute threat can be impaired by inattentional blindness and inappropriate intuitive responses. Badly designed technology makes it worse.
- Our perception of risk can be distorted by various cognitive biases, including availability bias, optimism bias, future discounting, loss aversion, fundamental attribution error, and risk compensation. Personality traits such as sensation-seeking and impulsivity can add to the mix.
- Our ability to manage crises and learn lesson from them can be impaired by other cognitive biases, including confirmation bias, illusory superiority bias, groupthink, sunk-cost bias, hindsight bias, and outcome bias.
- Bad sleep can seriously impair our ability to manage risks and make sound decisions.
- The distorting effects of psychological predispositions can be countered by understanding our biases and acquiring expertise through practice and experience.
- Other useful techniques for countering the effects of cognitive biases include devil's advocacy, the Delphi method, premortems, key assumptions checking, Bayes' Rule, and automated decision-support tools.

Rule 8: Cyber Is New Ways of Doing Old Things

The cyber domain brings distinctive problems. Nonetheless, its security is subject to the same fundamental principles as other forms of protective security, including the pre-eminence of the human dimension.

- Cyber security is the protection of digital systems, the data on them, and the services they provide from unauthorized access, harm, or misuse.
- Cyber technology provides threat actors with powerful new tools which are characterized by their massive scalability, low cost, ease of use, perceived lack of risk to the threat actors, plausible deniability, and transnational nature.
- The three broad categories of cyber risk are cyber espionage (gaining illicit access to data), cyber sabotage (overt disruption of systems), and cyber subversion (using digital systems to undermine democratic processes).
- The same fundamental principles of risk apply to cyber security as they do to other forms of security risk. The malicious activities for which cyber tools are used, including espionage, sabotage, subversion, and crime, pre-date the existence of computers.
- The human dimension is central to cyber security. Common attack methods such as phishing rely on exploiting human psychology.
- Cyber sabotage attacks on critical infrastructure are capable of causing catastrophic harm.
- Air gaps cannot be relied upon to protect digital systems.
- Cyber weapons escape and breed.
- Lies travel further and faster than truth on social media.
- Cyber terrorism does not (yet) exist.
- The main factor in most successful cyber attacks is the victim's vulnerability. Basic security precautions, such as strong passwords, updating software, correctly configuring networks, and managing access credentials, would prevent most attacks.
- The inadequacy of much cyber security underlines the importance of building cyber resilience.
- The impact of a successful cyber attack can be reduced through secure backup, data minimization, incident management, segmentation of systems and data, encryption, and pseudonymization.

Rule 9: Know What Good Looks Like

Good protective security has nine distinguishing characteristics: it is risk-based, well governed, holistic, understandable, regularly tested, well measured, layered, designed-in, and dynamic.

- Risk-based security is shaped according to an understanding of the threats, vulnerabilities, and impacts of the relevant security risks (as in Rule 2).
- Well-governed security has clear lines of responsibility, an integrated structure, good leadership, independent assurance, and sufficient bandwidth (as in Rule 10).

- Holistic security takes an integrated approach to physical, personnel, and cyber security. It considers all three dimensions in the round.
- Understandable security does not overwhelm the decision-makers and operators with complexity. Checklists can help.
- Regularly tested means routinely verifying that the security measures work as intended and identifying areas for improvement.
- Well-measured security is assessed using metrics that are valid and reliable. Measuring the right things imperfectly is better than measuring the wrong things precisely. Avoid spurious quantification.
- Layered security has two or more distinct layers of defence that provide opportunities to detect, delay, and respond to attacks.
- Designed-in security has been thought about from the outset. Security that is retrofitted to a finished structure or system is liable to be ugly, expensive, and less effective. Security by default is even better.
- Dynamic security presents threat actors with a moving target that is harder to hit.

Rule 10: Know Who's in Charge

Good security requires good governance, which means clear lines of responsibility, an integrated structure, good leadership, independent assurance, and sufficient bandwidth.

- Governance is the way in which an organization is structured, managed, and led. Good governance is essential for good security.
- Good governance has five essential attributes: clear lines of responsibility, an integrated structure, good leadership, independent assurance, and sufficient bandwidth.
- Clear lines of responsibility provide clarity about who is responsible for performing which functions, who has the authority and resources needed to do the work, and who is accountable for the outcomes.
- Accountable individuals should have skin in the game.
- An integrated structure is one that promotes a holistic approach to managing security risk by considering the physical, personnel, and cyber elements in the round.
- Good leadership is essential for promoting a good security culture and good security behaviour. Toxic leadership worsens the insider risk.
- Independent assurance means checking that all is as it should be. The guiding principle is to trust but verify.
- People must be allowed sufficient bandwidth to think and do their job properly.

GLOSSARY

. *The Glossary includes some terms that I have not used in the book but which readers might encounter elsewhere.*

3-2-1 rule (for secure data backup): Keep at least three copies of your data (the primary plus at least two backups); store the copies on at least two different types of storage device (e.g. hard disk and cloud); and keep at least one backup copy off-site.

active resilience: Growing progressively tougher by learning from adversity and becoming better able to cope with future stresses. See also *passive resilience*.

aftercare: The post-recruitment elements of *personnel security*. Aftercare is intended to mitigate the *insider risk* from people who already have authorized access to an organization's assets, including employees, contractors, and other third parties.

AI: Artificial Intelligence. A set of advanced general-purpose digital technologies that enable machines to perform highly complex tasks effectively. Common applications include search engines, spam filters, facial recognition, translation, digital assistants, and autonomous vehicles. See also *machine learning*.

ALARP: As Low as Reasonably Practicable (with reference to risk).

anonymization: Completely breaking the link between data and the personal identities of the people to whom it applies. Easier said than done.

APT: Advanced Persistent Threat. A euphemism for a nation state *threat actor* in the cyber domain. Formerly, a euphemism for China.

assurance: The process of actively verifying that all is as it should be.

attack surface: *Cyber security* term denoting the full range of potential vulnerabilities in a target.

authentication: Verifying the identity of a person, process, or device.

Bitcoin: One form of *cryptocurrency*. There are many others.

blockchain: A technology for securely storing data in a distributed digital ledger. Transactions are recorded in a peer-to-peer network, avoiding the need for a trusted central authority. Blockchain technology forms the basis of *cryptocurrencies* such as *Bitcoin*.

C2: Command and Control. The exercise of authority and direction in pursuit of a common goal. Not to be confused with C3 (Command, Control, and Communication), C4 (Command, Control, Communication, and Computing), C5 (Command, Control, Communication, Computing, and Collaboration), or many variants thereof.

capability (of *threat actors*): The practical ability (as distinct from *intention*) of *threat actors* to cause harm.

CAPSS: Cyber Assurance of Physical Security Systems. A standard produced by *CPNI*.

CBRN: Chemical, Biological, Radiological, and Nuclear.

CERT: Computer Emergency Response Team.

CIA: Confidentiality, Integrity and Availability. The holy trinity by which information security practitioners judge information security. (Also the Central Intelligence Agency.)

cloud: Somebody else's computers.

CNI: Critical National Infrastructure. Those critical elements of infrastructure (assets, facilities, systems, networks, or processes, and the essential workers who operate and facilitate them), the loss or compromise of which could result in (a) major detrimental impact on the availability, integrity, or delivery of essential services—including those services whose integrity, if compromised, could result in significant loss of life or casualties—taking into account significant economic or social impacts; and/or (b) significant impact on national security, national defence, or the functioning of the state.

complex system: A set of interacting components whose collective behaviour is greater than the sum of its parts. Businesses, organizations, terrorist groups, economies, human societies, and security crises are examples of complex systems.

CPNI: Centre for the Protection of National Infrastructure. The UK Government national authority on physical and personnel protective security.

cryptocurrency: A system of digital currency using *blockchain* technology. The best-known example is *Bitcoin*.

current risk: The level of security risk that applies with the existing protective security measures. Also referred to by risk specialists as *residual risk*.

cyber: Related in some way to digital electronic networks or systems.

cyber espionage: Covertly gaining illicit access to someone's data over a digital network.

cyber sabotage: Using digital systems to cause disruption or physical effects.

cyber security: The protection of digital systems, the data on them, and the services they provide from unauthorized access, harm, or misuse.

cyber subversion: The use of the *internet*, social media, or other digital systems to undermine established democratic processes—for example, by spreading propaganda or fake news.

Daesh: *Dowla al-Islamiya fi al-Iraq wa al-Sham*, otherwise known as ISIL, ISIS, or *IS*.

dark web or dark net: The vast number of *internet* sites that cannot be accessed by conventional search engines or web browsers.

DDoS: Distributed Denial of Service attack. A type of cyber attack in which *threat actors* attempt to overwhelm a system with more requests than it can handle, thereby blocking legitimate users from accessing it.

Delphi method: A structured process for eliciting and distilling the views of a large number of experts.

deterrence communications: Communications designed to deter and otherwise influence *threat actors*.

digital footprint: All of the information that is available online about an individual or an organization.

doxing: Publishing a potential victim's personal details online. More specifically, revealing the link between an individual's supposedly anonymous online identity and their real-world identity.

encryption: Cryptographic encoding of data to prevent unauthorized access.

FUD: Fear, Uncertainty, and Doubt.

GCHQ: Government Communications Headquarters.

GDPR: General Data Protection Regulation.

GNSS: Global Navigation Satellite Systems. *GPS* is one example.

governance: The way in which an organization is structured, managed, and led.

GPS: Global Positioning System. An example of a *GNSS*.

hacktivists: Hackers who are motivated by a particular cause or political issue.

HEAT: Hostile Environment Awareness Training.

heuristic: A simple procedure that helps to find adequate, though often imperfect answers to difficult questions.

holistic security: Protective security that considers physical, personnel, and *cyber security* in the round.

honeypot: A computer system or person used to lure or distract *threat actors*.

hostile reconnaissance: The physical or online processes by which *threat actors* collect information about a potential target.

humint: Human intelligence gathering operations. Recruiting and running covert human sources to collect secret intelligence.

HVM: Hostile Vehicle Mitigation. The use of vehicle security barriers to protect against attack by vehicles carrying bombs or vehicles used as weapons. See also *standoff*.

ICS: Industrial Control Systems. Electronic information systems used to control industrial processes. See also *SCADA*.

impact: The multi-dimensional consequences of a successful attack—for example, the physical, psychological, financial, and political harm caused by a terrorist attack.

insider: Someone who exploits, or intends to exploit, their authorized access for unauthorized purposes.

insider risk: The security risk arising from *insiders*.

intention (of *threat actors*): The desire (as distinct from *capability*) of *threat actors* to cause harm.

internet: A global computer network providing a variety of information and communication facilities, consisting of interconnected networks using standardized communication protocols. Or, to put it more simply, the means by which most digital devices and networks communicate.

IoT: The Internet of Things. The global collection of many billions of digital devices that are connected to the *internet*.

IS: (So-called) Islamic State ('so-called' because, although fervently Islamic, it is not really a state). Also known as ISIL (Islamic State of Iraq and the Levant), ISIS (Islamic State of Iraq and al-Sham), and *Daesh* (its slightly derogatory Arabic acronym).

machine learning: The ability of computers to learn without being explicitly programmed. See also *AI*.

malvertising: Online advertising containing *malware*.

malware: Malicious software. The main types of malware include viruses, worms, and Trojans.

MI5: Otherwise known as the Security Service. The UK agency responsible for keeping the country safe from threats to its national security, particularly terrorism and hostile foreign state activity.

NCSC: National Cyber Security Centre. The protective security arm of *GCHQ*.

NIST: National Institute of Standards and Technology. Leading US authority on standards and measurement.

NSA: National Security Agency. The US equivalent of *GCHQ*.

operational technology (OT): Digital technology (hardware and software) that monitors or controls physical devices, processes, or events. OT is distinct from the more familiar information technology (IT), which is principally concerned with processing data.

passive resilience: The ability to recover from a setback and return to normality. Protective security can increase passive resilience by reducing the *impact* of an attack. See also *active resilience*.

patching: Updating software to fix known vulnerabilities and bugs.

people security: Any way in which an understanding of human behaviour can be applied to improving protective security. Not to be confused with *personal security* or *personnel security*, and perhaps best avoided.

personal security: The protection of individuals against threats to their security in their private and professional lives. Not to be confused with *people security* or *personnel security*.

personnel security: The defensive measures by which an organization protects itself against *insider risk*. Not to be confused with *people security* or *personal security*.

phishing: The use of emails that appear to originate from a trusted source to deceive recipients into clicking on malicious links or attachments that contain *malware*.

PIRA: Provisional Irish Republican Army.

protective security: The means of mitigating risks that arise directly from the potentially harmful actions of people such as criminals, terrorists, hostile states, and *insiders*.

ransomware: A type of *malware* used by criminals to extort money. It works by encrypting the victim's data. The criminals offer to unlock the data in return for a ransom payment in *cryptocurrency*.

residual risk: The level of risk that remains after protective security measures have been applied. Equivalent to *current risk*.

resilience (in relation to protective security): The ability to prepare for, absorb, respond to, and recover from attacks and adapt to new conditions. See also *active resilience* and *passive resilience*.

risk: The amount of harm that is likely to arise if no further action is taken.

risk tolerance: The amount of risk that an individual or organization is willing to accept.

SCADA: Supervisory Control and Data Acquisition. A subset of Industrial Control Systems (*ICS*). SCADA systems are used to monitor and control industrial processes.

script kiddies: Unsophisticated hackers who are motivated mainly by curiosity and entertainment. They tend to use ready-made *malware* to conduct relatively crude cyber attacks, such as defacing websites.

secure by design: Designed from the ground up to be secure.

security culture: An organization's consistent tendency to behave in certain ways with regard to security.

security through obscurity: Improving the security of a potential target by masking its true significance or making it hard for *threat actors* to identify its vulnerabilities.

security through peculiarity: Improving the security of a potential target by using unusual or bespoke hardware or software.

shadow IT: Software or hardware used by people within an organization without the organization's knowledge or agreement.

SIEM: A *cyber security* term standing for Security Information and Event Management.

SOC: Security Operations Centre. Generally applied to a cyber hub that monitors the IT network. Sometimes referred to as a CSOC (Cyber SOC).

social engineering: A collection of techniques used by *threat actors* to deceive and manipulate people into performing actions or revealing confidential information.

standoff: The distance between a protected site and the closest point at which a terrorist bomb could be detonated. Standoff against vehicle bombs is generally enforced with vehicle security

barriers (otherwise known as hostile vehicle mitigation, or *HVM*).

STAR: Simulated Target Attack and Reconnaissance. A sophisticated form of penetration testing that uses threat intelligence and prior reconnaissance of the target to make the simulated attack more realistic.

strategy: Knowing where you are today, knowing where you want to be tomorrow, and knowing how to get there.

threat: The probability (likelihood) that *threat actors* will make a credible attempt to attack. Threat is a product of *capability* and *intention*.

threat actor: An adversary, enemy, or potential attacker; an individual, group, or other entity with the intent to attack one or more targets.

triage: Make an initial assessment of risks or threats and decide which ones are sufficiently credible and serious to require further action.

UAV: Unmanned Aerial Vehicle.

UKIC: The UK Intelligence Community, comprising *MI5*, *MI6*, and *GCHQ*, otherwise known as the security and intelligence agencies.

useful idiots: Russian term for ideologically sympathetic but naïve individuals who are unwittingly exploited to support the *threat actor*'s interests.

UVIED: Under-Vehicle Improvised Explosive Device.

VBIED: Vehicle-Borne Improvised Explosive Device.

vetting: A term used to denote personnel security in general, or the pre-employment screening elements of personnel security in particular.

vishing: Voice phishing. The use of telephones or voice messaging to trick people into revealing sensitive information, usually to facilitate fraud.

vulnerability: The gaps or weaknesses in the potential victim's protective security defences that could be exploited by *threat actors*. More precisely, the probability that *threat actors* would succeed if they were to attempt an attack.

watering hole attack: A cyber attack method in which the victim is infected with *malware* by visiting a compromised website.

wicked problem: A complex problem that is hard to describe, has many interdependent causes, and does not have a right answer. The problems generated by *complex systems* tend to be wicked.

zero-day malware/zero-day exploit: *Malware* that exploits a previously unknown software vulnerability for which there is currently no fix.

NOTES

Rule 1: Security Rules

1. A heuristic may be defined as a simple procedure that helps to find adequate, though often imperfect, answers to difficult questions (Kahneman, 2011).
2. Despite their differences, safety and security can complement one another. It may be easier to persuade an organization to pay more attention to its security if the security measures also bring safety benefits.
3. Heyman (1991).
4. Thomas Hobbes, *Leviathan* (1651).
5. Omand (2010), p. 14.
6. Andrew (2010), pp. 76–9.
7. Andrew (2010), pp. 174, 607.
8. Pinker (2012); Ministry of Defence (2014).
9. Hope-Hailey et al. (2012).
10. Omand (2010), p. 11.
11. Research has shown that a high level of trust within an organization is associated with greater job satisfaction and reduced turnover (Hope-Hailey et al., 2012).

Rule 2: Risk Is the Key

1. Strictly speaking, 'risk' can also refer to positive outcomes, such as winning money or completing a project on time, but for all practical purposes protective security is concerned only with negative outcomes.
2. See, for example, Fischhoff and Kadvany (2011).
3. See, for example, Slovic et al. (2004).
4. The UK national threat levels are: LOW (an attack is unlikely); MODERATE (an attack is possible, but not likely); SUBSTANTIAL (an attack is a strong possibility); SEVERE (an attack is highly likely); and CRITICAL (an attack is expected imminently). https://www.mi5.gov.uk/threat-levels.
5. Pedants like to point out that the probability of an event is meaningful only if you specify the period of time over which it is assessed. The probability of a terrorist attack occurring somewhere in the UK within the next ten minutes is vanishingly small, whereas the probability of one happening at some point over the next ten years is close to 100 per cent. The UK threat level is rather loosely defined in terms of 'the likelihood of an attack in the near term', which is generally taken to mean the next few weeks or months.

6. https://www.bbc.co.uk/news/world-middle-east-43527152.

7. Strictly speaking, impact encompasses the duration for which the consequences are felt. However, some experts find it helpful to break out duration as a distinct fourth component of risk (i.e. Risk = Threat x Vulnerability x Impact x Duration).

8. Some risk management aficionados insist that when a 'risk' materializes, it ceases to be a 'risk' and becomes an 'issue'. To avoid unnecessary confusion, I am not following this usage.

9. The risk chain can be expressed mathematically in terms of conditional probabilities.

10. https://www.gov.uk/government/publications/counter-terrorism-strategy-contest-2018.

11. Omand (2010), p. 91.

12. ONS (2018). The Office for National Statistics Crime Survey for England and Wales recorded approximately 10.6 million crimes in the year ending September 2017, including fraud and computer misuse but excluding crimes against businesses or non-households.

13. Fischhoff and Kadvany (2011), p. 63.

14. Cabinet Office (2017).

15. Some would argue that probabilities must be based on large numbers of empirical observations of similar past events. But the empirical data is simply not there for some of the most significant security risks. They involve single-event probabilities, which are unlike those associated with the risks of common diseases, house fires, or conventional crimes. Nonetheless, the probabilities of rare events can still be estimated using subjective judgements about likelihood. See Gigerenzer (2003).

16. Anderson (2012). The lawyer in question was at the time the UK's Independent Reviewer of Terrorism Legislation. He was using the argument to make a wider point about the need to scrutinize and reform counter-terrorism legislation.

17. The Westminster attack on 22 March 2017 killed five. The Manchester Arena bombing on 22 May left twenty-two dead. The London Bridge attack on 3 June killed eight. The Finsbury Mosque attack on 19 June killed one. The Parsons Green attack on 15 September injured dozens but there were no fatalities. I have excluded the attackers, most of whom also died, from the numbers killed.

18. https://www.mi5.gov.uk/news/director-general-andrew-parker-speech-to-bfv-symposium.

19. Scientists have explored the adaptive nature of security risk using a form of simulation called Stackelberg security games, in which one or more experts—or, more commonly, computer algorithms—play the role of defenders trying to protect a set of potential targets, while other experts or algorithms play the role of a threat actor planning to attack one of the targets. The attacker can see how the defender has allocated resources to protect the targets. See, for example, Tambe (2011).

20. Andrew (2010), pp. 828–32; Omand (2010), p. 21.

21. https://www.bbc.co.uk/news/magazine-18161870.

22. Hemmingby and Bjørgo (2016), pp. 20–7.

23. Hemmingby and Bjørgo (2016), p. 68.

24. Hemmingby and Bjørgo (2016), pp. 46, 57–8, 61.
25. Hemmingby (2017).
26. See, for example, Mitleton-Kelly (2003); Gribbin (2005); Cairney (2012); Holland (2014).
27. Gribbin (2005), pp. 56–7.
28. What Tolstoy actually wrote, in *Anna Karenina*, is: 'All happy families resemble each other; each unhappy family is unhappy in its own way.' The underlying concept is the same: there are far more ways of achieving unhappiness than happiness.
29. Hemmingby and Bjørgo (2016), p. 65.

Rule 3: Think Like an Attacker

1. Mullen et al. (2009); James et al. (2016).
2. Omand (2010), p. 312.
3. Omand (2010), p. 229.
4. Iraq: https://www.nytimes.com/2013/10/07/world/middleeast/deadly-bombing-at-elementary-school-playground-in-iraq.html; Peshawar: https://www.bbc.co.uk/news/world-asia-30491435.
5. https://www.ohchr.org/Documents/Countries/IQ/UNAMIReport1May31October2015.pdf.
6. Although this killing was ethically unconstrained by any reasonable standards, IS attempted to justify it as a 'fixed' punishment under Islamic jurisprudence, reflecting the murdered pilot's actions in dropping bombs.
7. Stenersen (2009).
8. Wilkening (2006). The anthrax spore has a lethality of 80–90 per cent when inhaled, making it one of the most intensively researched biological warfare agents.
9. https://www.bbc.co.uk/news/uk-35371344.
10. https://www.gov.uk/government/news/novichok-nerve-agent-use-in-salisbury-uk-government-response.
11. https://www.ncsc.gov.uk/news/advice-thwart-devastating-cyber-attacks-small-charities.
12. *Hamlet* 1:5. 'O villain, villain, smiling, damned villain! / My tables! Meet it is I set it down / That one may smile, and smile, and be a villain.'
13. See, for example, Houlihan and Giulianotti (2012).
14. By the summer of 2012 the UK national threat level had temporarily dropped one notch to SUBSTANTIAL ('an attack is a strong possibility'), which still signified a high level of threat. It soon went back up to SEVERE.
15. The distinction between intelligence and information is less apparent in some languages, which use the same word to signify both.
16. Omand (2010), p. 22.
17. Dimbleby (2016), pp. 209–12, 398–400.
18. Hemmingby and Bjørgo (2016), p. 45.
19. This is probably the most succinct of the many different definitions of a 'wicked' problem. See Rittel and Webber (1973); Camillus (2008).

20. Omand (2010), p. 250.
21. See Taleb (2010); Kahneman (2011), pp. 212, 218.
22. Camillus (2008).
23. Several years ago, the European Commission estimated that 6–7 per cent of western countries' GDP depended on satellite navigation and timing (Ministry of Defence, 2014).
24. There are estimated to be up to 30,000 large objects in low earth orbit and around 100 million small pieces of orbiting debris. GPS relies on thirty-one satellites. In 2007, China created a huge cloud of debris when it tested an anti-satellite missile by destroying an old weather satellite. See Lamb (2018).
25. Andrew (2010), p. 796.
26. https://www.nationalgrid.com/sites/default/files/documents/High%20Level%20Black%20Start%20Strategy.pdf.
27. Omand (2010), p. 69.
28. Andrew (2010), p. 654.
29. Andrew (2010), p. 705.
30. Andrew (2010), p. 772.
31. Hemmingby (2017). The attacks on individuals included the near-fatal stabbing of the British MP Stephen Timms in 2010 and the failed attack on the Danish cartoonist Kurt Westergaard, also in 2010.
32. There are many other cryptocurrencies besides Bitcoin, including Monero, Dash, Zcash, Ethereum, Cardano, and Ripple.
33. CSIS (2018). Identification is usually through IP address mapping or accidental leaks by web trackers.
34. https://www.bbc.co.uk/news/business-41035201.
35. https://maliciousaireport.com.
36. Ministry of Defence (2014).

Rule 4: There Are Three Ways to Reduce Risk

1. Many other, more sophisticated risk management schemes are available, especially in the cyber security domain. For example, the UK NCSC exhorts us to Understand/Reduce Risk/Respond/Nurture, while the US NIST advises us to Identify/Protect/Detect/Respond/Recover. The three-step Understand/Decide/Act process outlined here has the advantage of being the simplest possible formulation. By the same token, it is pretty broad-brush.
2. Omand (2010), p. 91.
3. See Adams et al. (2013); Ganin et al. (2016).
4. The UK government's current classification scheme has three main categories: OFFICIAL, SECRET, and TOP SECRET. They signify the increasing sensitivity of the information assets and the baseline security controls needed to defend them against applicable threats. OFFICIAL covers the majority of information created or processed by the public sector. SECRET covers very sensitive information, where the

effects of accidental or deliberate compromise would be likely, for example, to directly threaten an individual's life or cause serious damage to relations with friendly governments. TOP SECRET covers exceptionally sensitive information assets, the compromise of which would be likely, for example, to lead directly to widespread loss of life or threaten directly the internal stability of the UK (Cabinet Office, 2013).

5. Klahr et al. (2017).
6. Heal and Kunreuther (2007); Andrew (2010), pp. 746–8.
7. Risk management aficionados use the less self-explanatory term 'residual risk' to refer to the risk that remains after security has been applied (i.e. current risk in my terminology).
8. According to a more speculative suggestion, the development of life-extending medical technologies will make us even more risk-averse in the future. The idea is that as medical advances enable us to live longer and healthier lives, we will become even more averse to the risk of dying prematurely (Harari, 2015, pp. 430–1).
9. The 9/11 Commission (2004), pp. 154, 245.
10. Farrell et al. (2011).
11. Corera (2016), p. 289.
12. Hemmingby and Bjørgo (2016), pp. 52–4.
13. Babuta and Krasodomski-Jones (2018).
14. *The Times*, 29 January 2018. See also Hsu (2018). The locational data was collected by Strava, a 'social network for athletes'.
15. https://www.japantimes.co.jp/news/2017/08/29/national/communications-ministry-build-decoy-networks-bid-lure-cyberattackers/#.WxP7kC2ZPUI.
16. Honeynet Project (2004).
17. Corera (2016), pp. 83–4.
18. https://www.bbc.co.uk/news/technology-42225214.
19. Westminster (22 March), Manchester Arena (22 May), and London Bridge (3 June).
20. Andrew (2010), p. 651.
21. There are some notable exceptions. In particular, dissident republican terrorists in Northern Ireland have continued to deploy UVIEDs against security personnel.
22. https://eandt.theiet.org/content/articles/2017/10/online-censorship-who-are-the-gatekeepers-of-our-digital-lives.

Rule 5: Build Resilience

1. See, for example, Reggiani (2013); Ganin et al. (2016); Massaro et al. (2018).
2. National Research Council (2012).
3. Taleb (2012).
4. Taleb (2012), pp. 10, 32.
5. Shakespeare's line is from *As You Like It*.
6. https://www.veritas.com/news-releases/2018-03-15-veritas-study-shows-that-organizations-are-moving-to-the-cloud-without-evaluating-the-impact-of-a-cloud-outage.

7. *The M-Trends 2018* report by the cyber security company FireEye found that the global median dwell time in 2017 was 101 days, where dwell time was defined as the number of days from first evidence of compromise that an attacker is present on a victim network before detection. Dwell times varied between less than a week and several years. https://www.fireeye.com/content/dam/collateral/en/mtrends-2018.pdf.

8. See, for example, Neave et al. (2017).

9. Gormley and Gormley (2012); van Bennekom et al. (2015).

10. Neave et al. (2019); Sweeten et al. (2018).

11. Neave et al. (2019).

12. https://e-estonia.com/estonia-to-open-the-worlds-first-data-embassy-in-luxembourg.

13. https://www.iii.org/press-release/terrorism-and-insurance-13-years-after-9-11-the-threat-of-terrorist-attack-remains-real-090914.

14. Andrew (2010), pp. 782–3.

15. https://www.poolre.co.uk/20-years-since-the-manchester/.

16. https://www.munichre.com/topics-online/en/2018/01/cyber-insurance.

17. Klahr et al. (2017).

18. Barrett and Martin (2014), ch. 8.

19. Beal et al. (2003).

20. Andrew (2010), p. 82.

21. Walker et al. (2011).

22. London Chamber of Commerce and Industry (2016).

23. https://www.apa.org/helpcenter/road-resilience.aspx.

24. Barrett and Martin (2014), p. 168.

25. Barrett and Martin (2014), p. 169.

26. Seery (2011); Barrett and Martin (2014).

27. Put in different terms, coping represents passive resilience; post-traumatic stress represents the breakdown of passive resilience; and 'post-traumatic growth', as some psychologists call it, represents active resilience. See Taleb (2012), p. 41.

28. Coutou (2002).

29. Chamorro-Premuzic and Lusk (2017).

30. Reggiani (2013).

Rule 6: It's All About People

1. https://www.nextgov.com/ideas/2016/07/succeed-cyberspace-dont-forget-human-element/129939.

2. West (2008).

3. Stajano and Wilson (2011).

4. https://www.cpni.gov.uk/reducing-insider-risk.

5. https://www.thetimes.co.uk/article/home-office-man-falsified-records-for-hundreds-of-illegal-immigrants-8px5prc2g.

6. https://www.bbc.co.uk/news/uk-12788224.

7. Corera (2016), p. 290.
8. SANS (2017).
9. HM Government (2014).
10. https://4iq.com/wp-content/uploads/2018/05/2018_IdentityBreachReport_4iQ.pdf.
11. MoJ (2010). UK Ministry of Justice figures showed that in 2006, an estimated 24 per cent of males and 6 per cent of females between the ages of ten and fifty-two in England and Wales had at least one conviction for a 'standard list' offence. The proportion was even higher in the past: 33 per cent of males (and 9 per cent of females) born in 1953 were convicted of at least one 'standard list' offence.
12. Kahneman (2011), p. 225.
13. CIPD (2015).
14. Vrij et al. (2015).
15. CIPD (2015).
16. Vrij (2008).
17. Vrij et al. (2015).
18. Vrij et al. (2015).
19. Paulhus and Williams (2002).
20. Furnham et al. (2013).
21. Hogan and Hogan (2001); Taylor et al. (2014).
22. Furnham and Taylor (2011).
23. Andrew (2010), pp. 714–24.
24. Andrew (2010), p. 714.
25. See, for example, Legg et al. (2015); Agrafiotis et al. (2017).
26. Big Data (capital 'B', capital 'D') is sometimes defined by three distinguishing features—*volume, variety,* and *velocity.* Other definitions incorporate two additional 'Vs'—namely, *veracity* and *value.* See, for example, De Mauro et al. (2015).
27. Lamb (2017).
28. Ford (1995).
29. https://www.bbc.co.uk/news/world-asia-42850194.
30. NCSC (2016).
31. West (2008).
32. Andrew (2010), p. 843.
33. Dietz and Den Hartog (2006); Hope-Hailey et al. (2012).
34. Hope-Hailey et al. (2012).
35. Botsman (2017); Greenfield (2018).

Rule 7: Everyone Is Biased

1. Martin (2005); Hughes (2012); Barrett and Martin (2014); Bond (2017).
2. Chabris and Simons (2011).
3. Drew et al. (2013).
4. My 'semi-automatic' is what psychologist Daniel Kahneman would call 'fast' thinking, which he famously contrasts with the 'slow' thinking of consciously analysing

a problem. Kahneman's 'fast' thinking includes expert intuition and heuristic intuition. See Kahneman (2011).

5. Robinson and Bridges (2011). See also *New Scientist*, 10 May 2017.
6. *New Scientist*, 15 August 2015, pp. 28–33.
7. https://www.ncsc.gov.uk/guidance/password-guidance-simplifying-your-approach. The US NIST also changed its advice after recognizing that its previous policies were incompatible with humans.
8. Psychologists draw a distinction between fear and anxiety. Fear is a state of apprehension and physiological arousal triggered by the presence of a specific and imminent threat to wellbeing. Anxiety is a more diffuse state associated with less specific or less tangible threats. Walking alone on a dark street late at night might induce anxiety about the risk of being mugged, whereas coming face-to-face with a knife-wielding mugger would trigger fear. Anxiety can be enduring, whereas fear typically starts when the threat appears and ends soon after the threat goes away. See Barrett and Martin (2014), p. 15.
9. Preston and Harris (1965).
10. Dunning et al. (2003).
11. Kahneman (2011), p. 255.
12. Hemmingby and Bjørgo (2016), pp. 41–2.
13. BASE stands for Buildings, Antennas, Spans (bridges), and Earth (as in cliffs), for these are the things from which BASE jumpers like to jump.
14. Barrett and Martin (2014), p. 132.
15. Fischhoff and Kadvany (2011), p. 12.
16. Loss aversion is one of the main principles of Prospect Theory, the highly influential and evidence-based psychological theory formulated by Daniel Kahneman and Amos Tversky. See Kahneman (2011).
17. Various experiments have estimated the so-called loss aversion ratio (i.e. the degree to which losses weigh more heavily than gains) to be between 1.5 and 2.5. See Kahneman (2011), p. 284.
18. The psychologist Daniel Kahneman won a Nobel Prize in economics for revealing how this asymmetry, along with other forms of cognitive bias, influences the behaviour of national economies.
19. Martin (2006), pp. 40–1.
20. See, for example, Gamble and Walker (2016).
21. Barrett and Martin (2014), pp. 133–4.
22. Martin (2008).
23. Ronay and von Hippel (2010).
24. Kahneman (2011), pp. 202–4.
25. Martin (2010); Barrett and Martin (2014).
26. Sicard et al. (2001).
27. Barrett and Martin (2014), ch. 4; Martin (2010), pp. 65–6.
28. Linstone and Turoff (2011); Markmann et al. (2013). The Delphi method was developed in the 1950s to help the US government think about national security issues.

29. Kahneman (2011), pp. 264–5.
30. See, for example, US Government (2009); Heuer (1999).
31. Barrett and Martin (2014), ch. 9.
32. Hemmingby and Bjørgo (2016), p. 54.
33. Bayesian methods interpret a statement about probability (likelihood) as the degree of confidence in the truth of the statement. Bayes' Rule tells us the probability that an existing judgement (J) is still correct after we have received new evidence (E). The revised probability that J is still true is given by the prior probability modified by a factor X, where X is the probability that the new evidence E would have emerged if J were really true. The more incongruous and surprising the new evidence, the less confident we should be that our prior judgement was correct. See Martin and Bateson (2007), pp. 143–4; Omand (2010), p. 154.

Rule 8: Cyber Is New Ways of Doing Old Things

1. https://www.oecd-forum.org/users/85359-william-below-and-leigh-wolfrom/posts/30529-the-cyber-insurance-market-responding-to-a-risk-with-few-boundaries.
2. This definition is based on a UK government definition of cyber security—see HMG (2017), NCSS.
3. Gartner estimated that 8.4 billion IoT devices were in use in 2017, rising to 20.4 billion by 2020. https://www.gartner.com/newsroom/id/3598917.
4. Anthony (2017); Botsman (2017), p. 172.
5. https://www.wired.com/story/dont-gift-internet-connected-toys/?mod=djem-CybersecruityPro&tpl=cy.
6. Federal Trade Commission. (2018).
7. https://www.bbc.co.uk/news/business-41192163.
8. The cheap stuff sells for as little as $1, while customized ransomware can cost $1,000 or more. The median cost of all products was $10.50. https://www.carbonblack.com/resource/the-ransomware-economy.
9. ODNI (2017).
10. The US DARPA agency is running an Enhanced Attribution Program to do just that.
11. HM Government (2017).
12. Joinson (2007); Nguyen et al. (2012).
13. ONS (2018); CSIS (2018).
14. The information security profession uses a parallel terminology of Confidentiality, Integrity, and Availability (CIA). Using these categories, cyber espionage may be regarded as an assault on the confidentiality of information; cyber sabotage as an assault on its integrity and availability; and cyber subversion as an assault on its integrity.
15. Corera (2016), p. 193.
16. https://www.wired.com/2016/10/inside-cyberattack-shocked-us-government.
17. https://www.bbc.co.uk/news/uk-23098867.

18. USTR (2018), p. 153.
19. https://www.bbc.co.uk/news/uk-41622903.
20. See, for example, https://www.wombatsecurity.com/state-of-the-phish.
21. Ashenden and Lawrence (2013).
22. Stanton et al. (2016). See also https://www.nist.gov/news-events/news/2016/10/secur ity-fatigue-can-cause-computer-users-feel-hopeless-and-act-recklessly.
23. World Economic Forum (2018).
24. CSIS (2018).
25. See, for example, Zetter (2014).
26. Young and Leveson (2014).
27. Corera (2016), p. 284.
28. Corera (2016), pp. 276–8.
29. Corera (2016), pp. 280–2.
30. Corera (2016), p. 277.
31. Corera (2016), pp. 1–2. The undersea cables were used for telegraphy, which relied on a form of digital communication (dots and dashes), therefore arguably making it a cyber system of sorts.
32. https://www.ncsc.gov.uk/news/russian-military-almost-certainly-responsible-destructive-2017-cyber-attack.
33. Corera (2016), pp. 301–2.
34. SWIFT stands for the Society for Worldwide Interbank Financial Telecommunication. The SWIFT messaging platform is used by some 11,000 banks and other institutions around the world.
35. CSIS (2018).
36. Galeotti (2016).
37. Stajano and Wilson (2011).
38. Committee on Standards in Public Life (2017).
39. MI5: https://www.mi5.gov.uk/news/director-general-andrew-parker-speech-to-bfv-symposium; GCHQ: https://www.bbc.co.uk/news/technology-43738953.
40. ODNI (2017).
41. https://www.bbc.co.uk/news/world-us-canada-43092085.
42. https://www.bbc.co.uk/news/technology-36284447.
43. Vosoughi et al. (2018). The MIT researchers analysed the diffusion of 126,000 verified and false stories on Twitter between 2006 and 2017. Each story was classified as true or false using information from six independent fact-checking organizations.
44. Babuta and Krasodomski-Jones (2018).
45. Committee on Standards in Public Life (2017).
46. James et al. (2016).
47. For more about what might or might not constitute cyber terrorism, see Jarvis and Macdonald (2014).
48. Martin et al. (2017); Klahr et al. (2017).
49. Klahr et al. (2017).

50. https://info.digitalshadows.com/FileSharingDataExposureResearch-HomePage.html.
51. https://cyber.dhs.gov/bod/17-01. The UK NCSC issued similar advice.
52. Adams et al. (2013).
53. CAST (2017).
54. Corera (2016), p. 74.

Rule 9: Know What Good Looks Like

1. https://www.schneier.com/blog/archives/2013/03/phishing_has_go.html.
2. Gawande (2011) gives a masterly account of the power of the checklist.
3. Haynes et al. (2009). The nineteen-item surgical checklist reduced the rate of post-operative complications from 11 per cent to 7 per cent and reduced the mortality rate from 1.5 per cent to 0.8 per cent. An added benefit of surgical checklists is improving teamwork.
4. In statistical terms, a valid metric is free from systematic errors and a reliable metric is free from random errors. In the example of the precise and reliable clock set to the wrong time, the measurement is high in systematic error (i.e. inaccurate) but low in random error. See Martin and Bateson (2007), pp. 72–3.
5. Omand (2010), p. 91.
6. https://www.cpni.gov.uk/personnel-security-maturity-model.
7. https://www.cpni.gov.uk/cyber-assurance-physical-security-systems-capss-0.
8. https://www.bbc.co.uk/news/world-europe-34818994.
9. https://www.nytimes.com/2017/05/09/world/europe/hackers-came-but-the-french-were-prepared.html.
10. Anderson and Moore (2009).
11. Bartlett (2015), p. 6.
12. Corera (2016), p. 83.
13. Corera (2016), pp. 76–7.
14. Andrew (2010), p. 393.
15. The UK National Cyber Security Strategy (HM Government, 2017) includes a specific objective for the majority of new online products and services to be 'secure by default' (in the narrow sense) by 2021.
16. Adams et al. (2013) discuss how the science of cybernetics can be applied to break the 'cyber cycle'.

Rule 10: Know Who's in Charge

1. Official guidance on governance in UK central government defines corporate governance as 'the way in which organisations are directed, controlled and led' (HM Treasury and Cabinet Office, 2011).
2. For a comprehensive coverage of corporate governance, see Leblanc (2016).
3. Strategy is an overused word which sometimes appears to mean little more than aping the methods allegedly used by Sun-Tzu or some other successful general.

What it should mean, in simple terms, is knowing where you are today, knowing where you want to be tomorrow, and knowing how to get there. The all-important *how* part is sometimes forgotten. Strategy is a continuing process, not a state.

4. A different scheme, which comes from project management methodology, distinguishes between the people who are variously Responsible, Accountable, Consulted, and Informed; hence the acronym RACI.

5. The definitions are my own but consistent with most others. There are plenty of others in circulation. 'Accountability' in its original and narrowest sense means being called to explain one's actions. It has come to mean being scrutinized by those in authority and subject to blame if the account is judged unsatisfactory. The meaning of 'responsibility' has also evolved beyond being tasked to do something; a broader definition includes acting freely and in line with professional, ethical, or moral standards. For more on these debates, see, for example, Bovens (1998) or Mulgan (2000).

6. When someone is given the authority to make decisions, they should also be told the limits on their authority, to prevent them overstepping (or understepping) the mark.

7. Klahr et al. (2017).

8. https://www.pwc.co.uk/assets/pdf/2015-isbs-executive-summary-02.pdf.

9. HM Government (2017). The survey covered FTSE 350 companies.

10. For detailed accounts of the WannaCry incident and its causes and implications, see NAO (2017), Department of Health and Social Care (2018), and Smart (2018).

11. Most of the NHS devices infected by WannaCry were running on unpatched Windows 7 and about 5 per cent were still on Windows XP.

12. Smart (2018).

13. Smart (2018).

14. Martin et al. (2017).

15. HM Government (2017).

16. NAO (2017).

17. NAO (2017).

18. Department of Health and Social Care (2018).

19. https://ico.org.uk/about-the-ico/news-and-events/news-and-blogs/2016/10/talktalk-gets-record-400-000-fine-for-failing-to-prevent-october-2015-attack.

20. HM Government (2017).

21. Hall (2015).

22. http://www.rcmp-grc.gc.ca/en/independent-investigation-death-michael-zehaf-bibeau; http://www.ourcommons.ca/Content/Newsroom/Articles/2015-06-03-Summary-e.pdf.

23. https://www.csoonline.com/article/3169912/leadership-management/secrets-of-successful-cisos-infographic.html.

24. https://medium.com/@_rob_sloan/cyber-matters-barclays-aims-for-holistic-security-with-new-division-50ae9008a806.

25. The principal organizations responsible for building venues and staging the Games were the International Olympic Association (IOC), the Olympic Delivery Authority (ODA), and the London Organising Committee of the Olympic and Paralympic Games (LOCOG).

26. Tett (2016), pp. 121–6.

27. Barrett and Martin (2014), pp. 118–22.

28. Botsman (2017), p. 3, quoting the Financial Crisis Inquiry Commission.

29. https://www.iia.org.uk/resources/audit-committees/governance-of-risk-three-lines-of-defence.

REFERENCES

Adams, M.D., Hitefield, S.D., Hoy, B., Fowler, M.C., and Clancy, T.C. (2013). Application of cybernetics and control theory for a new paradigm in cybersecurity. arXiv:1311.0257v1 [cs.CR], 1 November 2013.

Agrafiotis, I., Erola, A., Goldsmith, M., and Creese, S. (2017). Formalising policies for insider-threat detection: A tripwire grammar. *Journal of Wireless Mobile Networks, Ubiquitous Computing, and Dependable Applications, 8, 26–43.*

Anderson, D. (2012). *The Terrorism Acts in 2011: Report of the Independent Reviewer on the operation of the Terrorism Act 2000 and Part 1 of the Terrorism Act 2006.* London: The Stationery Office. https://terrorismlegislationreviewer.independent.gov.uk/wp-content/uploads/2013/04/report-terrorism-acts-2011.pdf.

Anderson, R. and Moore, T. (2009). Information security: Where computer science, economics and psychology meet. *Philosophical Transactions of the Royal Society A, 367,* 2717–27.

Andrew, C. (2010). *The defence of the realm: The authorized history of MI5.* London: Penguin.

Anthony, S. (2017). Internet-connected vibrator with built-in webcam fails penetration testing. *Ars Technica,* 6 April 2017.

Ashenden, D. and Lawrence, D. (2013). Can we sell security like soap? A new approach to behaviour change. *Proceedings of the 2013 New Security Paradigms Workshop.* doi.org/10.1145/2535813.2535823.

Babuta, A. and Krasodomski-Jones, A. (2018). *The personal security of individuals in British public life.* London: RUSI. https://rusi.org/publication/occasional-papers/personal-security-individuals-british-public-life.

Barrett, E. and Martin, P. (2014). *Extreme: Why some people thrive at the limits.* Oxford: Oxford University Press.

Bartlett, J. (2015). *The dark net.* London: Windmill Books.

Beal, D.J., Cohen, R.R., Burke, M.J., and McLendon, C.L. (2003). Cohesion and performance in groups: A meta-analytic clarification of construct relations. *Journal of Applied Psychology, 88, 989–1004.*

Bond, M. (2017). In the face of danger. *New Scientist,* 13 May 2017, 32–5.

Botsman, R. (2017). *Who can you trust? How technology brought us together—and why it could drive us apart.* London: Portfolio Penguin.

Bovens, M. (1998). *The quest for responsibility: Accountability and citizenship in complex organisations.* Cambridge: Cambridge University Press.

Cabinet Office. (2013). *Government security classifications.* April 2014. Version 1.0. October 2013. https://www.gov.uk.

Cabinet Office. (2017). *National risk register of civil emergencies.* London: Cabinet Office. https://www.gov.uk/government/publications/national-risk-register-of-civil-emergencies-2017-edition.

Cairney, P. (2012). Complexity theory in political science and public policy. *Political Studies Review,* 10, 346–58.

Camillus, J.C. (2008). Strategy as a wicked problem. *Harvard Business Review,* May 2008, 1–10.

CAST. (2017). *CRASH report on application security.* Cast Research Labs. https://www.castsoftware.com/resources/research-library?research#research.

Chabris, C. and Simons, D. (2011). *The invisible gorilla: And other ways our intuition deceives us.* London: HarperCollins.

Chamorro-Premuzic, T. and Lusk, D. (2017). The dark side of resilience. *Harvard Business Review,* 16 August 2017.

CIPD. (2015). *A head for hiring: The behavioural science of recruitment and selection.* Research report. August 2015.

Committee on Standards in Public Life. (2017). *Intimidation in public life: A review by the Committee on Standards in Public Life.* Cm 9543. UK Parliament. December 2017.

Corera, G. (2016). *Cyberspies: The secret history of surveillance, hacking, and digital espionage.* New York: Pegasus.

Coutu, D.L. (2002). How resilience works. *Harvard Business Review,* May 2002, 46–55.

CSIS. (2018). *Economic impact of cybercrime—no slowing down.* Washington DC: Center for Strategic and International Studies. February 2018. https://www.csis.org/analysis/economic-impact-cybercrime.

De Mauro, A., Greco, M., and Grimaldi, M. (2015). What is big data? A consensual definition and a review of key research topics. *AIP Conference Proceedings,* 1644, 97–104. doi.org/10.1063/1.4907823.

Department of Health and Social Care. (2018). *Securing cyber resilience in health and care: A progress update.* https://www.gov.uk/dh.

Dietz, G. and Den Hartog, D.N. (2006). Measuring trust inside organisations. *Personnel Review,* 35, 557–88.

Dimbleby, J. (2016). *The battle of the Atlantic: How the allies won the war.* London: Penguin.

Drew, T., Vö, M.L.-H., and Wolfe, J.M. (2013). The invisible gorilla strikes again. *Psychological Science,* 24, 1848–53.

Dunning, D., Johnson, K., Ehrlinger, J., and Kruger, J. (2003). Why people fail to recognize their own incompetence. *Current Directions in Psychological Science,* 12, 83–7.

Farrell, G., Tilley, N., Tseloni, A., and Mailley, J. (2011). The crime drop and the security hypothesis. *Journal of Research in Crime and Delinquency,* 48, 147–75.

Federal Trade Commission. (2018). *Electronic toy maker VTech settles FTC allegations that it violated children's privacy law and the FTC Act.* Press release, 8 January 2018. https://www.ftc.gov/news-events/press-releases/2018/01/electronic-toy-maker-vtech-settles-ftc-allegations-it-violated.

Fischhoff, B. and Kadvany, J. (2011). *Risk: A very short introduction.* Oxford: Oxford University Press.

Ford, C.V. (1995). *Lies! Lies!! Lies!!! The psychology of deceit.* Washington DC: American Psychiatric Press.

Furnham, A., Richards, S.C., and Paulhus, D.L. (2013). The Dark Triad of personality: A 10-year review. *Social and Personality Psychology Compass, 7*, 199–216.

Furnham, A. and Taylor, J. (2011). *Bad apples: Identify, prevent and manage negative behaviour at work.* Basingstoke: Palgrave Macmillan.

Galeotti, M. (2016). *Putin's hydra: Inside Russia's intelligence services.* London: European Council on Foreign Relations. https://www.ecfr.eu.

Gamble, T. and Walker, I. (2016). Wearing a bicycle helmet can increase risk taking and sensation seeking in adults. *Psychological Science, 27*, 289–94.

Ganin, A.A., Massaro, E., Gutfraind, A., Steen, N., Keisler, J.M., Kott, A., Mangoubi, R., and Linkov, I. (2016). Operational resilience: Concepts, design and analysis. *Scientific Reports, 6*, 19540. doi.org/10.1038/srep19540.

Gawande, A. (2011). *The checklist manifesto: How to get things right.* London: Profile Books.

Gigerenzer, G. (2003). *Reckoning with risk: Learning to live with uncertainty.* London: Penguin.

Gormley, C.J. and Gormley, S.J. (2012). Data hoarding and information clutter: The impact on cost, life span of data, effectiveness, sharing, productivity and knowledge management culture. *Issues in Information Systems, 13*, 90–5.

Greenfield, A. (2018). China's dystopian tech could be contagious. *The Atlantic*, 14 February 2018.

Gribbin, J. (2005). *Deep simplicity: Chaos, complexity and the emergence of life.* London: Penguin.

Hall, K. (2015). Cyber security buck stops with me, says Dido Harding. *The Register*, 16 December 2015.

Harari, Y.N. (2015). *Sapiens: A brief history of mankind.* London: Vintage.

Haynes, A.B., Weiser, T.G., Berry, W.R., et al. (2009). A surgical safety checklist to reduce morbidity and mortality in a global population. *New England Journal of Medicine, 360*, 491–9.

Heal, G. and Kunreuther, H. (2007). Modeling interdependent risks. *Risk Analysis, 27*, 621–34.

Hemmingby, C. (2017). Exploring the continuum of lethality: Militant Islamists' targeting preferences in Europe. *Perspectives on Terrorism, 11*, 25–41.

Hemmingby, C. and Bjørgo, T. (2016). *The dynamics of a terrorist targeting process: Anders B. Breivik and the 22 July attacks in Norway.* London: Palgrave Macmillan.

Heuer, R.J. (1999). *The psychology of intelligence analysis.* Washington DC: Center for the Study of Intelligence.

Heyman, S.J. (1991). The first duty of government: Protection, liberty and the fourteenth amendment. *Duke Law Journal, 41*, 507–71.

HM Government. (2014). *Security policy framework.* July 2014. https://www.gov.uk/government/publications/security-policy-framework/hmg-security-policy-framework.

HM Government. (2017). *FTSE 350 cyber governance health check report 2017.* July 2017. https://www.gov.uk.

HM Government. (2017). *National Cyber Security Strategy 2016–2021.* https://www.gov.uk.

HM Treasury and Cabinet Office. (2011). *Corporate governance in central government departments: Code of good practice 2011.* https://www.gov.uk.

Hogan, R. and Hogan, J. (2001). Assessing leadership: A view from the dark side. *International Journal of Selection and Assessment, 9,* 40–51.

Holland, J.H. (2014). *Complexity: A very short introduction.* Oxford: Oxford University Press.

Honeynet Project. (2004). *Know your enemy: Learning about security threats.* 2nd edition. Boston, MA: Addison-Wesley Professional. https://www.honeynet.org.

Hope-Hailey, V., Searle, R., and Dietz, G. (2012). *Where has all the trust gone?* London: CIPD.

Houlihan, B. and Giulianotti, R. (2012). Politics and the London 2012 Olympics: The (in)security games. *International Affairs, 88,* 701–17.

Hsu, J. (2018). The Strava heat map and the end of secrets. *Wired,* 29 January 2018.

Hughes, V. (2012). The roots of resilience. *Nature, 490,* 165–7.

James, D.V., Farnham, F.R., Sukhwal, S., Jones, K., Carlisle, J., and Henley, S. (2016). Aggressive/intrusive behaviours, harassment and stalking of members of the United Kingdom parliament: A prevalence study and cross-national comparison. *The Journal of Forensic Psychiatry & Psychology, 27,* 177–97.

Jarvis, L. and Macdonald, S. (2014). What is cyberterrorism? Findings from a survey of researchers. *Terrorism and Political Violence, 27,* 657–78.

Joinson, A. (2007). Disinhibition and the internet. In *Psychology and the internet* (2nd edn), ed. by J. Gackenbach. London: Academic Press, 75–92.

Kahneman, D. (2011). *Thinking, fast and slow.* London: Allen Lane.

Klahr, R., Shah, J.N., Finnerty, K., Chhatralia, K., and Rossington, T. (2017). *Cyber security among charities. Findings from qualitative research.* Department for Digital, Culture, Media & Sport. August 2017. https://www.gov.uk/government/publications/cyber-security-in-charities.

Klahr, R., Shah, J.N., Sheriffs, P., Rossington, T., and Pestell, G. (2017). *Cyber security breaches survey 2017. Main report.* Department for Culture, Media & Sport. April 2017. https://www.gov.uk/government/statistics/cyber-security-breaches-survey-2017.

Lamb, H. (2017). Putin's 'psychological firewall' induces Russians to self-censor online, study finds. *Engineering & Technology, 12,* 20.

Lamb, H. (2018). Space agencies turn focus on small space debris. *Engineering & Technology, 13,* 48–9.

Leblanc, R. (ed.) (2016). *The handbook of board governance: A comprehensive guide for public, private, and not-for-profit board members.* Hoboken, NJ: John Wiley.

Legg, P.A., Buckley, O., Goldsmith, M., and Creese, S. (2015). Automated insider threat detection system using user and role-based profile assessment. *IEEE Systems Journal, 11,* 503–12.

Linstone, H.A. and Turoff, M. (2011). Delphi: A brief look backward and forward. *Technological Forecasting & Social Change, 78,* 1712–19.

London Chamber of Commerce and Industry. (2016). *Living on the edge: Housing London's blue light emergency services.* June 2016.

Markmann, C., Darkow, I.-L., and von der Gracht, H. (2013). A Delphi-based risk analysis: Identifying and assessing future challenges for supply chain security in a multi-stakeholder environment. *Technological Forecasting & Social Change, 80*, 1815–33.

Martin, G., Martin, P., Hankin, C., Darzi, A., and Kinross, J. (2017). Cybersecurity and healthcare: How safe are we? BMJ 2017;358:j3179.

Martin, P. (2005). *The sickening mind: Brain, behaviour, immunity and disease*. London: Harper Perennial.

Martin, P. (2006). *Making happy people: The nature of happiness and its origins in childhood*. London: Harper Perennial.

Martin, P. (2008). *Sex, drugs and chocolate: The science of pleasure*. London: Fourth Estate.

Martin, P. (2010). *Counting sheep: The science and pleasures of sleep and dreams* (reissued edition). London: Flamingo.

Martin, P. and Bateson, P. (2007). *Measuring behaviour: An introductory guide*. 3rd edition. Cambridge: Cambridge University Press.

Massaro, E., Ganin, A., Perra, N., Linkov, I., and Vespignani, A. (2018). Resilience management during large-scale epidemic outbreaks. *Scientific Reports, 8*, 1859. doi. org/10.1038/s41598-018-19706-2.

Ministry of Defence. (2014). *Global strategic trends—out to 2045*. 5th edition. https://www.gov.uk/government/publications/global-strategic-trends-out-to-2045.

Mitleton-Kelly, E. (ed.) (2003). *Complex systems and evolutionary perspectives on organisations: The application of complexity theory to organisations*. Oxford: Pergamon.

MoJ. (2010). *Conviction histories of offenders between the ages of 10 and 52*. Ministry of Justice Statistics Bulletin, 15 July 2010. https://assets.publishing.service.gov.uk/government/uploads/system/uploads/attachment_data/file/217474/criminal-histories-bulletin.pdf.

Mulgan, R. (2000). 'Accountability': An ever-expanding concept? *Public Administration, 78*, 555–73.

Mullen, P.E., James, D.V., Reid Meloy, J., et al. (2009). The fixated and the pursuit of public figures. *The Journal of Forensic Psychiatry & Psychology, 20*, 33–47.

NAO. (2017). *Investigation: WannaCry cyber attack and the NHS*. Report by the Comptroller and Auditor General. National Audit Office, October 2017.

National Research Council. (2012). *Disaster resilience: A national imperative*. Washington DC: National Academies Press.

NCSC. (2016). Security governance introduction. https://www.ncsc.gov.uk.

Neave, N., Caiazza, R., Hamilton, C., McInnes, L., Saxton, T.K., Deary, V., and Wood, M. (2017). The economic costs of hoarding behaviours in local authority/housing association tenants and private home owners in the north-east of England. *Public Health, 148*, 137–9.

Neave, N., McKellar, K., Sillence, E., and Briggs, P. (2019). Digital hoarding behaviours: Measurement and evaluation. Under review. *Computers in Human Behavior*.

Nguyen, M., Bin, Y.S., and Campbell, A. (2012). Comparing online and offline self-disclosure: A systematic review. *Cyberpsychology, Behavior, and Social Networking, 15*, 103–11.

The 9/11 Commission. (2004). *Final report of the National Commission on terrorist attacks upon the United States*. New York: W. W. Norton.

ODNI. (2017). *Assessing Russian activities and intentions in recent US elections*. Intelligence Community Assessment ICA 2017-01D, 6 January 2017.

Omand, D. (2010). *Securing the state*. London: Hurst & Co.

ONS. (2018). *Crime in England and Wales: Year ending September 2017*. Statistical bulletin. 25 January 2018. https://www.ons.gov.uk/peoplepopulationandcommunity/crimeandjustice/bulletins/crimeinenglandandwales/yearendingseptember2017.

Paulhus, D. and Williams, K. (2002). The Dark Triad of personality. *Journal of Research in Personality*, 36, 557–63.

Pinker, S. (2012). *The better angels of our nature: A history of violence and humanity*. London: Penguin.

Preston, C.E. and Harris, S. (1965). Psychology of drivers in traffic accidents. *Journal of Applied Psychology*, 49, 284–8.

Reggiani, A. (2013). Network resilience for transport security: Some methodological considerations. *Transport Policy*, 28, 63–8.

Rittel, H.W.J. and Webber, M.M. (1973). Dilemmas in a general theory of planning. *Policy Sciences*, 4, 155–69.

Robinson, S.J. and Bridges, N.K. (2011). Survival: Mind and brain. *The Psychologist*, 24, 30–3.

Ronay, R. and von Hippel, W. (2010). The presence of an attractive woman elevates testosterone and physical risk taking in young men. *Social Psychological and Personality Science*, 1, 57–64.

SANS. (2017). *Defending against the wrong enemy: 2017 SANS insider threat survey*. SANS Institute. https://www.sans.org.

Seery, M.D. (2011). Resilience: A silver lining to experiencing adverse life events? *Current Directions in Psychological Science*, 20, 390–4.

Sicard, B., Jouve, E., and Blin, O. (2001). Risk propensity assessment in military special operations. *Military Medicine*, 166, 871–4.

Slovic, P., Finucane, M.L., Peters, E., and MacGregor, D.G. (2004). Risk as analysis and risk as feelings: Some thoughts about affect, reason, risk, and rationality. *Risk Analysis*, 24, 311–22.

Smart, W. (2018). *Lessons learned review of the WannaCry ransomware cyber attack*. Department of Health and Social Care, February 2018. https://www.dh.gov.uk.

Stajano, F. and Wilson, P. (2011). Understanding scam victims: Seven principles for systems security. *Communications of the ACM*, 54, 70–5.

Stanton, B., Theofanos, M.F., Prettyman, S., and Furman, S. (2016). Security fatigue. *IT Professional*, 18, 26–32. doi.org/10.1109/MITP.2016.84.

Stenersen, A. (2009). Al-Qaeda's thinking on CBRN: A case study. In *Unconventional weapons and international terrorism: Challenges and new approaches*, ed. by M. Ranstorp and M. Normark. London: Routledge, 50–64.

Sweeten, G., Sillence, E., and Neave, N. (2018). Digital hoarding behaviours: Underlying motivations and potential negative consequences. *Computers in Human Behavior*, 85, 54–60.

Taleb, N.N. (2010). *The black swan: The impact of the highly improbable*. London: Penguin.

Taleb, N.N. (2012). *Antifragile*. London: Allen Lane.

Tambe, M. (2011). *Security and game theory: Algorithms, deployed systems, lessons learned.* Cambridge: Cambridge University Press.

Taylor, J., Furnham, A., and Breeze, J. (2014). *Revealed: Using remote personality profiling to influence, negotiate and motivate.* Basingstoke: Palgrave Macmillan.

Tett, G. (2016). *The silo effect: Why every organisation needs to disrupt itself to survive.* London: Abacus.

US Government. (2009). *A tradecraft primer: Structured analytic techniques for improving intelligence analysis.* https://www.cia.gov/library/publications/publications-rss-up dates/tradecraft-primer-may-4-2009.html.

USTR. (2018). *Findings of the investigation into China's acts, policies, and practices related to technology transfer, intellectual property, and innovation under Section 301 of the Trade Act of 1974.* Washington DC: Executive Office of the President.

van Bennekom, M.J., Blom, R.M., Vulink, N., and Denys, D. (2015). A case of digital hoarding. *BMJ Case Reports.* doi.org/10.1136/bcr-2015-210814.

Vosoughi, S., Roy, D., and Aral, S. (2018). The spread of true and false news online. *Science, 359,* 1146–51.

Vrij, A. (2008). *Detecting lies and deceit: Pitfalls and opportunities.* 2nd edition. Chichester: Wiley.

Vrij, A., Fisher, R.P., and Blank, H. (2015). A cognitive approach to lie detection: A meta-analysis. *Legal and Criminological Psychology, 22,* 1–21.

Walker, W.E., Giddings, J., and Armstrong, S. (2011). Training and learning for crisis management using a virtual simulation/gaming environment. *Cognition, Technology & Work, 13,* 163–73.

West, R. (2008). The psychology of security. *Communications of the ACM, 51,* 34–41.

Wilkening, D.A. (2006). Sverdlovsk revisited: Modeling human inhalation anthrax. *PNAS, 103,* 7589–94.

World Economic Forum. (2018). *The global risks report 2018.* 13th edition. Geneva: World Economic Forum. https://www.weforum.org/reports/the-global-risks-report-2018.

Young, W. and Leveson, N.G. (2014). An integrated approach to safety and security based on systems theory. *Communications of the ACM, 57,* 31–5.

Zetter, K. (2014). An unprecedented look at Stuxnet, the world's first digital weapon. *Wired,* 3 November 2014.

ABOUT THE AUTHOR

Paul Martin is a security practitioner with thirty years' experience in the national security arena. During a career in UK government service from 1986 to 2013, he held a variety of senior positions, including advising on the protection of critical national infrastructure and leading national security preparations for the London 2012 Olympics. He was awarded a CBE in 2013 for his services to defence. From 2013 to 2016 he was the Director of Security for the UK Parliament, with responsibility for its physical, personnel, and cyber security.

Paul was educated at the University of Cambridge, where he graduated in natural sciences and took a PhD in behavioural biology, and Stanford University, where he was a Harkness Fellow. He subsequently lectured and researched at the University of Cambridge and was a Fellow of Wolfson College Cambridge before leaving academia to join government service. In the margins of his national security career he continued to write about behavioural science, as the author or co-author of books including: *Measuring Behaviour*; *The Sickening Mind*; *Design for a Life*; *Counting Sheep*; *Making Happy People*; *Play, Playfulness, Creativity and Innovation*; and *Extreme*.

He is an Honorary Principal Research Fellow at Imperial College London, a Fellow of the Institution of Engineering and Technology, and a Distinguished Fellow of the Royal United Services Institute for Defence and Security Studies (RUSI).

INDEX